KVM Virtualization Cookbook

Learn how to effectively use KVM in production

Konstantin Ivanov

Packt>

BIRMINGHAM - MUMBAI

KVM Virtualization Cookbook

First published: June 2017

Production reference: 1140617

Published by Packt Publishing Ltd.
Livery Place
35 Livery Street
Birmingham
B3 2PB, UK.

ISBN 978-1-78829-467-6

www.packtpub.com

Credits

Author
Konstantin Ivanov

Reviewer
Jay Payne

Acquisition Editor
Rahul Nair

Content Development Editor
Devika Battike

Technical Editor
Prachi Sawant

Production Coordinator
Aparna Bhagat

Copy Editor
Dipti Mankame

Project Coordinator
Judie Jose

Proofreader
Safis Editing

Indexer
Rekha Nair

Graphics
Kirk D'Penha

About the Author

Konstantin Ivanov is a Linux systems engineer, an open source developer, and a technology blogger who has been designing, configuring, deploying, and administering large-scale, highly available Linux environments for more than 15 years.

His interests include large distributed systems and task automation, along with solving technical challenges involving multiple technology stacks.

Konstantin received two master of science in computer science degrees from universities in Bulgaria and the United States, specializing in system and network security and software engineering.

In his spare time, he loves writing technology blogs and spending time with his two boys.

To my amazing wife, Deepa, my trusty companion through the many long days of writing.

About the Reviewer

Jay Payne has been a database administrator 5 at Rackspace for over 10 years, working on the design, development, implementation, and operation of storage systems.

Previously, Jay worked on billing and support systems for hosting companies. For the last 20 years, he has primarily focused on the data life cycle, from database architecture, administration, operations, and reporting to disaster recovery and compliance. He has domain experience in hosting, finance, billing, and customer-support industries.

www.PacktPub.com

For support files and downloads related to your book, please visit `www.PacktPub.com`.

Did you know that Packt offers eBook versions of every book published, with PDF and ePub files available? You can upgrade to the eBook version at `www.PacktPub.com` and as a print book customer, you are entitled to a discount on the eBook copy. Get in touch with us at `service@packtpub.com` for more details.

At `www.PacktPub.com`, you can also read a collection of free technical articles, sign up for a range of free newsletters and receive exclusive discounts and offers on Packt books and eBooks.

Mapt

`https://www.packtpub.com/mapt`

Get the most in-demand software skills with Mapt. Mapt gives you full access to all Packt books and video courses, as well as industry-leading tools to help you plan your personal development and advance your career.

Why subscribe?

- Fully searchable across every book published by Packt
- Copy and paste, print, and bookmark content
- On demand and accessible via a web browser

Customer Feedback

Thanks for purchasing this Packt book. At Packt, quality is at the heart of our editorial process. To help us improve, please leave us an honest review on this book's Amazon page at `https://www.amazon.com/dp/178829467X`.

If you'd like to join our team of regular reviewers, you can e-mail us at `customerreviews@packtpub.com`. We award our regular reviewers with free eBooks and videos in exchange for their valuable feedback. Help us be relentless in improving our products!

Table of Contents

Preface	1
Chapter 1: Getting Started with QEMU and KVM	7
Introduction	7
Installing and configuring QEMU	8
Getting ready	8
How to do it...	8
How it works...	9
Managing disk images with qemu-img	10
Getting ready	11
How to do it...	11
How it works...	12
There's more...	12
Preparing images for OS installation with qemu-nbd	13
Getting ready	13
How to do it...	14
How it works...	16
Installing a custom OS on the image with debootstrap	17
Getting ready	17
How to do it...	18
How it works...	22
Resizing an image	23
Getting ready	23
How to do it...	23
How it works...	29
Using pre-existing images	30
Getting ready	30
How to do it...	31
How it works...	32
There's more...	32
See also	33
Running virtual machines with qemu-system-*	33
Getting ready	34
How to do it...	36
How it works...	36

Starting the QEMU VM with KVM support   37
   Getting ready   38
   How to do it...   39
   How it works...   39
   There's more...   40
Connecting to a running instance with VNC   40
   Getting ready   41
   How to do it...   41
   How it works...   44

Chapter 2: Using libvirt to Manage KVM   45

Introduction   45
Installing and configuring libvirt   46
   Getting ready   46
   How to do it...   46
   How it works...   48
Defining KVM instances   49
   Getting ready   49
   How to do it...   50
   How it works...   51
   There's more...   52
Starting, stopping, and removing KVM instances   55
   Getting ready   55
   How to do it...   56
   How it works...   57
Inspecting and editing KVM configs   58
   Getting ready   58
   How to do it...   58
   How it works...   61
Building new KVM instances with virt-install and using the console   62
   Getting ready   63
   How to do it...   63
   How it works...   66
Managing CPU and memory resources in KVM   66
   Getting ready   67
   How to do it...   67
   How it works...   69
   There's more...   70
Attaching block devices to virtual machines   71
   Getting ready   71

How to do it...	71
How it works...	74
Sharing directories between a running VM and the host OS	75
Getting ready	76
How to do it...	76
How it works...	78
There's more...	78
Autostarting KVM instances	79
Getting ready	80
How to do it...	80
How it works...	81
Working with storage pools	82
Getting ready	83
How to do it...	83
How it works...	85
There's more...	86
Managing volumes	88
Getting ready	88
How to do it...	88
How it works...	91
Managing secrets	92
Getting ready	92
How to do it...	92
How it works...	94
Chapter 3: KVM Networking with libvirt	95
Introduction	95
The Linux bridge	96
Getting ready	96
How to do it...	98
How it works...	100
There's more...	103
The Open vSwitch	105
Getting ready	106
How to do it...	106
How it works...	109
There's more...	110
Configuring NAT forwarding network	111
Getting ready	111
How to do it...	111

How it works...	116
Configuring bridged network	118
Getting ready	118
How to do it...	119
How it works...	120
Configuring PCI passthrough network	121
Getting ready	121
How to do it...	122
How it works...	125
Manipulating network interfaces	126
Getting ready	127
How to do it...	127
How it works...	129

Chapter 4: Migrating KVM Instances — 131

Introduction	131
Manual offline migration using an iSCSI storage pool	132
Getting ready	133
How to do it...	133
How it works...	142
There's more...	143
Manual offline migration using GlusterFS shared volumes	144
Getting ready	145
How to do it...	145
How it works...	149
Online migration using the virsh command with shared storage	149
Getting ready	150
How to do it...	150
How it works...	151
There's more...	152
Offline migration using the virsh command and local image	154
Getting ready	154
How to do it...	155
How it works...	156
Online migration using the virsh command and local image	156
Getting ready	156
How to do it...	157
How it works...	158

Chapter 5: Monitoring and Backup of KVM Virtual Machines — 159

Introduction   159
Resource usage collection with libvirt   160
  Getting ready   160
  How to do it...   160
  How it works...   163
  There's more...   164
Monitoring KVM instances with Sensu   169
  Getting ready   169
  How to do it...   170
  How it works...   177
  There's more...   178
Simple KVM backups with tar and rsync   181
  Getting ready   181
  How to do it...   182
  How it works...   183
Creating snapshots   184
  Getting ready   187
  How to do it...   187
  How it works...   189
Listing snapshots   190
  Getting ready   190
  How to do it...   190
  How it works...   191
Inspecting snapshots   191
  Getting ready   192
  How to do it...   192
  How it works...   194
Editing snapshots   194
  Getting ready   194
  How to do it...   194
  How it works...   195
Reverting snapshots   195
  Getting ready   195
  How to do it...   196
  How it works...   197
Deleting snapshots   197
  Getting ready   197
  How to do it...   198
  How it works...   199

Chapter 6: Deploying KVM Instances with OpenStack	201
Introduction	201
Preparing the host for the OpenStack deployment	202
Getting ready	203
How to do it...	203
How it works...	204
Installing and configuring the OpenStack Keystone identity service	205
Getting ready	205
How to do it...	205
How it works...	213
Installing and configuring the OpenStack Glance image service	214
Getting ready	214
How to do it...	214
How it works...	220
Installing and configuring the OpenStack Nova compute service	221
Getting ready	221
How to do it...	222
How it works...	227
Installing and configuring the OpenStack Neutron networking service	228
Getting ready	229
How to do it...	229
How it works...	241
Building and inspecting KVM instances with OpenStack	241
Getting ready	242
How to do it...	242
How it works...	249
Stopping KVM instances with OpenStack	250
Getting ready	250
How to do it...	250
How it works...	252
Terminating KVM instances with OpenStack	252
Getting ready	252
How to do it...	253
How it works...	255
Chapter 7: Using Python to Build and Manage KVM Instances	257
Introduction	257
Installing and using the Python libvirt library	258
Getting ready	258

How to do it...   258
How it works...   260
Defining KVM instances with Python   260
Getting ready   261
How to do it...   261
How it works...   264
There's more...   265
Starting, stopping, and deleting KVM instances with Python   268
Getting ready   268
How to do it...   269
How it works...   270
There's more...   270
Inspecting KVM instances with Python   273
Getting ready   274
How to do it...   274
How it works...   276
There's more...   276
Building a simple REST API server with libvirt and bottle   280
Getting ready   281
How to do it...   281
How it works...   284
There's more...   287

Chapter 8: Kernel Tuning for KVM Performance   291

Introduction   291
Tuning the kernel for low I/O latency   293
Getting ready   294
How to do it...   294
How it works...   296
Memory tuning for KVM guests   297
Getting ready   297
How to do it...   297
How it works...   301
CPU performance options   302
Getting ready   302
How to do it...   302
How it works...   304
NUMA tuning with libvirt   305
Getting ready   306
How to do it...   306

How it works...	308
There is more...	309
Tuning the kernel for network performance	310
Getting ready	311
How to do it...	311
How it works...	315
Index	319

Preface

The foundation of most modern cloud deployments is some sort of virtualization technology, such as Kernel-based Virtual Machine (KVM). KVM has been part of the mainstream Linux kernel since version 2.6.20, released in February 2007, and since then has enjoyed wide system adoption.

Virtualization in general not only provides a way to fully utilize server resources, but also allows greater multitenancy, along with running various workloads on the same system.

The OpenStack cloud operating system uses KVM as its default compute driver, providing a centralized way of managing the lifecycle of virtual machines: from building, resizing, and migrating to pausing and terminating.

This book is about KVM and how to build and manage virtual machines in the most efficient way. Unlike containerization solutions such as Docker, KVM is designed to run an entire operating system rather than a single process. Although containerization has its advantages, full virtualization provides extra security by having the hypervisor layer between the guest OS and the host and added stability by running different guest kernels (kernel panic of the guest instance will not bring the entire host down) or entirely different operating systems.

This book takes a rather direct and pragmatic step-by-step approach--you will learn how to create custom guest images, install and configure QEMU and libvirt, resize and migrate instances, deploy monitoring, and provision guests using OpenStack and Python.

What this book covers

Chapter 1, *Getting Started with QEMU and KVM*, provides recipes for installing and configuring QEMU, creating and managing disk images, and running virtual machines with the qemu-system utility.

Chapter 2, *Using libvirt to Manage KVM*, covers everything that is needed to install, configure, and run KVM instances using libvirt. You will learn what packages and tools are required, along with different ways of configuring virtual machines using XML definition files. By the end of this chapter, you will have a Linux system with running KVM instances.

Chapter 3, *KVM Networking with libvirt*, will present recipes for working with the Linux Bridge and Open vSwitch and will demonstrate how to connect KVM instances using NAT, bridged, and PCI pass-through networking.

Chapter 4, *Migrating KVM Instances,* will show examples on how to perform offline and online migration of running KVM virtual machines.

Chapter 5, *Monitoring and Backup of KVM Virtual Machines,* will present examples on how to deploy complete monitoring systems with Sensu and Uchiwa and demonstrate how to create snapshots to use as backups.

Chapter 6, *Deploying KVM Instances with OpenStack,* demonstrates how to provision KVM instances with OpenStack. It begins by introducing the various components that make OpenStack and how to use the LXC Nova driver to automatically provision virtual machines.

Chapter 7, *Using Python to Build and Manage KVM Instances,* will present recipes for building, starting, and managing the lifecycle of KVM instances using the Python libvirt library. We will also see examples on how to build a simple RESTful API to work with KVM.

Chapter 8, *Kernel Tuning for KVM Performance,* shows recipes for tuning the host OS for better I/O, CPU, memory, and network utilization. The presented examples can also be used inside the KVM instances, depending on their workload.

What you need for this book

A beginner-level knowledge of Linux and the command line is required to follow along and run the recipes. Some Python experience is required to fully understand and be able to run the examples in Chapter 7, *Using Python to Build and Manage KVM Instances.*

Most recipes in this book have been tested on bare metal servers with processors supporting virtualization and the latest version of Ubuntu Linux.

Who this book is for

This book is for anyone who is curious about virtualization with KVM--from Linux administrators who are looking for in-depth understanding of how KVM can be deployed and managed in large scale production environments to software developers that need a quick and easy way to prototype code in isolated guests. A DevOps engineer is most likely the best job title for those who want to read the book from cover to cover and try all examples.

Sections

In this book, you will find several headings that appear frequently (Getting ready, How to do it, How it works, There's more, and See also).

To give clear instructions on how to complete a recipe, we use these sections as follows:

Getting ready

This section tells you what to expect in the recipe, and describes how to set up any software or any preliminary settings required for the recipe.

How to do it...

This section contains the steps required to follow the recipe.

How it works...

This section usually consists of a detailed explanation of what happened in the previous section.

There's more...

This section consists of additional information about the recipe in order to make the reader more knowledgeable about the recipe.

See also

This section provides helpful links to other useful information for the recipe.

Conventions

In this book, you will find a number of styles of text that distinguish between different kinds of information. Here are some examples of these styles, and an explanation of their meaning.

Code words in text, database table names, folder names, filenames, file extensions, pathnames, dummy URLs, user input, and Twitter handles are shown as follows:" Managing disk images with `qemu-img`."

A block of code is set as follows:

```
import libvirt
from bottle import run, request, get, post, HTTPResponse
def libvirtConnect():
try:
conn = libvirt.open('qemu:///system')
except libvirt.libvirtError:
conn = None
return conn
```

Any command-line input or output is written as follows:

```
root@kvm:~# apt-get update
```

New terms and important words are shown in bold. Words that you see on the screen, in menus or dialog boxes for example, appear in the text like this: "The **memory_check** for the KVM instance is now showing in the Uchiwa dashboard."

> Warnings or important notes appear in a box like this.

> Tips and tricks appear like this.

Reader feedback

Feedback from our readers is always welcome. Let us know what you think about this book-what you liked or disliked. Reader feedback is important for us as it helps us develop titles that you will really get the most out of.

To send us general feedback, simply e-mail feedback@packtpub.com, and mention the book's title in the subject of your message.

If there is a topic that you have expertise in and you are interested in either writing or contributing to a book, see our author guide at www.packtpub.com/authors.

Customer support

Now that you are the proud owner of a Packt book, we have a number of things to help you to get the most from your purchase.

Downloading the example code

You can download the example code files for this book from your account at `http://www.p` `acktpub.com`. If you purchased this book elsewhere, you can visit `http://www.packtpub.c` `om/support` and register to have the files e-mailed directly to you.

You can download the code files by following these steps:

1. Log in or register to our website using your e-mail address and password.
2. Hover the mouse pointer on the **SUPPORT** tab at the top.
3. Click on **Code Downloads & Errata**.
4. Enter the name of the book in the **Search** box.
5. Select the book for which you're looking to download the code files.
6. Choose from the drop-down menu where you purchased this book from.
7. Click on **Code Download**.

You can also download the code files by clicking on the **Code Files** button on the book's webpage at the Packt Publishing website. This page can be accessed by entering the book's name in the **Search** box. Please note that you need to be logged in to your Packt account.

Once the file is downloaded, please make sure that you unzip or extract the folder using the latest version of:

- WinRAR / 7-Zip for Windows
- Zipeg / iZip / UnRarX for Mac
- 7-Zip / PeaZip for Linux

The code bundle for the book is also hosted on GitHub at `https://github.com/PacktPubl` `ishing/KVM-Virtualization-Cookbook`. We also have other code bundles from our rich catalog of books and videos available at `https://github.com/PacktPublishing/`. Check them out!

Downloading the color images of this book

We also provide you with a PDF file that has color images of the screenshots/diagrams used in this book. The color images will help you better understand the changes in the output. You can download this file from `https://www.packtpub.com/sites/default/files/down loads/KVMVirtualizationCookbook_ColorImages.pdf`.

Errata

Although we have taken every care to ensure the accuracy of our content, mistakes do happen. If you find a mistake in one of our books-maybe a mistake in the text or the code-we would be grateful if you could report this to us. By doing so, you can save other readers from frustration and help us improve subsequent versions of this book. If you find any errata, please report them by visiting `http://www.packtpub.com/submit-errata`, selecting your book, clicking on the **Errata Submission Form** link, and entering the details of your errata. Once your errata are verified, your submission will be accepted and the errata will be uploaded to our website or added to any list of existing errata under the Errata section of that title.

To view the previously submitted errata, go to `https://www.packtpub.com/books/conten t/support` and enter the name of the book in the search field. The required information will appear under the **Errata** section.

Piracy

Piracy of copyrighted material on the Internet is an ongoing problem across all media. At Packt, we take the protection of our copyright and licenses very seriously. If you come across any illegal copies of our works in any form on the Internet, please provide us with the location address or website name immediately so that we can pursue a remedy.

Please contact us at `copyright@packtpub.com` with a link to the suspected pirated material.

We appreciate your help in protecting our authors and our ability to bring you valuable content.

Questions

If you have a problem with any aspect of this book, you can contact us at `questions@packtpub.com`, and we will do our best to address the problem.

1
Getting Started with QEMU and KVM

In this chapter, we will cover the following topics:

- Installing and configuring QEMU
- Managing disk images with qemu-img
- Preparing images for OS installation with qemu-nbd
- Installing a custom OS on the image with debootstrap
- Resizing an image
- Using pre-existing images
- Running virtual machines with qemu-system-*
- Starting the QEMU VM with KVM support
- Connecting to a running instance with VNC

Introduction

Quick Emulator (**QEMU**) is the main component of the QEMU/KVM virtualization technology suit. It provides hardware virtualization and processor emulation. QEMU runs in userspace and, without the need for kernel, drivers can still provide fast system emulation. QEMU supports two operating modes:

- Full system emulation, where QEMU emulates an entire computer system, including the CPU type and peripherals
- User mode emulation, where QEMU can run a process that has been compiled on a different CPU architecture natively

In this book, we are going to focus on full system emulation with the hardware acceleration support provided by the **Kernel-based Virtual Machine (KVM)** hypervisor.

In this chapter, we will start by installing QEMU on Linux, then explore various examples of building, managing, and using disk images for the virtual instances. We will then have an in-depth look at running QEMU in full system emulation mode, using the provided binaries. We will see examples of using the KVM kernel module to accelerate the QEMU processes. Finally, we are going to end the chapter with details on how to connect to the virtual machines we started earlier, using VNC clients.

Installing and configuring QEMU

In this recipe, we will look at installing QEMU on a single server with the provided distribution packages. For production environments, we recommend using precompiled, packaged versions of QEMU for easier and more consistent deployments. However, we are going to see an example of how to compile QEMU from source, in case you need a certain version that you might want to package later.

Getting ready

Depending on your Linux distribution, the package name and installation commands will differ. You can use your system's package manager, such as `apt`, `dnf`, or `yum` to search for any packages containing the QEMU string and get familiar with what is available for your particular Linux variant. The source code can be downloaded from the official QEMU project website at `http://www.qemu-project.org/download/#source`.

How to do it...

Perform the following steps to install QEMU from packages on Ubuntu/Debian and RHEL/CentOS distributions:

1. On Ubuntu/Debian distributions, update your packages index:

    ```
    root@kvm:~# apt-get update
    ```

2. Install the package:

    ```
    root@kvm:~# apt-get install -y qemu
    ```

3. On CentOS/RHEL distributions execute:

```
root@kvm:~# yum install qemu-kvm
```

To install from source, execute the following:

1. Download the archive first:

```
root@kvm:~#cd /usr/src && wget
http://download.qemu-project.org/qemu-2.8.0.tar.xz
```

2. Extract the files from the archive:

```
root@kvm:/usr/src# tar xvJf qemu-2.8.0.tar.xz && cd qemu-
2.8.0
```

3. Configure and compile the source code:

```
root@kvm:/usr/src/qemu-2.8.0# ./configure
root@kvm:/usr/src/qemu-2.8.0# make && make install
```

How it works...

Installing QEMU is quite trivial, as we just saw. Let's have a look at what the QEMU metapackage installed on Ubuntu looks like:

```
root@kvm:~# dpkg --list | grep qemu
ii ipxe-qemu 1.0.0+git-20150424.a25a16d-1ubuntu1 all PXE boot firmware -
ROM images for qemu
ii qemu 1:2.5+dfsg-5ubuntu10.8 amd64 fast processor emulator
ii qemu-block-extra:amd64 1:2.5+dfsg-5ubuntu10.8 amd64 extra block backend
modules for qemu-system and qemu-utils
ii qemu-slof 20151103+dfsg-1ubuntu1 all Slimline Open Firmware -- QEMU
PowerPC version
ii qemu-system 1:2.5+dfsg-5ubuntu10.8 amd64 QEMU full system emulation
binaries
ii qemu-system-arm 1:2.5+dfsg-5ubuntu10.8 amd64 QEMU full system emulation
binaries (arm)
ii qemu-system-common 1:2.5+dfsg-5ubuntu10.8 amd64 QEMU full system
emulation binaries (common files)
ii qemu-system-mips 1:2.5+dfsg-5ubuntu10.8 amd64 QEMU full system emulation
binaries (mips)
ii qemu-system-misc 1:2.5+dfsg-5ubuntu10.8 amd64 QEMU full system emulation
binaries (miscelaneous)
ii qemu-system-ppc 1:2.5+dfsg-5ubuntu10.8 amd64 QEMU full system emulation
binaries (ppc)
```

```
ii qemu-system-sparc 1:2.5+dfsg-5ubuntu10.8 amd64 QEMU full system
emulation binaries (sparc)
ii qemu-system-x86 1:2.5+dfsg-5ubuntu10.8 amd64 QEMU full system emulation
binaries (x86)
ii qemu-user 1:2.5+dfsg-5ubuntu10.8 amd64 QEMU user mode emulation binaries
ii qemu-user-binfmt 1:2.5+dfsg-5ubuntu10.8 amd64 QEMU user mode binfmt
registration for qemu-user
ii qemu-utils 1:2.5+dfsg-5ubuntu10.8 amd64 QEMU utilities
root@kvm:~#
```

From the preceding output, we can see that there are few packages involved. If you are interested, you can read the individual description to get more familiar with what each package provides.

It's worth mentioning that all binaries provided from the earlier-mentioned packages start with the prefix QEMU. You can use tab completion to see the list of available executables:

```
root@kvm:~# qemu-
qemu-aarch64 qemu-io qemu-mips64el qemu-ppc64 qemu-sparc32plus qemu-system-
lm32 qemu-system-mipsel qemu-system-sh4 qemu-system-xtensa
qemu-alpha qemu-m68k qemu-mipsel qemu-ppc64abi32 qemu-sparc64 qemu-system-
m68k qemu-system-moxie qemu-system-sh4eb qemu-system-xtensaeb
qemu-arm qemu-make-debian-root qemu-mipsn32 qemu-ppc64le qemu-system-
aarch64 qemu-system-microblaze qemu-system-or32 qemu-system-sparc qemu-
tilegx
qemu-armeb qemu-microblaze qemu-mipsn32el qemu-s390x qemu-system-alpha
qemu-system-microblazeel qemu-system-ppc qemu-system-sparc64 qemu-unicore32
qemu-cris qemu-microblazeel qemu-nbd qemu-sh4 qemu-system-arm qemu-system-
mips qemu-system-ppc64 qemu-system-tricore qemu-x86_64
qemu-i386 qemu-mips qemu-or32 qemu-sh4eb qemu-system-cris qemu-system-
mips64 qemu-system-ppc64le qemu-system-unicore32
qemu-img qemu-mips64 qemu-ppc qemu-sparc qemu-system-i386 qemu-system-
mips64el qemu-system-ppcemb qemu-system-x86_64
root@kvm:~#
```

We can see that there's a single executable for each CPU architecture type that can be emulated.

Managing disk images with qemu-img

To run virtual machines, QEMU needs images to store the filesystem of the guest OS. The image itself is a type of file, and it represents the guest filesystem residing on a virtual disk. QEMU supports various images and provides tools to create and manage them. In this recipe, we are going to build a blank disk image with the qemu-img utility.

Getting ready

To use this recipe, we need to have the `qemu-img` utility installed. If you followed the steps in the first recipe, you should have that covered. To check what image types are supported on your Linux distribution, run the following command:

```
root@kvm:~# qemu-img -h | grep Supported
Supported formats: bochs vvfat rbd vpc parallels tftp ftp ftps raw https
qcow dmg http qcow2 quorum null-aio cloop vdi iscsi null-co vhdx blkverify
file vmdk host_cdrom blkdebug host_device sheepdog qed nbd
root@kvm:~#
```

From the preceding output, we can see that there are many supported images on the test system that we are using. Make sure that your QEMU version supports the raw image type, as it's the default and that is what we are going to use in this recipe. One of the most commonly used image type is `qcow2`, which supports copy on write, compression, encryption, and snapshotting. We are going to leverage that in later recipes.

> Please note that even though QEMU supports multiple formats, that does not necessarily mean that you can run virtual machines on them. However, `qemu-img` can be used to convert different images to raw and `qcow2` formats. For best performance, use raw or `qcow2` image formats.

How to do it...

Perform the following steps to create a blank raw image of a specified size and to verify that the file was created on the host:

1. Create a raw image named `debian.img` with size of 10 GB:

   ```
   root@kvm:~# qemu-img create -f raw debian.img 10G
   Formatting 'debian.img', fmt=raw size=10737418240
   root@kvm:~#
   ```

2. Check that the file was created:

   ```
   root@kvm:~# ls -lah debian.img
   -rw-r--r-- 1 root root 10G Feb 10 16:58 debian.img
    root@kvm:~#
   ```

3. Examine the file type:

```
root@kvm:~# file -s debian.img
debian.img: data
root@kvm:~#
```

4. Obtain more information about the image:

```
root@kvm:~# qemu-img info debian.img
image: debian.img
file format: raw
virtual size: 10G (10737418240 bytes)
disk size: 0
root@kvm:~#
```

How it works...

The `qemu-img` utility allows us to create, convert, and modify guest images.

In step 1, we used the `-f` flag specifying the image format; in this case, `raw`, the name of the image to be created and the size in gigabytes.

In step 4, we used the `info` subcommand to gather additional information about the existing image. Note how the disk size is showing as currently being zero. This is due to the fact that this is a blank image, not containing a filesystem. We are going to create one in the next recipe.

There's more...

In this recipe, we listed the supported disk image formats by QEMU. The following is a brief description of the most common types that you might encounter:

- `raw`: Raw disk image format. This is the default format and can be one of the fastest file-based formats. If you format this image with a filesystem that supports holes, for example, EXT3, then only sectors that have data will use space. The main drawback of the raw images is the lack of features, making them ideal for testing and quick prototyping.
- `qcow2`: As we mentioned in the previous section, this is one of the most feature-rich formats. It supports VM snapshots, compression, and encryption for the price of slightly reduced performance.

- qcow: This is an older QEMU image format that supports backing files, compact image files, encryption, and compression.
- dmg: This is the Mac disk image format. The Mac disk image provides secure password protection and compression, and it is most commonly used to distribute software, rather than running virtual machines.
- nbd: The network block device, typically used for accessing remote storage devices.
- vdi: This disk format is used by the Oracle VirtualBox software and can be used to run virtual machines on various CPU platforms.
- vmdk: This is the VMware disk image type, where a single virtual hard disk can span multiple files.
- vhdx: Microsoft Hyper-V uses this image format. It provides large storage capacity, data corruption protection during power failures and read/write optimization for larger disk images.

In this book, we are going to use the raw and qcow2 disk formats, as they provide the best performance and toolset for running and manipulating them.

Preparing images for OS installation with qemu-nbd

In the previous recipe, we created a blank raw image. In this recipe, we are going to make a partition and a filesystem on it, getting the image ready for full guest OS installation. When creating the partition and file system, you should consider the type of load that the virtual instance will create. If your applications running inside VM are IO bound, you might consider XFS for the image filesystem. For this recipe, we are going to use EXT4, as most Linux distributions support it out of the box.

Getting ready

For this recipe, we are going to use the following tools:

- qemu-nbd
- sfdisk
- The nbd kernel module
- mkfs

Most Linux distributions should already have the tools installed. If that's not the case, consult your distribution's documentation on how to install them.

How to do it...

Perform the following steps outlined to partition and create a filesystem on the blank image:

1. Load the nbd kernel module:

```
root@kvm:~# modprobe nbd
root@kvm:~#
```

2. Using the qemu-nbd tool, associate the blank image file to the /dev/nbd0 block device:

```
root@kvm:~# qemu-nbd --format=raw --connect=/dev/nbd0
debian.img
root@kvm:~#
```

3. Create two partitions on the block device. One will be used for swap, and the other as the root partition for the guest OS:

```
root@kvm:~# sfdisk /dev/nbd0 << EOF
>,1024,82
>;
>EOF
Checking that no-one is using this disk right now ...
OK
Disk /dev/nbd0: cannot get geometry

Disk /dev/nbd0: 1305 cylinders, 255 heads, 63 sectors/track

sfdisk: ERROR: sector 0 does not have an msdos signature
 /dev/nbd0: unrecognized partition table type
Old situation:
No partitions found
New situation:
Units = cylinders of 8225280 bytes, blocks of 1024 bytes, counting
from 0

  Device Boot Start End #cyls #blocks Id System
/dev/nbd0p1 0+ 1023 1024- 8225279+ 82 Linux swap / Solaris
/dev/nbd0p2 1024 1304 281 2257132+ 83 Linux
/dev/nbd0p3 0 - 0 0 0 Empty
/dev/nbd0p4 0 - 0 0 0 Empty
```

```
Warning: no primary partition is marked bootable (active)
This does not matter for LILO, but the DOS MBR will not boot this
disk.
Successfully wrote the new partition table

Re-reading the partition table ...

If you created or changed a DOS partition, /dev/foo7, say, then use
dd(1)
to zero the first 512 bytes: dd if=/dev/zero of=/dev/foo7 bs=512
count=1
(See fdisk(8).)
root@kvm:~#
```

4. List the available block devices after the partitioning:

```
root@kvm:~# ls -la /dev/nbd0*
brw-rw---- 1 root disk 43, 0 Feb 10 18:24 /dev/nbd0
brw-rw---- 1 root disk 43, 1 Feb 10 18:24 /dev/nbd0p1
brw-rw---- 1 root disk 43, 2 Feb 10 18:24 /dev/nbd0p2
root@kvm:~#
```

5. Create the swap partition:

```
root@kvm:~# mkswap /dev/nbd0p1
Setting up swapspace version 1, size = 508 KiB (520192 bytes)
no label, UUID=c246fe39-1bc5-4978-967c-806264771d69
root@kvm:~#
```

6. Make the EXT4 filesystem on the root partition:

```
root@kvm:~# mkfs.ext4 /dev/nbd0p2
mke2fs 1.42.13 (17-May-2015)
Discarding device blocks: failed - Input/output error
Creating filesystem with 2620928 4k blocks and 655360 inodes
Filesystem UUID: 2ffa23de-579a-45ad-abbc-2a179de67f11
Superblock backups stored on blocks:
    32768, 98304, 163840, 229376, 294912, 819200, 884736, 1605632

Allocating group tables: done
Writing inode tables: done
Creating journal (32768 blocks): done
Writing superblocks and filesystem accounting information: done
root@kvm:~#
```

How it works...

We take advantage of the functionality that the `nbd` kernel module provides by allowing us to associate a raw image file to a block device using the `qemu-nbd` utility. To get more information about the kernel module run the following code:

```
root@kvm:~# modinfo nbd
filename: /lib/modules/4.4.0-62-generic/kernel/drivers/block/nbd.ko
license: GPL
description: Network Block Device
srcversion: C67096AF2AE3C738DBE0B7E
depends:
intree: Y
vermagic: 4.4.0-62-generic SMP mod_unload modversions
parm: nbds_max:number of network block devices to initialize (default: 16)
(int)
parm: max_part:number of partitions per device (default: 0) (int)
root@kvm:~#
```

We can examine the block device metadata created in step 2 by running the following command:

```
root@kvm:~# file -s /dev/nbd0
/dev/nbd0: x86 boot sector
root@kvm:~#
```

After creating the two new partitions in step 3, the type of the image file has changed. Let's examine it again:

```
root@kvm:~# file -s debian.img
debian.img: x86 boot sector
root@kvm:~#
```

> We chose to use the `sfdisk` utility to create the partitions, but you can use the `fdisk` utility interactively instead if you prefer. The end result will be the same.

Now that we have an image file that contains two partitions and a filesystem, we can proceed with installing the guest OS in the next recipe.

Installing a custom OS on the image with debootstrap

In this recipe, we are going to use the `debootstrap` utility to install a Debian distribution on the raw image we prepared in the previous two recipes. The `debootstrap` command is used to bootstrap a basic Debian system using a specific public mirror. By the end of this recipe, we should have an image containing an entire Linux distribution, ready for QEMU execution.

Getting ready

We are going to need the following in order to complete this recipe:

- The block devices created in the previous recipe
- The `debootstrap` utility
- The `chroot` utility

To ensure that the swap and root block devices are still present on the system, run the following:

```
root@kvm:~# ls -la /dev/nbd0*
brw-rw---- 1 root disk 43, 0 Feb 10 18:24 /dev/nbd0
brw-rw---- 1 root disk 43, 1 Feb 10 18:24 /dev/nbd0p1
brw-rw---- 1 root disk 43, 2 Feb 10 18:24 /dev/nbd0p2
root@kvm:~#
```

If that's not the case, please refer to the *Preparing images for OS installation with qemu-nbd* recipe on how to associate the raw image with the `/deb/nbd0` block device.

To install the `debootstrap` utility, if not already present on your system, execute the following code:

```
root@kvm:~# apt install -y debootstrap
...
Setting up debootstrap (1.0.78+nmu1ubuntu1.2) ...
root@kvm:~#
```

How to do it...

Follow these steps outlined to install a new Debian Linux distribution on the raw image:

1. Mount the root partition from the **Network Block Device** (**NBD**) device and ensure that it was mounted successfully:

   ```
   root@kvm:~# mount /dev/nbd0p2 /mnt/
   root@kvm:~# mount | grep mnt
   /dev/nbd0p2 on /mnt type ext4 (rw)
   root@kvm:~#
   ```

2. Install the latest stable Debian distribution on the root partition mounted on /mnt from the specified public repository:

   ```
   root@kvm:~# debootstrap --arch=amd64 --include="openssh-server vim"
   stable /mnt/ http://httpredir.debian.org/debian/
   ...
   I: Base system installed successfully.
   root@kvm:~#
   ```

3. Ensure the root filesystem was created, by listing all the files at the mounted location:

   ```
   root@kvm:~# ls -lah /mnt/
   total 100K    drwxr-xr-x 22 root root 4.0K Feb 10 17:19 .
   drwxr-xr-x 23 root root 4.0K Feb 10 15:29 ..
   drwxr-xr-x 2 root root 4.0K Feb 10 17:19 bin
   drwxr-xr-x 2 root root 4.0K Dec 28 17:42 boot
   drwxr-xr-x 4 root root 4.0K Feb 10 17:18 dev
   drwxr-xr-x 55 root root 4.0K Feb 10 17:19 etc
   drwxr-xr-x 2 root root 4.0K Dec 28 17:42 home
   drwxr-xr-x 12 root root 4.0K Feb 10 17:19 lib
   drwxr-xr-x 2 root root 4.0K Feb 10 17:18 lib64
   drwx------ 2 root root 16K Feb 10 17:06 lost+found
   drwxr-xr-x 2 root root 4.0K Feb 10 17:18 media
   drwxr-xr-x 2 root root 4.0K Feb 10 17:18 mnt
   drwxr-xr-x 2 root root 4.0K Feb 10 17:18 opt
   drwxr-xr-x 2 root root 4.0K Dec 28 17:42 proc
   drwx------ 2 root root 4.0K Feb 10 17:18 root
   drwxr-xr-x 4 root root 4.0K Feb 10 17:19 run
   drwxr-xr-x 2 root root 4.0K Feb 10 17:19 sbin
   drwxr-xr-x 2 root root 4.0K Feb 10 17:18 srv
   drwxr-xr-x 2 root root 4.0K Apr 6 2015 sys
   drwxrwxrwt 2 root root 4.0K Feb 10 17:18 tmp
   drwxr-xr-x 10 root root 4.0K Feb 10 17:18 usr
   drwxr-xr-x 11 root root 4.0K Feb 10 17:18 var
   ```

```
root@kvm:~#
```

4. Bind and mount the devices directory from the host to the image filesystem:

```
root@kvm:~# mount --bind /dev/ /mnt/dev
root@kvm:~#
```

5. Ensure that the nbd devices are now present inside the mount location:

```
root@kvm:~# ls -la /mnt/dev/ | grep nbd0
brw-rw---- 1 root disk 43, 0 Feb 10 18:24 nbd0
brw-rw---- 1 root disk 43, 1 Feb 10 18:26 nbd0p1
brw-rw---- 1 root disk 43, 2 Feb 10 18:26 nbd0p2
root@kvm:~#
```

6. Change the directory namespace to be the root filesystem of the image and ensure the operation succeeded:

```
root@kvm:~# chroot /mnt/
root@kvm:/# pwd
/
root@kvm:/#
```

7. Check the distribution version inside the chroot environment:

```
root@kvm:/# cat /etc/debian_version
8.7
root@kvm:/#
```

8. Mount the proc and sysfs virtual filesystems inside the chrooted environment:

```
root@kvm:/# mount -t proc none /proc
root@kvm:/# mount -t sysfs none /sys
root@kvm:/#
```

9. While still inside the chrooted location, install the Debian kernel metapackage and the grub2 utilities:

```
root@kvm:/# apt-get install -y --force-yes linux-image-amd64 grub2
```

If asked to select target device for GRUB to install on, do not select any and just continue.

10. Install GRUB on the root device:

```
root@kvm:/# grub-install /dev/nbd0 --force
Installing for i386-pc platform.
grub-install: warning: this msdos-style partition label has no
post-MBR gap; embedding won't be possible.
grub-install: warning: Embedding is not possible. GRUB can only be
installed in this setup by using blocklists. However, blocklists
are UNRELIABLE and their use is discouraged..
Installation finished. No error reported.
root@kvm:/#
```

11. Update the GRUB configs and the initrd image:

```
root@kvm:/# update-grub2
Generating grub configuration file ...
Found linux image: /boot/vmlinuz-3.16.0-4-amd64
Found initrd image: /boot/initrd.img-3.16.0-4-amd64
done
root@kvm:/#
```

12. Change the root password of the guest:

```
root@kvm:/# passwd
Enter new UNIX password:
Retype new UNIX password:
passwd: password updated successfully
root@kvm:/#
```

13. Allow access to the pseudo Terminal inside the new guest OS:

```
root@kvm:/# echo "pts/0" >> /etc/securetty
root@kvm:/#
```

14. Change the systemd run level to the multi-user level:

```
root@kvm:/# systemctl set-default multi-user.target
Created symlink from /etc/systemd/system/default.target to
/lib/systemd/system/multi-user.target.
root@kvm:/#
```

15. Add the root mountpoint to the `fstab` file, so it can persist reboots:

    ```
    root@kvm:/# echo "/dev/sda2 / ext4 defaults,discard 0 0" >
    /etc/fstab
    ```

16. Unmount the following filesystems as we are done using them for now:

    ```
    root@kvm:/# umount /proc/ /sys/ /dev/
    ```

17. Exit the chrooted environment:

    ```
    root@kvm:/# exit
    exit
    root@kvm:~#
    ```

18. Install GRUB on the root partition of the block device associated with the raw image:

    ```
    root@kvm:~# grub-install /dev/nbd0 --root-directory=/mnt --
    modules="biosdisk part_msdos" --force
    Installing for i386-pc platform.
    grub-install: warning: this msdos-style partition label has no
    post-MBR gap; embedding won't be possible.
    grub-install: warning: Embedding is not possible. GRUB can only be
    installed in this setup by using blocklists. However, blocklists
    are UNRELIABLE and their use is discouraged..
    Installation finished. No error reported.
    root@kvm:~#
    ```

19. Update the GRUB configuration file to reflect the correct block device for the guest image:

    ```
    root@kvm:~# sed -i 's/nbd0p2/sda2/g' /mnt/boot/grub/grub.cfg
    root@kvm:~#
    ```

20. Unmount the nbd0 device:

    ```
    root@kvm:~# umount /mnt
    root@kvm:~#
    ```

21. Disassociate the nbd0 device from the raw image:

    ```
    root@kvm:~# qemu-nbd --disconnect /dev/nbd0
    /dev/nbd0 disconnected
    root@kvm:~#
    ```

How it works...

A lot has happened in the previous section, so let's step through the commands and talk a little bit more about what exactly was performed and why.

In step 1, we mounted the root partition we created earlier on the /dev/nbd0p2 device to /mnt, so we can use it. Once mounted, in step 2, we installed an entire Debian distribution on that device using the mount-point as the target.

In order to install the GRUB boot loader on the root partition of the image, we bind and mounted the /dev directory from the host filesystem to the image filesystem in /mnt in step 4.

Then in step 6, we used the chroot tool to change our directory namespace to be /mnt, so we can perform operations, as we are directly on the new OS.

In step 8, we mounted the proc and sysfs virtual filesystems inside the image because the GRUB bootloader tool expect them.

In step 9, we proceeded to install the kernel source and GRUB tools in preparation of installing the bootloader on the boot partition and in step 10 we installed the bootloader.

In step 11, the GRUB configuration files were generated and the boot ramdisk image was updated.

In steps 12, 13, and 14, we changed the root password and ensured we get access to the pseudo Terminal, so we can log into the VM later and change the run-level from the default graphical interface to the multiuser.

Since the fstab file is empty right after installing the Debian OS on the image, we have to add the root mount point, or the VM will not be able to start. This was accomplished in step 15.

In steps 16 and 17, we performed some cleaning up by unmounting the filesystems we mounted earlier and exited the chroot environment.

Back on the host filesystem in step 18, we installed GRUB on the nbd0 device by specifying the mounted location of the image.

In step 19, we updated the GRUB config device name to be sda2 because this is the name that will appear inside the virtual machine once we start it. The nbd0p2 name is only present while we have the association between the raw image and the network block device on the host OS. From the VM perspective, the second partition inside the image we created by is named sda2 by default.

And finally, in steps 20 and 21, we performed some cleaning by removing the mount point and disassociating the raw image from the network block device nbd0.

Resizing an image

In this recipe, we are going to examine how to resize an existing raw image, the partitions hosted on it and the filesystem on top of the partitions. We are going to be using the raw image that we build in the previous recipes, which contains a swap and a root partition with an EXT4 filesystem formatted on it.

Getting ready

For this recipe, we are going to use the following tools:

- qemu-img
- losetup
- tune2fs
- e2fsck
- kpartx
- fdisk
- resize2fs

Most of the utilities should already be installed on Ubuntu with the exception of kpartx. To install it, run the following:

```
root@kvm:~# apt install kpartx
```

How to do it...

The next steps demonstrate how to add additional space to the raw image we created earlier, extend the root partition, and resize the filesystem. By the end of this recipe, the original raw image filesystem size should have changed from 10G to 20G.

1. Obtain the current size of the image:

```
root@kvm:~# qemu-img info debian.img
image: debian.img
file format: raw
```

```
virtual size: 10G (10737418240 bytes)
disk size: 848M
root@kvm:~#
```

2. Add additional 10 GB to the image:

```
root@kvm:~# qemu-img resize -f raw debian.img +10GB
Image resized.
root@kvm:~#
```

Please note that not all image types support resizing. In order to resize such an image, you will need to convert it to raw image first using the qemu-img convert command.

3. Check the new size of the image:

```
root@kvm:~# qemu-img info debian.img
image: debian.img
file format: raw
virtual size: 20G (21474836480 bytes)
disk size: 848M
root@kvm:~#
```

4. Print the name of the first unused loop device:

```
root@kvm:~# losetup -f
/dev/loop0
root@kvm:~#
```

5. Associate the first unused loop device with the raw image file:

```
root@kvm:~# losetup /dev/loop1 debian.img
root@kvm:~#
```

6. Read the partition information from the associated loop device and create the device mappings:

```
root@kvm:~# kpartx -av /dev/loop1
add map loop1p1 (252:0): 0 1024 linear 7:1 2048
add map loop1p2 (252:1): 0 20967424 linear 7:1 4096
root@kvm:~#
```

7. Examine the new device maps, representing the partitions on the raw image:

```
root@kvm:~# ls -la /dev/mapper
total 0
drwxr-xr-x 2 root root 100 Mar 9 19:10 .
drwxr-xr-x 20 root root 4760 Mar 9 19:10 ..
crw------- 1 root root 10, 236 Feb 10 23:25 control
lrwxrwxrwx 1 root root 7 Mar 9 19:10 loop1p1
lrwxrwxrwx 1 root root 7 Mar 9 19:10 loop1p2
root@kvm:~#
```

8. Obtain some information from the root partition mapping:

```
root@kvm:~# tune2fs -l /dev/mapper/loop1p2
tune2fs 1.42.13 (17-May-2015)
Filesystem volume name: <none>
Last mounted on: /
Filesystem UUID: 96a73752-489a-435c-8aa0-8c5d1aba3e5f
Filesystem magic number: 0xEF53
Filesystem revision #: 1 (dynamic)
Filesystem features: has_journal ext_attr resize_inode dir_index
filetype needs_recovery extent flex_bg sparse_super
 large_file huge_file uninit_bg dir_nlink extra_isize     Filesystem
flags: signed_directory_hash
Default mount options: user_xattr acl
Filesystem state: clean
Errors behavior: Continue
Filesystem OS type: Linux
Inode count: 655360
Block count: 2620928
Reserved block count: 131046
Free blocks: 2362078
Free inodes: 634148
First block: 0
Block size: 4096
Fragment size: 4096
Reserved GDT blocks: 639
Blocks per group: 32768
Fragments per group: 32768
Inodes per group: 8192
Inode blocks per group: 512
Flex block group size: 16
Filesystem created: Fri Feb 10 23:29:01 2017
Last mount time: Thu Mar 9 19:09:25 2017
Last write time: Thu Mar 9 19:08:23 2017
Mount count: 12
Maximum mount count: -1
Last checked: Fri Feb 10 23:29:01 2017
```

```
Check interval: 0 (<none>)
Lifetime writes: 1621 MB
Reserved blocks uid: 0 (user root)
Reserved blocks gid: 0 (group root)
First inode: 11
Inode size: 256
Required extra isize: 28
Desired extra isize: 28
Journal inode: 8
Default directory hash: half_md4
Directory Hash Seed: f101cccc-944e-4773-8644-91ebf4bd4f2d
Journal backup: inode blocks
root@kvm:~#
```

9. Check the filesystem on the root partition of the mapped device:

```
root@kvm:~# e2fsck /dev/mapper/loop1p2
e2fsck 1.42.13 (17-May-2015)
/dev/mapper/loop1p2: recovering journal    Setting free blocks
count to 2362045 (was 2362078)    /dev/mapper/loop1p2: clean,
21212/655360 files, 258883/2620928 blocks
root@kvm:~#
```

10. Remove the journal from the root partition device:

```
root@kvm:~# tune2fs -O ^has_journal /dev/mapper/loop1p2
tune2fs 1.42.13 (17-May-2015)
root@kvm:~#
```

11. Ensure that the journaling has been removed:

```
root@kvm:~# tune2fs -l /dev/mapper/loop1p2 | grep "features"
Filesystem features: ext_attr resize_inode dir_index filetype
extent flex_bg sparse_super large_file huge_file uninit_bg
dir_nlink extra_isize
root@kvm:~#
```

12. Remove the partition mappings:

```
root@kvm:~# kpartx -dv /dev/loop1
del devmap : loop1p2
del devmap : loop1p1
root@kvm:~#
```

13. Detach the loop device from the image:

```
root@kvm:~# losetup -d /dev/loop1
root@kvm:~#
```

14. Associate the raw image with the network block device:

```
root@kvm:~# qemu-nbd --format=raw --connect=/dev/nbd0 debian.img
root@kvm:~#
```

15. Using `fdisk`, list the available partitions, then delete the root partition, recreate it, and write the changes:

```
root@kvm:~# fdisk /dev/nbd0

Command (m for help): p

Disk /dev/nbd0: 21.5 GB, 21474836480 bytes
255 heads, 63 sectors/track, 2610 cylinders, total 41943040 sectors
Units = sectors of 1 * 512 = 512 bytes
Sector size (logical/physical): 512 bytes / 512 bytes
I/O size (minimum/optimal): 512 bytes / 512 bytes
Disk identifier: 0x00000000

 Device Boot Start End Blocks Id System
/dev/nbd0p1 1 16450559 8225279+ 82 Linux swap / Solaris
/dev/nbd0p2 16450560 20964824 2257132+ 83 Linux

Command (m for help): d
Partition number (1-4): 2

Command (m for help): n
Partition type:
 p primary (1 primary, 0 extended, 3 free)
 e extended
Select (default p): p
Partition number (1-4, default 2): 2
First sector (16450560-41943039, default 16450560):
Using default value 16450560
Last sector, +sectors or +size{K,M,G} (16450560-41943039, default
41943039):
Using default value 41943039

Command (m for help): w
The partition table has been altered!

Calling ioctl() to re-read partition table.
```

```
Syncing disks.
root@kvm:~#
```

16. Associate the first unused loop device with the raw image file, like we did in step 5:

```
root@kvm:~# losetup /dev/loop1 debian.img
```

17. Read the partition information from the associated loop device and create the device mappings:

```
root@kvm:~# kpartx -av /dev/loop1
add map loop1p1 (252:2): 0 1024 linear 7:1 2048
add map loop1p2 (252:3): 0 41938944 linear 7:1 4096
root@kvm:~#
```

18. After the partitioning is complete, perform a filesystem check:

```
root@kvm:~# e2fsck -f /dev/mapper/loop1p2
e2fsck 1.42.13 (17-May-2015)
Pass 1: Checking inodes, blocks, and sizes
Pass 2: Checking directory structure
Pass 3: Checking directory connectivity
Pass 4: Checking reference counts
Pass 5: Checking group summary information
/dev/mapper/loop1p2: 21212/655360 files (0.2% non-contiguous),
226115/2620928 blocks
root@kvm:~#
```

19. Resize the filesystem on the root partition of the mapped device:

```
root@kvm:~# resize2fs /dev/nbd0p2
resize2fs 1.42.13 (17-May-2015)
Resizing the filesystem on /dev/mapper/loop1p2 to 5242368 (4k)
blocks.
The filesystem on /dev/mapper/loop1p2 is now 5242368 (4k) blocks
long.
root@kvm:~#
```

20. Create the filesystem journal because we removed it earlier:

```
root@kvm:~# tune2fs -j /dev/mapper/loop1p2
tune2fs 1.42.13 (17-May-2015)
Creating journal inode: done
root@kvm:~#
```

21. Remove the device mappings:

```
root@kvm:~# kpartx -dv /dev/loop1
del devmap : loop1p2
del devmap : loop1p1
root@kvm:~# losetup -d /dev/loop1
root@kvm:~#
```

How it works...

Resizing an image for VM can be somewhat involving, as we saw from all the steps in the previous section. Things can get complicated when there are multiple Linux partitions inside the same image, even more so if we are not using **Logical Volume Management (LVM)**. Let's step through all the commands we ran earlier and explain in more details why we ran them and what they do.

In step 1, we confirmed the current size of the image being 10 GB.

In step 2, we added 10 GB at the end of the image and confirm the new image size in step 3.

Recall that the image we built from earlier recipes contains two partitions, swap and root. We need a way to manipulate them individually. Particularly, we would like to allocate the extra space we added in step 2 to the root partition. To do that we need to expose it as a block device that we can easily manipulate with standard disk and filesystem utilities. We accomplished that using the losetup command in step 5, resulting in a mapping between the image and a new block device named /dev/loop1. In step 6, we exposed the individual partitions as two new device mappings. The /dev/mapper/loop1p2 is the root partition that we would like to append the unused disk space to.

Before we can resize the partitioned on the loop device, we need to check the integrity of the filesystem on it, and this is what we did in step 9. Because we are using a journaling filesystem, we need to remove the journal prior to resizing. We do that in step 10 and made sure that the has_journal attribute is not showing after running the tune2fs command in step 11.

Now, we need to work directly on the main block device and not the individual partitions. We remove the mappings in steps 12 and 13 and associated a new block device with the image file using the qemu nbd command in step 14. The new /dev/nbd0 block device now represents the entire disk of the guest VM and it's a direct mapping to what's inside the raw image. We can use this block device just like any other regular disk, most importantly we can use tools such as fdisk to examine and manipulate the partitions residing on it.

In step 15, we use the `fdisk` utility to delete the root partition and recreate it. This does not destroy any filesystem data, but changes the metadata, allocating the extra space we added earlier as part of the root partition.

Now that the block device has all the disk space allocated to the root partition, we need to extend the filesystem that is on top of it. We do that by first recreating the individual partition mappings like we did earlier, to expose the root partition directly so that we can yet again manipulate it. We do that in steps 16 and 17.

In steps 18 and 19, we check the integrity of the root file system, then we resize it to the maximum available disk space on the root partition that it resides.

Finally, in step 20, we remove the mappings again. Now the image, the root partition inside the image, and the EXT4 filesystem on top of the Linux partition have been resized to 20 GB.

You can check the new root partition size by starting a new QEMU instance using the image. We are going to do just that in a separate recipe in this chapter.

Using pre-existing images

In the *Installing a custom OS on the image with debootstrap* recipe, we saw how to use the `debootstrap` command to install Debian on an image we built. Most Linux vendors provide already built images of their distributions for various architectures. Installable images are also available for manually installing the guest OS. In this recipe, we are going to demonstrate how to obtain and examine CentOS and Debian images that have already been built. In a later recipe, we are going to show how to start QEMU/KVM instances using those same images.

Getting ready

For this recipe, we are going to need QEMU installed on the host OS. For instructions on how to install QEMU, please refer to the *Installing and configuring QEMU* recipe from this chapter. We are also going to need the `wget` utility to download the images from the upstream public repositories.

How to do it...

To obtain Debian Wheezy images for use with QEMU and KVM, perform the following:

1. Download the image using `wget`:

```
root@kvm:~tmp# wget
https://people.debian.org/~aurel32/qemu/amd64/debian_wheezy_amd64_s
tandard.qcow2
--2017-03-09 22:07:20-- 2    Resolving people.debian.org
(people.debian.org)... 2001:41c8:1000:21::21:30, 5.153.231.30
Connecting to people.debian.org
(people.debian.org)|2001:41c8:1000:21::21:30|:443... connected.
HTTP request sent, awaiting response... 200 OK    Length: 267064832
(255M)    Saving to: 'debian_wheezy_amd64_standard.qcow2'
debian_wheezy_amd64_standard.qcow2 100% .
 [===================================>] 254.69M 35.8MB/s in 8.3s
2017-03-09 22:07:29 (30.9 MB/s) -
'debian_wheezy_amd64_standard.qcow2' saved [267064832/267064832]
root@kvm:~#
```

2. Inspect the type of the image:

```
root@kvm:~# qemu-img info debian_wheezy_amd64_standard.qcow2
image: debian_wheezy_amd64_standard.qcow2
file format: qcow2
virtual size: 25G (26843545600 bytes)
disk size: 261M
cluster_size: 65536
Format specific information:
compat: 1.1
lazy refcounts: false
refcount bits: 16
corrupt: false
root@kvm:~#
```

To download CentOS images run the following commands:

1. Download the image using wget:

```
root@kvm:/tmp# wget
https://cloud.centos.org/centos/7/images/CentOS-7-x86_64-GenericClo
ud.qcow2    --2017-03-09 22:11:34--
https://cloud.centos.org/centos/7/images/CentOS-7-x86_64-GenericClo
ud.qcow2    Resolving cloud.centos.org (cloud.centos.org)...
2604:4500::2a8a, 136.243.75.209    Connecting to cloud.centos.org
(cloud.centos.org)|2604:4500::2a8a|:443... connected.    HTTP
```

```
request sent, awaiting response... 200 OK    Length: 1361182720
(1.3G)    Saving to: 'CentOS-7-x86_64-GenericCloud.qcow2'
CentOS-7-x86_64-GenericCloud.qcow2
100%[========================================>] 1.27G 22.3MB/s in
54s
2017-03-09 22:12:29 (24.0 MB/s) - 'CentOS-7-x86_64-
GenericCloud.qcow2' saved [1361182720/1361182720]
FINISHED --2017-03-09 22:12:29--    Total wall clock time: 54s
Downloaded: 1 files, 1.3G in 54s (24.0 MB/s)
root@kvm:/tmp#
```

2. Inspect the type of the image:

```
root@kvm:~# qemu-img info CentOS-7-x86_64-GenericCloud.qcow2
image: CentOS-7-x86_64-GenericCloud.qcow2
file format: qcow2
virtual size: 8.0G (8589934592 bytes)
disk size: 1.3G
cluster_size: 65536
Format specific information:
compat: 0.10
refcount bits: 16
root@kvm:~#
```

How it works...

There are many public repositories on the Internet that provide images of various types, most commonly qcow2 for use with QEMU/KVM. In the previous section, we used the official CentOS repository to obtain the image and an another one containing prebuilt images for Debian.

Both images are in the qcow2 format, as we confirmed in step 2.

There's more...

So far, we've only seen how to build, examine, manipulate, and download images. In the next recipe, we are going to focus on how to actually use the images to start QEMU/KVM instances.

See also

Examine the following links to get more information about what prebuilt images are available for the listed distributions:

- Official Ubuntu images: `https://uec-images.ubuntu.com/releases/`
- Official CentOS images: `https://cloud.centos.org/centos/`
- Official Debian images: `http://cdimage.debian.org/cdimage/openstack/`
- Official Fedora images: `https://alt.fedoraproject.org/cloud/`
- Official openSUSE images: `http://download.opensuse.org/repositories/Cloud:/Images:/`

Running virtual machines with qemu-system-*

In this recipe, we are going to demonstrate how to start virtual machines with QEMU. QEMU provides binaries that can emulate different CPU architectures using either custom or prebuilt images for the guest OS.

If you completed the *Installing and configuring QEMU* recipe, you should have a host that contains the following binaries:

```
root@kvm:~# ls -la /usr/bin/qemu-system-*
-rwxr-xr-x 1 root root 8868848 Jan 25 12:49 /usr/bin/qemu-system-aarch64
-rwxr-xr-x 1 root root 7020544 Jan 25 12:49 /usr/bin/qemu-system-alpha
-rwxr-xr-x 1 root root 8700784 Jan 25 12:49 /usr/bin/qemu-system-arm
-rwxr-xr-x 1 root root 3671488 Jan 25 12:49 /usr/bin/qemu-system-cris
-rwxr-xr-x 1 root root 8363680 Jan 25 12:49 /usr/bin/qemu-system-i386
-rwxr-xr-x 1 root root 3636640 Jan 25 12:49 /usr/bin/qemu-system-lm32
-rwxr-xr-x 1 root root 6982528 Jan 25 12:49 /usr/bin/qemu-system-m68k
-rwxr-xr-x 1 root root 3652224 Jan 25 12:49 /usr/bin/qemu-system-microblaze
-rwxr-xr-x 1 root root 3652224 Jan 25 12:49 /usr/bin/qemu-system-microblazeel
-rwxr-xr-x 1 root root 8132992 Jan 25 12:49 /usr/bin/qemu-system-mips
-rwxr-xr-x 1 root root 8356672 Jan 25 12:49 /usr/bin/qemu-system-mips64
-rwxr-xr-x 1 root root 8374336 Jan 25 12:49 /usr/bin/qemu-system-mips64el
-rwxr-xr-x 1 root root 8128896 Jan 25 12:49 /usr/bin/qemu-system-mipsel
-rwxr-xr-x 1 root root 3578592 Jan 25 12:49 /usr/bin/qemu-system-moxie
-rwxr-xr-x 1 root root 3570848 Jan 25 12:49 /usr/bin/qemu-system-or32
-rwxr-xr-x 1 root root 8701760 Jan 25 12:49 /usr/bin/qemu-system-ppc
-rwxr-xr-x 1 root root 9048000 Jan 25 12:49 /usr/bin/qemu-system-ppc64
lrwxrwxrwx 1 root root 17 Jan 25 12:49 /usr/bin/qemu-system-ppc64le ->
```

```
qemu-system-ppc64
-rwxr-xr-x 1 root root 8463680 Jan 25 12:49 /usr/bin/qemu-system-ppcemb
-rwxr-xr-x 1 root root 6894528 Jan 25 12:49 /usr/bin/qemu-system-sh4
-rwxr-xr-x 1 root root 6898624 Jan 25 12:49 /usr/bin/qemu-system-sh4eb
-rwxr-xr-x 1 root root 4032000 Jan 25 12:49 /usr/bin/qemu-system-sparc
-rwxr-xr-x 1 root root 7201696 Jan 25 12:49 /usr/bin/qemu-system-sparc64
-rwxr-xr-x 1 root root 3704704 Jan 25 12:49 /usr/bin/qemu-system-tricore
-rwxr-xr-x 1 root root 3554912 Jan 25 12:49 /usr/bin/qemu-system-unicore32
-rwxr-xr-x 1 root root 8418656 Jan 25 12:49 /usr/bin/qemu-system-x86_64
-rwxr-xr-x 1 root root 3653024 Jan 25 12:49 /usr/bin/qemu-system-xtensa
-rwxr-xr-x 1 root root 3642752 Jan 25 12:49 /usr/bin/qemu-system-xtensaeb
root@kvm:~#
```

Each command can start a QEMU-emulated instance for the specific CPU architecture. For this recipe, we are going to be using the `qemu-system-x86_64` utility.

Getting ready

To complete this recipe, you will need the following:

- The QEMU binaries, provided after following the *Installing and configuring QEMU* recipe
- The custom raw Debian image we built in the *Installing a custom OS on the image with debootstrap* recipe
- The CentOS `qcow2` image we downloaded in the *Using pre-existing images* recipe

Let's have a look at what CPU architectures QEMU supports on the host system:

```
root@kvm:~# qemu-system-x86_64 --cpu help
x86 qemu64 QEMU Virtual CPU version 2.5+
x86 phenom AMD Phenom(tm) 9550 Quad-Core Processor
x86 core2duo Intel(R) Core(TM)2 Duo CPU T7700 @ 2.40GHz
x86 kvm64 Common KVM processor
x86 qemu32 QEMU Virtual CPU version 2.5+
x86 kvm32 Common 32-bit KVM processor
x86 coreduo Genuine Intel(R) CPU T2600 @ 2.16GHz
x86 486
x86 pentium
x86 pentium2
x86 pentium3
x86 athlon QEMU Virtual CPU version 2.5+
x86 n270 Intel(R) Atom(TM) CPU N270 @ 1.60GHz
x86 Conroe Intel Celeron_4x0 (Conroe/Merom Class Core 2)
x86 Penryn Intel Core 2 Duo P9xxx (Penryn Class Core 2)
x86 Nehalem Intel Core i7 9xx (Nehalem Class Core i7)
```

```
x86 Westmere Westmere E56xx/L56xx/X56xx (Nehalem-C)
x86 SandyBridge Intel Xeon E312xx (Sandy Bridge)
x86 IvyBridge Intel Xeon E3-12xx v2 (Ivy Bridge)
x86 Haswell-noTSX Intel Core Processor (Haswell, no TSX)
x86 Haswell Intel Core Processor (Haswell)
x86 Broadwell-noTSX Intel Core Processor (Broadwell, no TSX)
x86 Broadwell Intel Core Processor (Broadwell)
x86 Opteron_G1 AMD Opteron 240 (Gen 1 Class Opteron)
x86 Opteron_G2 AMD Opteron 22xx (Gen 2 Class Opteron)
x86 Opteron_G3 AMD Opteron 23xx (Gen 3 Class Opteron)
x86 Opteron_G4 AMD Opteron 62xx class CPU
x86 Opteron_G5 AMD Opteron 63xx class CPU
x86 host KVM processor with all supported host features (only available in
KVM mode)

Recognized CPUID flags:
fpu vme de pse tsc msr pae mce cx8 apic sep mtrr pge mca cmov pat pse36 pn
clflush ds acpi mmx fxsr sse sse2 ss ht tm ia64 pbe
pni|sse3 pclmulqdq|pclmuldq dtes64 monitor ds_cpl vmx smx est tm2 ssse3 cid
fma cx16 xtpr pdcm pcid dca sse4.1|sse4_1 sse4.2|sse4_2 x2apic movbe popcnt
tsc-deadline aes xsave osxsave avx f16c rdrand hypervisor
fsgsbase tsc_adjust bmi1 hle avx2 smep bmi2 erms invpcid rtm mpx avx512f
rdseed adx smap pcommit clflushopt clwb avx512pf avx512er avx512cd
syscall nx|xd mmxext fxsr_opt|ffxsr pdpe1gb rdtscp lm|i64 3dnowext 3dnow
lahf_lm cmp_legacy svm extapic cr8legacy abm sse4a misalignsse
3dnowprefetch osvw ibs xop skinit wdt lwp fma4 tce nodeid_msr tbm topoext
perfctr_core perfctr_nb
invtsc
xstore xstore-en xcrypt xcrypt-en ace2 ace2-en phe phe-en pmm pmm-en
kvmclock kvm_nopiodelay kvm_mmu kvmclock kvm_asyncpf kvm_steal_time
kvm_pv_eoi kvm_pv_unhalt kvmclock-stable-bit
npt lbrv svm_lock nrip_save tsc_scale vmcb_clean flushbyasid decodeassists
pause_filter pfthreshold
xsaveopt xsavec xgetbv1 xsaves
arat
root@kvm:~#
```

From the preceding output, we can see the list of CPUs that we can pass as parameters to
the -cpu flag in order to emulate that CPU type inside our virtual machine.

How to do it...

To start a new virtual machine using the `qemu-system` utility, perform the following steps:

1. Start a new QEMU virtual machine using the `x86_64` CPU architecture:

    ```
    root@kvm:~# qemu-system-x86_64 -name debian -vnc 146.20.141.254:0 -
    cpu Nehalem -m 1024 -drive     format=raw,index=2,file=debian.img -
    daemonize
    root@kvm:~#
    ```

2. Ensure that the instance is running:

    ```
    root@kvm:~# pgrep -lfa qemu
    3527 qemu-system-x86_64 -name debian -vnc 146.20.141.254:0 -m 1024
    -drive format=raw,index=2,file=debian.img -daemonize
    root@kvm:~#
    ```

3. Terminate the Debian QEMU instance:

    ```
    root@kvm:~# pkill qemu
    root@kvm:~#
    ```

4. Start a new QEMU instance using the prebuilt CentOS image:

    ```
    root@kvm:~# qemu-system-x86_64 -vnc 146.20.141.254:0 -m 1024 -hda
    CentOS-7-x86_64-GenericCloud.qcow2 -daemonize
    root@kvm:~#
    ```

5. Ensure that the instance is running:

    ```
    root@kvm:~# pgrep -lfa qemu
    3546 qemu-system-x86_64 -vnc 146.20.141.254:0 -m 1024 -hda
    CentOS-7-x86_64-GenericCloud.qcow2 -daemonize
    root@kvm:~#
    ```

6. Terminate the CentOS QEMU instance:

    ```
    root@kvm:~# pkill qemu
    root@kvm:~#
    ```

    > Make sure to replace the IP address of the `-vnc` parameter with the one from your host machine.

How it works...

How to start a virtual machine with QEMU/KVM depends greatly on the type of image and how the partitions are structured inside that image.

We used two different image types with different partitioning schemes to demonstrate this concept.

In step 1, we used the `qemu-system-x86_64` command to emulate a `x86_64` CPU architecture, specifically we passed the `-cpu Nehalem` flag, emulating the Nehalem CPU model. We passed the IP address of our host as a parameter to the `-vnc` flag. This starts a VNC server in the VM so that we can later use a VNC client to connect to the QEMU instance. We specified the amount of memory to be allocated to the instance, in this case, 1GB with the `-m` flag. We instructed QEMU that we are going to use a raw image with the `format=raw` option and the name and location of the actual image with the `file=debian.img` parameter.

Recall that this raw image contains two partitions with the second partition containing the root filesystem where the bootloader is located. This is very important to remember because we need to specify from what partition index the guest OS should load. We do that with the `index=2` flag. Finally, we pass the `-daemonize` parameter to background the QEMU process.

In step 4, we started another QEMU instance, this time using the `qcow2` CentOS image we downloaded earlier. We did not have to specify from what partition we need to boot from this this time because most prebuilt images use the first partition, or only have one partition. We also used the `-hda` flag instead of the `-drive` parameter, just to demonstrate that both options can be used with the same result. The `-hda` flag tells QEMU the first disk for the instance should be loaded from the filename that follows it.

Starting the QEMU VM with KVM support

In this recipe, we are going to start a QEMU virtual machine with KVM acceleration. **Kernel-based Virtual Machine (KVM)** is a full virtualization technology for CPU architectures that support virtualization extensions. For Intel-based processors, this is the Intel VT, and for AMD CPUS, it is the AMD-V hardware extension. The main parts of KVM are two loadable kernel modules, named `kvm.ko`, which provides the main virtualization functionality, and a second kernel module that is processor specific, `kvm-intel.ko` and `kvm-amd.ko` for both main CPU vendors.

QEMU is the userspace component to create virtual machines, where KVM resides in kernel space. If you completed the *Running virtual machines with qemu-system-** recipe, you might note that the difference between running a KVM virtual machine and running a nonaccelerated QEMU instance is just a single command-line option.

Getting ready

In order to start a KVM instance, you will need the following:

- The QEMU binaries, provided after following the *Installing and configuring QEMU* recipe
- The custom raw Debian image we built in the *Installing a custom OS on the image with debootstrap* recipe
- Processor that supports virtualization
- The KVM kernel modules

To check whether your CPU supports virtualization, run the following code:

```
root@kvm:~# cat /proc/cpuinfo | egrep "vmx|svm" | uniq
flags : fpu vme de pse tsc msr pae mce cx8 apic sep mtrr pge mca cmov pat
pse36 clflush dts acpi mmx fxsr sse sse2 ss ht tm pbe syscall nx pdpe1gb
rdtscp lm constant_tsc arch_perfmon pebs bts rep_good nopl xtopology
nonstop_tsc aperfmperf eagerfpu pni pclmulqdq dtes64 monitor ds_cpl vmx smx
est tm2 ssse3 sdbg fma cx16 xtpr pdcm pcid dca sse4_1 sse4_2 x2apic movbe
popcnt tsc_deadline_timer aes xsave avx f16c rdrand lahf_lm abm epb
tpr_shadow vnmi flexpriority ept vpid fsgsbase tsc_adjust bmi1 avx2 smep
bmi2 erms invpcid cqm xsaveopt cqm_llc cqm_occup_llc dtherm arat pln pts
root@kvm:~#
```

The presence of the `vmx` (for Intel) or `svm` (for AMD) flags indicate that your CPU supports the virtualization extensions.

> The flags from the `cpuinfo` command output simply mean that your processor supports virtualization; however, make sure that this feature is enabled in the BIOS of your system; otherwise, the KVM instance will fail to start.

To manually load the KVM kernel module and ensure that it's been loaded, run the following code:

```
root@kvm:~# modprobe kvm
root@kvm:~# lsmod | grep kvm
kvm                    455843  0
root@kvm:~#
```

How to do it...

To start a KVM instance, ensure that it's running and finally terminate it, execute the following:

1. Start a QEMU instance with KVM support:

    ```
    root@kvm:~# qemu-system-x86_64 -name debian -vnc 146.20.141.254:0 -
    m 1024 -drive format=raw,index=2,file=debian.img -enable-kvm -
    daemonize
    root@kvm:~#
    ```

2. Ensure that the instance is running:

    ```
    root@kvm:~# pgrep -lfa qemu
    4895 qemu-system-x86_64 -name debian -vnc 146.20.141.254:0 -m 1024
    -drive format=raw,index=2,file=debian.img -enable-kvm -daemonize
    root@kvm:~#
    ```

3. Terminate the instance:

    ```
    root@kvm:~# pkill qemu
    root@kvm:~#
    ```

How it works...

To start a QEMU/KVM virtual machine, all we had to do differently from what we performed in the *Installing and configuring QEMU* recipe is pass the `-enable-kvm` flag to the `qemu-system-x86_64` command.

In step 1, we specified a name for the VM with the −name flag, provided the IP address of our physical host to the −vnc flag, enabling VNC access for the virtual instance, allocated 1 GB of memory with the −m flag, specified the partition where the bootloader is located with the index=2 parameter, the image format, and name, and finally we enabled KVM hardware acceleration with the −enable−kvm parameter and deamonized the process with the −daemonize flag.

In step 2, we ensured that the instance is running and we terminated it in step 3.

There's more...

As an alternative to directly running the qemu−system−* commands, on Ubuntu systems there's the qemu−kvm package that provides the /usr/bin/kvm binary. This file is a wrapper to the qemu−system−x86_64 command, and it passes the −enable−kvm parameter to it automatically.

To install the package and use the kvm command instead, run the following:

```
root@kvm:~# apt install qemu-kvm
. . .
root@kvm:~# kvm −name debian −vnc 146.20.141.254:0 −cpu Nehalem −m 1024 −
drive format=raw,index=2,file=debian.img −daemonize
root@kvm:~# pgrep −lfa qemu
25343 qemu-system-x86_64 −enable-kvm −name debian −vnc 146.20.141.254:0 −
cpu Nehalem −m 1024 −drive format=raw,index=2,file=debian.img −daemonize
root@kvm:~#
```

You might have noted that starting and stopping QEMU/KVM instances is somewhat of a manual process, especially having to kill the instance process in order to stop it. In Chapter 2, *Using libvirt to Manage KVM*, we are going to walk you through a set of recipes that will make managing the life cycle of KVM virtual machines much easier, with the userspace tools that the libvirt package provides.

Connecting to a running instance with VNC

In this recipe, we are going to connect to a running KVM instance using a VNC client. Once connected, we are going to log in and check the CPU type and available memory of the instance. We've already seen how to start QEMU/KVM instances with VNC support in the previous recipes, but we are going to do it again, in case you are not reading this book from cover to cover.

Virtual Network Computing (**VNC**) uses the **Remote Frame Buffer** (**RFB**) protocol to remotely control another system. It relays the screen from the remote computer back to the client, allowing the full keyboard and mouse control.

There are many different VNC client and server implementations, but for this recipe, we are going to use a freely available version named chicken of the VNC for macOS. You can download the client from `https://sourceforge.net/projects/cotvnc/`.

Getting ready

In order to complete this recipe, you will need the following:

- The QEMU binaries, provided after following the *Installing and configuring QEMU* recipe
- The custom raw Debian image we built in the *Installing a custom OS on the image with debootstrap* recipe
- A processor that supports virtualization
- The loaded KVM kernel modules
- The chicken of the VNC client, installed, as described in the previous section

How to do it...

1. Start a new KVM-accelerated `qemu` instance:

```
root@kvm:~# qemu-system-x86_64 -name debian -vnc 146.20.141.254:0 -
cpu Nehalem -m 1024 -drive format=raw,index=2,file=debian.img -
daemonize
root@kvm:~#
```

2. Ensure that the instance is running:

```
root@kvm:~# pgrep -lfa qemu
4987 qemu-system-x86_64 -name debian -vnc 146.20.141.254:0 -cpu
Nehalem -m 1024 -drive format=raw,index=2,file=debian.img -
daemonize
root@kvm:~#
```

3. Start the VNC client and connect to the VNC server on the IP address and display port you specified in step 1:

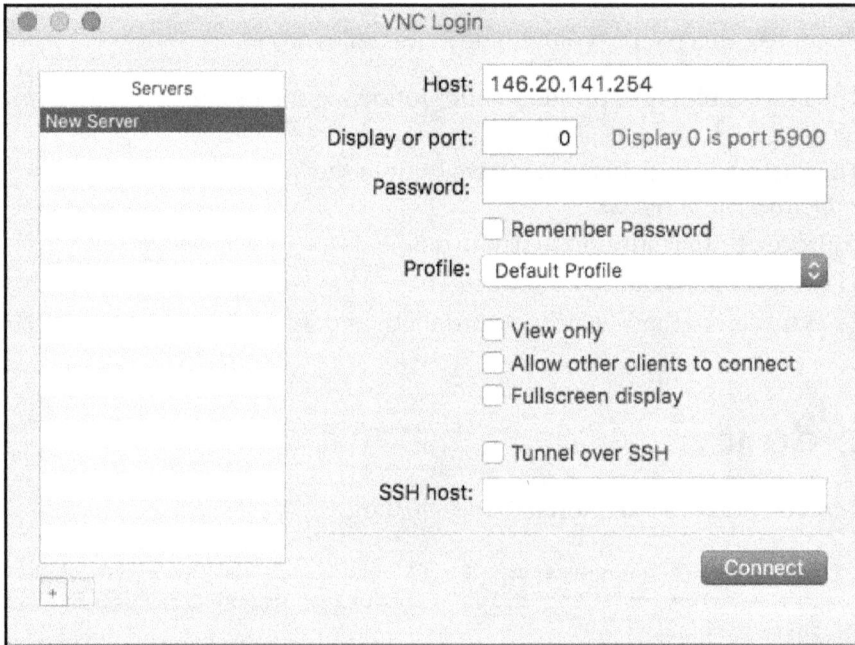

The VNC login screen

4. Log in to the instance using the root user, then check the CPU type and available memory as shown here:

```
● ● ●                                                    QEMU (debian)

Debian GNU/Linux 8 server-23 tty1

server-23 login: root
Password:
Last login: Fri Mar 10 15:05:26 UTC 2017 on tty1
Linux server-23 3.16.0-4-amd64 #1 SMP Debian 3.16.39-1 (2016-12-30) x86_64

The programs included with the Debian GNU/Linux system are free software;
the exact distribution terms for each program are described in the
individual files in /usr/share/doc/*/copyright.

Debian GNU/Linux comes with ABSOLUTELY NO WARRANTY, to the extent
permitted by applicable law.
root@server-23:~# lscpu
Architecture:          x86_64
CPU op-mode(s):        32-bit, 64-bit
Byte Order:            Little Endian
CPU(s):                1
On-line CPU(s) list:   0
Thread(s) per core:    1
Core(s) per socket:    1
Socket(s):             1
NUMA node(s):          1
Vendor ID:             GenuineIntel
CPU family:            6
Model:                 26
Model name:            Intel Core i7 9xx (Nehalem Class Core i7)
Stepping:              3
CPU MHz:               2593.788
BogoMIPS:              5187.57
L1d cache:             32K
L1i cache:             32K
L2 cache:              4096K
NUMA node0 CPU(s):     0
root@server-23:~# free -m
             total       used       free     shared    buffers     cached
Mem:          1000         59        941          4          5         27
-/+ buffers/cache:         26        973
Swap:            0          0          0
root@server-23:~# _
```

VNC session

How it works...

In step 1, we started a new QEMU instance with KVM acceleration and enabled a VNC server on it with the specified IP address and display port. We specified the amount of available memory and the CPU model name.

In step 4, we logged in the instance using the root user and the password we created when building the image, then obtained the CPU information by running the `lscpu` command. Note how the CPU model name matches what we specified with the `-cpu` flag when we started the virtual machine. Next, we checked the allocated memory with the `free` command, which also matches what we previously specified with the `-m` parameter.

2
Using libvirt to Manage KVM

In this chapter, we will cover the following topics:

- Installing and configuring libvirt
- Defining KVM instances
- Starting, stopping, and removing KVM instances
- Inspecting and editing KVM configs
- Building new KVM instances with virt-install and using the console
- Managing CPU and memory resources in KVM
- Attaching block devices to virtual machines
- Sharing directories between a running VM and the host OS
- Autostarting KVM instances
- Working with storage pools
- Managing volumes
- Managing secrets

Introduction

In the previous chapter, we saw examples of provisioning virtual machines using the QEMU toolset and the KVM kernel modules. The QEMU commands are convenient for quickly starting virtual instances; however, they don't provide an easy way of configuring and administering the life cycle of the virtual machines.

In this chapter, we are going to work with the libvirt toolset. Libivrt provides various userspace commands and language bindings in order to build, configure, start, stop, migrate, terminate, and do other functions to manage your virtual machines. It provides support for different virtualization technologies, such as QEMU/KVM, XEN, and containers with LXC.

We will start by installing and configuring the libvirt tools, then move on to creating virtual machines using the XML configuration files that libvirt supports and explore many of the functionalities that the toolkit provides in order to manage the life cycle of KVM instances. All the recipes in this chapter are going to be in the context of building highly available, multitenant environments.

Installing and configuring libvirt

In this recipe, we are going to install libvirt from packages provided by the Linux distribution of choice and see what configuration files and options are available for configuring it. As with any other production-ready tools, we recommend using packages for your production environment for ease and consistency of deployment; however, compiling the latest version from the source is also an option if the packages from your Linux vendor are older.

Getting ready

Depending on your Linux distribution, the package name and installation commands will differ. You can use your system's package manager, such as apt, dnf, or yum to search for any packages containing the libvirt string and get familiar with what is available for your particular Linux variant. The source code can be downloaded from the official libvirt project website at http://www.qemu-project.org/download/#source.

How to do it...

To install libvirt from packages and source follow the following steps:

1. On Ubuntu, install the package by running:

```
root@kvm:~# apt update && apt install libvirt-bin
root@kvm:~#
```

2. Ensure that the `libvirt` daemon is running by executing:

```
root@kvm:~# pgrep -lfa libvirtd
36667 /usr/sbin/libvirtd
root@kvm:~#
```

3. Examine the default configuration:

```
root@kvm:~# cat /etc/libvirt/libvirtd.conf | grep -vi "#"
  | sed '/^$/d'
  unix_sock_group = "libvirtd"
  unix_sock_ro_perms = "0777"
  unix_sock_rw_perms = "0770"
  auth_unix_ro = "none"
  auth_unix_rw = "none"
  root@kvm:~#
```

4. Disable the security driver in QEMU by editing the qemu configuration file as follows:

```
root@kvm:~# vim /etc/libvirt/qemu.conf
. . .
security_driver = "none"
. . .
root@kvm:~#
```

5. Restart the `libvirt` daemon:

```
root@kvm:~# /etc/init.d/libvirt-bin restart
libvirt-bin stop/waiting
libvirt-bin start/running, process 1158
root@kvm:~#
```

> Depending on your Linux distribution, the name of the `libvirt` service may be different. On RHEL/CentOS, the name of the service is `libvirtd`; to restart it, run `service libvirtd restart`.

6. Examine all configuration files in the `libvirt` directory:

```
root@kvm:~# ls -la /etc/libvirt/
total 76
drwxr-xr-x 5 root root 4096 Mar 22 14:27 .
drwxr-xr-x 90 root root 4096 Mar 21 23:17 ..
drwxr-xr-x 2 root root 4096 Feb 5 2016 hooks
-rw-r--r-- 1 root root 518 Feb 5 2016 libvirt.conf
-rw-r--r-- 1 root root 13527 Feb 5 2016 libvirtd.conf
```

```
-rw-r--r-- 1 root root 1176 Feb 5 2016 lxc.conf
drwxr-xr-x 2 root root 4096 Mar 21 23:16 nwfilter
drwxr-xr-x 3 root root 4096 Mar 21 23:57 qemu
-rw------- 1 root root 16953 Mar 21 23:18 qemu.conf
-rw-r--r-- 1 root root 2170 Feb 5 2016 qemu-lockd.conf
-rw-r--r-- 1 root root 2213 Feb 5 2016 virtlockd.conf
-rw-r--r-- 1 root root 1217 Feb 5 2016 virt-login-shell.conf
root@kvm:~#
```

How it works...

In step 1, we installed the package on Ubuntu. The postinstall script started the `libvirt` daemon after the package was successfully installed. We verified that in step 2.

In step 3, we examined the main configuration file for the service-side daemon - `libvirtd`. The process runs on the host OS and manages tasks for the virtual machines, such as configuration, life cycle management, migration, storage, and networking, as we are going to see later in this chapter. The userspace tools provided by the package we installed communicate with the daemon by sending requests on a local Unix domain socket. The default options we saw in step 3 are sufficient for the recipes in this chapter, but the configuration file is rather large. We encourage you to go through it and get familiar with the rest of the available configuration options. The file is very well documented.

In step 4, we disabled the security driver for QEMU. By default on RHEL/CentOS systems, QEMU is configured to use SELinux. Ubuntu distributions use **AppArmor**. For simplicity, we disable that functionality in this step; however, in production, you should take advantage of the extra security that a mandatory access control system such as SELinux provides.

Any change to the `libvirt` configuration file requires a restart. We restart the `libvirt` service in step 5.

There are few important configuration files that we need to be familiar, which are listed in step 6:

- `libvirt.conf` is the client-side configuration file for the `virsh` command that we are going to use in this recipe. We can specify URI aliases in it. The defaults should be sufficient.
- `libvirtd.conf` is the server-side configuration file, as we saw in step 3. It provides various security options, request limits, and logging controls. For the purpose of this book, the defaults are sufficient.

- `qemu.conf` is the main configuration file for the QEMU driver that `libvirt` uses. We can configure options such as the VNC server address, the security driver that we saw in step 4 and the user and group for the QEMU process.
- Once we create a QEMU/KVM virtual machine, the `/etc/libvirt/qemu/` directory will contain the XML configuration definition for that instance, as we are going to see in the following recipes.
- Finally, the `/etc/libvirt/qemu/networks/` directory contains configuration files for the networking. We are going to explore those in more detail later in this chapter.

Defining KVM instances

In this recipe, we are going to define a virtual instance by creating a simple XML configuration file that `libvirt` can use to build the virtual machine. We are going to describe some of the XML schema blocks and look at examples of how to generate the XML definition file using the `virt-install` command rather than writing it manually.

Getting ready

For this recipe, we are going to need the following:

- The QEMU binaries, provided after following the *Installing and configuring QEMU* recipe from `Chapter 1`, *Getting Started with QEMU and KVM*.
- The custom raw Debian image we built in the *Installing a custom OS on the image with debootstrap* recipe from the previous chapter.

> You can use your own virtual machine image or download one from the Internet, as we showed in the *Using pre-existing images* recipe in `Chapter 1`, *Getting Started with QEMU and KVM*.

How to do it...

To define a new KVM virtual machine, run the commands outlined here:

1. List all virtual machines on the host OS:

```
root@kvm:~# virsh list --all
 Id Name State
----------------------------------------------------

root@kvm:~#
```

2. Create the following XML definition file:

```
root@kvm:~# cat kvm1.xml
<domain type='kvm' id='1'>
 <name>kvm1</name>
 <memory unit='KiB'>1048576</memory>
 <vcpu placement='static'>1</vcpu>
 <os>
   <type arch='x86_64' machine='pc-i440fx-trusty'>hvm</type>
   <boot dev='hd'/>
 </os>
 <on_poweroff>destroy</on_poweroff>
 <on_reboot>restart</on_reboot>
 <on_crash>restart</on_crash>
 <devices>
   <emulator>/usr/bin/qemu-system-x86_64</emulator>
   <disk type='file' device='disk'>
     <driver name='qemu' type='raw'/>
     <source file='/tmp/debian.img'/>
     <target dev='hda' bus='ide'/>
     <alias name='ide0-0-0'/>
     <address type='drive' controller='0' bus='0' target='0'
unit='0'/>
   </disk>
   <interface type='network'>
     <source network='default'/>
     <target dev='vnet0'/>
     <model type='rtl8139'/>
     <alias name='net0'/>
     <address type='pci' domain='0x0000' bus='0x00' slot='0x03'
function='0x0'/>
   </interface>
   <graphics type='vnc' port='5900' autoport='yes'
listen='146.20.141.158'>
     <listen type='address' address='146.20.141.158'/>
   </graphics>
```

```
      </devices>
      <seclabel type='none'/>
    </domain>
    root@kvm:~#
```

3. Define the virtual machine:

```
    root@kvm:~# virsh define kvm1.xml
    Domain kvm1 defined from kvm1.xml

    root@kvm:~#
```

4. List all instances in all states:

```
    root@kvm:~# virsh list --all
     Id Name State
    ----------------------------------------------------------
     - kvm1 shut off

    root@kvm:~#
```

How it works...

In step 1, we used the virsh command and supplied all argument to list all active and inactive instances. As expected, we started with no instances defined.

In step 2, we created a definition file for a new KVM instance. We used a small subsection of the available XML schema attributes to set the following options:

- The root element of the XML file is required for all virtual machine definitions and is named **domain**. It has two attributes--type and id. We specified kvm as the type and an id as 1 because this is our first KVM virtual machine. All other attributes are defined under the domain root element.
- We specified a name for the instance with the name attribute.
- The memory attribute defines the available memory to the VM, in our case, 1 GB.
- The vcpu element defines the maximum number of virtual CPUs allocated for the guest OS. We specified 1, and we used the optional attribute placement that indicates the CPU placement mode; in this example, static. Static placement indicates that the virtual instance will be pinned to all the available physical CPUs.

- The OS element defines the architecture of the VM with the use of the type element. The `hvm` option indicates that we are going to use full virtualization, which is going to be KVM, as specified in the domain type attribute we saw earlier. We specify the boot device the VM will start from with the `<boot dev>` element.
- The next three elements specify the action to be taken when the guest requests a power off, reboot or it crashes. In our example, the VM will be destroyed when the guest OS is powered off and restarted when the guest reboots or crashes.
- The largest section of the XML definition is the devices section, where we use various XML elements to describe devices provided to the guest OS. The emulator element specifies the path to the emulator binary. We are going to use the same QEMU emulator binary `qemu-system-x86_64` we used in Chapter 1, *Getting Started with QEMU and KVM*. In the last few sections of the devices attribute, we define the type of virtual disk we are using, in this example, the raw image we built in the previous chapter. In a similar fashion, we describe the VNC server that the guest should start and the network interface inside the guest OS.

With the `config` file in place, we defined the instance in step 3, using the image we created earlier in `/tmp`.

Once a new instance has been defined, it does not automatically start by default. We can see that the status of the new instance is `shut off` in step 4.

> For information on all of the available XML elements and their attributes, please refer to the official documentation at `http://libvirt.org/format domain.html`.

There's more...

Configuring a virtual machine by writing the XML file, can be quite tedious and error-prone. An easier way of creating the VM from an existing image, or from an installation media (which can be physical, virtual, or a network location), is using the `virt-install` tool. Lets see an example of creating the same KVM instance using that tool.

1. We start by installing the package:

```
root@kvm:~# apt install virtinst
...
root@kvm:~#
```

2. Next, we define and start the new instance by invoking the `virt-install` command (if an instance with the same name already exist, you'll need to destroy and undefine it first):

```
root@kvm:~# virt-install --name kvm1 --ram 1024 --disk
path=/tmp/debian.img,format=raw --graphics
vnc,listen=146.20.141.158 --noautoconsole --hvm --import

Starting install...
Creating domain... | 0 B 00:00
Domain creation completed. You can restart your domain by running:
 virsh --connect qemu:///system start kvm1
root@kvm:~#
```

3. The new VM has now been defined and started. To confirm, execute:

```
root@kvm:~# virsh list --all
 Id Name State
----------------------------------------------------------
 10 kvm1 running

root@kvm:~#
```

4. We can see the virtual machine definition file that was automatically generated by running the following code:

```
root@kvm:~# cat /etc/libvirt/qemu/kvm1.xml
<!--
WARNING: THIS IS AN AUTO-GENERATED FILE. CHANGES TO IT ARE LIKELY
TO BE
OVERWRITTEN AND LOST. Changes to this xml configuration should be
made using:
 virsh edit kvm1
or other application using the libvirt API.
-->

<domain type='kvm'>
 <name>kvm1</name>
 <uuid>c3892cbf-812a-2448-7ad2-098ea8381066</uuid>
 <memory unit='KiB'>1048576</memory>
 <currentMemory unit='KiB'>1048576</currentMemory>
 <vcpu placement='static'>1</vcpu>
 <os>
    <type arch='x86_64' machine='pc-i440fx-trusty'>hvm</type>
    <boot dev='hd'/>
 </os>
 <features>
```

```
        <acpi/>
        <apic/>
        <pae/>
   </features>
   <clock offset='utc'/>
   <on_poweroff>destroy</on_poweroff>
   <on_reboot>restart</on_reboot>
   <on_crash>restart</on_crash>
   <devices>
     <emulator>/usr/bin/qemu-system-x86_64</emulator>
     <disk type='file' device='disk'>
       <driver name='qemu' type='raw'/>
       <source file='/tmp/debian.img'/>
       <target dev='hda' bus='ide'/>
       <address type='drive' controller='0' bus='0' target='0'
unit='0'/>
     </disk>
     <controller type='usb' index='0'>
       <address type='pci' domain='0x0000' bus='0x00' slot='0x01'
function='0x2'/>
     </controller>
     <controller type='pci' index='0' model='pci-root'/>
     <controller type='ide' index='0'>
       <address type='pci' domain='0x0000' bus='0x00' slot='0x01'
function='0x1'/>
     </controller>
     <interface type='network'>
       <mac address='52:54:00:59:e3:4e'/>
       <source network='default'/>
       <model type='rtl8139'/>
       <address type='pci' domain='0x0000' bus='0x00' slot='0x03'
function='0x0'/>
     </interface>
     <serial type='pty'>
       <target port='0'/>
     </serial>
     <console type='pty'>
       <target type='serial' port='0'/>
     </console>
     <input type='mouse' bus='ps2'/>
     <input type='keyboard' bus='ps2'/>
     <graphics type='vnc' port='-1' autoport='yes'
listen='146.20.141.158'>
       <listen type='address' address='146.20.141.158'/>
     </graphics>
     <video>
       <model type='cirrus' vram='9216' heads='1'/>
       <address type='pci' domain='0x0000' bus='0x00' slot='0x02'
```

```
function='0x0'/>
   </video>
   <memballoon model='virtio'>
     <address type='pci' domain='0x0000' bus='0x00' slot='0x04'
function='0x0'/>
   </memballoon>
 </devices>
</domain>
root@kvm:~#
```

Starting, stopping, and removing KVM instances

In the previous recipe, we saw how to define new KVM virtual machine by either manually writing the XML definition file or using the `virt-install` tool to define the instance for us.

If you define a new instance from an XML file, by default the instance will not start automatically. In this recipe, we will see how to start an instance that was previously configured.

Getting ready

For this recipe, we are going to need the following:

- The QEMU binaries, provided after following the *Installing and configuring QEMU* recipe from `Chapter 1`, *Getting Started with QEMU and KVM*.
- The custom raw Debian image we built in the *Installing a custom OS on the image with debootstrap* recipe from the previous chapter.
- The virsh tool provided by completing the *Installing and configuring libvirt* recipe.
- The defined instance from the *Defining KVM instances* recipe in a `shut off` state.

How to do it...

The following steps outline the process of listing, starting, and stopping KVM instances using the `virsh` command:

1. List all instances in all states:

```
root@kvm:~# virsh list --all
 Id Name State
----------------------------------------------------------
 - kvm1 shut off
root@kvm:~#
```

2. Start the newly defined instance and verify its status:

```
root@kvm:~# virsh start kvm1
Domain kvm1 started

root@kvm:~#
root@kvm:~# virsh list --all
 Id Name State
----------------------------------------------------------
 1 kvm1 running

root@kvm:~#
```

3. Examine the running process for the virtual machine:

```
root@kvm:~# pgrep -lfa qemu
1686 /usr/bin/qemu-system-x86_64 -name kvm1 -S -machine pc-i440fx-
trusty,accel=kvm,usb=off -m 1024 -realtime mlock=off -smp
1,sockets=1,cores=1,threads=1 -uuid a9dfd1a1-7dd1-098e-a926-
db9526785a9e -no-user-config -nodefaults -chardev
socket,id=charmonitor,path=/var/lib/libvirt/qemu/kvm1.monitor,serve
r,nowait -mon chardev=charmonitor,id=monitor,mode=control -rtc
base=utc -no-shutdown -boot strict=on -device piix3-usb-
uhci,id=usb,bus=pci.0,addr=0x1.0x2 -drive
file=/tmp/debian.img,if=none,id=drive-ide0-0-0,format=raw -device
ide-hd,bus=ide.0,unit=0,drive=drive-
ide0-0-0,id=ide0-0-0,bootindex=1 -netdev tap,fd=24,id=hostnet0 -
device
rtl8139,netdev=hostnet0,id=net0,mac=52:54:00:ce:dd:f2,bus=pci.0,add
r=0x3 -chardev pty,id=charserial0 -device isa-
serial,chardev=charserial0,id=serial0 -vnc 146.20.141.158:0 -device
cirrus-vga,id=video0,bus=pci.0,addr=0x2 -device virtio-balloon-
pci,id=balloon0,bus=pci.0,addr=0x4
root@kvm:~#
```

4. Terminate the VM and ensure its status changed from running to `shut off`:

```
root@kvm:~# virsh destroy kvm1
Domain kvm1 destroyed

root@kvm:~# virsh list --all
 Id Name State
----------------------------------------------------
 - kvm1 shut off

root@kvm:~#
```

5. Remove the instance definition:

```
root@kvm:~# virsh undefine kvm1
Domain kvm1 has been undefined

root@kvm:~# virsh list --all
 Id Name State
----------------------------------------------------

root@kvm:~#
```

How it works...

In step 1, we list all defined instances, regardless of their state. From the output, we can see that we currently have one instance that we defined in the earlier recipe.

In step 2, we started the virtual machine and ensured its status had changed to running.

If you completed the *Running Virtual Machines with qemu-system-** recipe from Chapter 1, *Getting Started with QEMU and KVM*, you might note that the XML definition for this VM is very similar to all the command-line options we used to start the QEMU instance. We can see the similarities of how the new instance was started in step 3. The main difference is the larger number of parameters that `libvirt` passed to the QEMU executable.

Finally, in steps 4 and 5, we stopped the VM and removed its definition file. The raw image we used for the VM is still available however and can be used again.

Inspecting and editing KVM configs

In this recipe, we are going to use the `virsh` tool to inspect and edit the configuration for an existing virtual machine. As we saw earlier, once we define and start a KVM instance, `libvirt` creates the XML definition file in the `/etc/libvirt/qemu/` directory. We can dump the guest configuration to disk, for inspection, or to back it up. With the `virsh` command we can also perform updates to the configuration in place, as we will see later in this recipe.

Getting ready

For this recipe, we are going to need the following:

- The QEMU binaries, provided after following the *Installing and configuring QEMU* recipe from Chapter 1, *Getting Started with QEMU and KVM*
- The custom raw Debian image we built in the *Installing custom OS on the image with debootstrap* recipe from the previous chapter, or any other virtual machine image, in either `raw` or `qcow2` format
- The `virsh` tool provided by completing the *Installing and configuring libvirt* recipe
- A running `libvirt` KVM instance

How to do it...

The following steps outline the process of inspecting and editing the XML definition of a KVM instance:

1. Ensure that you have a running KVM instance with libvirt, if not, follow the steps in the previous recipe:

```
root@kvm:~# virsh list
 Id Name State
----------------------------------------------------------
 11 kvm1 running

root@kvm:~#
```

2. Dump the instance configuration file to **standard output** (**stdout**). For more information on stdout refer to folllowing link:

```
https://en.wikipedia.org/wiki/Standard_streams
```

```
root@kvm:~# virsh dumpxml kvm1
<domain type='kvm' id='11'>
 <name>kvm1</name>
 <uuid>9eb9a2e9-abb2-54c5-5cb3-dc86728e70fc</uuid>
 <memory unit='KiB'>1048576</memory>
 <currentMemory unit='KiB'>1048576</currentMemory>
 <vcpu placement='static'>1</vcpu>
 <resource>
   <partition>/machine</partition>
 </resource>
 <os>
   <type arch='x86_64' machine='pc-i440fx-trusty'>hvm</type>
   <boot dev='hd'/>
 </os>
 <features>
   <acpi/>
   <apic/>
 <pae/>
 </features>
 <clock offset='utc'/>
 <on_poweroff>destroy</on_poweroff>
 <on_reboot>restart</on_reboot>
 <on_crash>restart</on_crash>
 <devices>
   <emulator>/usr/bin/qemu-system-x86_64</emulator>
   <disk type='file' device='disk'>
     <driver name='qemu' type='raw'/>
     <source file='/tmp/debian.img'/>
     <target dev='hda' bus='ide'/>
     <alias name='ide0-0-0'/>
     <address type='drive' controller='0' bus='0' target-'0'
unit='0'/>
   </disk>
   <controller type='usb' index='0'>
     <alias name='usb0'/>
     <address type='pci' domain='0x0000' bus='0x00' slot='0x01'
function='0x2'/>
   </controller>
   <controller type='pci' index='0' model='pci-root'>
     <alias name='pci.0'/>
   </controller>
   <controller type='ide' index='0'>
     <alias name='ide0'/>
```

```
        <address type='pci' domain='0x0000' bus='0x00' slot='0x01'
function='0x1'/>
    </controller>
    <interface type='network'>
      <mac address='52:54:00:d1:70:df'/>
      <source network='default'/>
      <target dev='vnet0'/>
      <model type='rt18139'/>
     <alias name='net0'/>
      <address type='pci' domain='0x0000' bus='0x00' slot='0x03'
function='0x0'/>
    </interface>
    <serial type='pty'>
      <source path='/dev/pts/0'/>
      <target port='0'/>
      <alias name='serial0'/>
    </serial>
    <console type='pty' tty='/dev/pts/0'>
      <source path='/dev/pts/0'/>
      <target type='serial' port='0'/>
      <alias name='serial0'/>
    </console>
    <input type='mouse' bus='ps2'/>
    <input type='keyboard' bus='ps2'/>
    <graphics type='vnc' port='5900' autoport='yes'
listen='146.20.141.158'>
      <listen type='address' address='146.20.141.158'/>
    </graphics>
    <video>
      <model type='cirrus' vram='9216' heads='1'/>
      <alias name='video0'/>
      <address type='pci' domain='0x0000' bus='0x00' slot='0x02'
function='0x0'/>
    </video>
    <memballoon model='virtio'>
      <alias name='balloon0'/>
      <address type='pci' domain='0x0000' bus='0x00' slot='0x04'
function='0x0'/>
    </memballoon>
  </devices>
  <seclabel type='none'/>
</domain>

root@kvm:~#
```

3. Save the configuration to a new file, as follows:

```
root@kvm:~# virsh dumpxml kvm1 > kvm1.xml
root@kvm:~# head kvm1.xml
<domain type='kvm' id='11'>
 <name>kvm1</name>
 <uuid>9eb9a2e9-abb2-54c5-5cb3-dc86728e70fc</uuid>
 <memory unit='KiB'>1048576</memory>
 <currentMemory unit='KiB'>1048576</currentMemory>
 <vcpu placement='static'>1</vcpu>
 <resource>
   <partition>/machine</partition>
 </resource>
 <os>
root@kvm:~#
```

4. Edit the configuration in place and change the available memory for the VM:

```
root@kvm:~# virsh edit kvm1
Domain kvm1 XML configuration edited.

root@kvm:~#
```

How it works...

Libvirt provides two main ways to manipulate the configuration definitions of the virtual instances. We can either dump the config from an existing instance, as we did in steps 2 and 3, or edit the XML definition in place, as we did in step 4.

Saving the current configuration to a file is a convenient way to back up the VM definition. It also provides a way of defining a new instance by editing the saved file and just changing the name and ID of the virtual machine. We can then use that file to start a new VM on the same, or a different host, assuming that the filesystem or image is also available. We are going to see examples of migrating and backing up virtual machines with libvirt in later recipes.

When making changes in place, as shown in step 4, the default system $EDITOR will be used. Once in the editing mode, note that the XML file contains information about the current state of the virtual instance. The `<uuid>` and `<currentMemory>` attributes are such examples. If you would like to change the available memory for the VM, after updating the `<memory>` attribute, you might need to delete the `<currentMemory>` stanza. If there are any issues with the edit, libvirt will complain with an error message and present the following options:

```
root@kvm:~# virsh edit kvm1
error: XML error: current memory '1048576k' exceeds maximum '524288k'
Failed. Try again? [y,n,f,?]:n
Domain kvm1 XML configuration not changed.
root@kvm:~#
```

Also keep in mind that, if you would like to create a new instance from the dump of an existing one, you will need to change the `<name>` and delete the `<uuid>` attributes, as the latter will be autogenerated once the new instance has been defined.

Building new KVM instances with virt-install and using the console

In the *Connecting to the running instance with VNC* recipe from Chapter 1, *Getting Started with QEMU and KVM,* you learned how to connect to a QEMU/KVM virtual machine that was running a VNC server. This is a great way to connect to an instance that is being installed or in the process of booting in order to interact with it.

So far, we've used the custom raw image that we created earlier, which contains an installation of Debian. Recall from Chapter 1, *Getting Started with QEMU and KVM,* that we used the `debootstrap` command to install the OS inside the image file. In this recipe, we are going to use the `virt-install` tool to install a new Linux distribution, using the provided upstream Internet repository, as the source of the installation and then use the `virsh` command to attach to the running instance, using the console.

Getting ready

For this recipe, we are going to need the following:

- The `virsh` command
- The `virt-install` command
- Internet connectivity in order to download the installation files

How to do it...

To build a new KVM instance and connect to it using the console, perform the following steps:

1. Install a new KVM virtual machine using the official Debian repository:

```
root@kvm:~# virt-install --name kvm1 --ram 1024 --extra-args="text
console=tty0 utf8 console=ttyS0,115200" --graphics
vnc,listen=146.20.141.158 --hvm --
location=http://ftp.us.debian.org/debian/dists/stable/main/installe
r-amd64/ --disk path=/tmp/kvm1.img,size=8

Retrieving file MANIFEST... | 3.3 kB 00:00 ...
Retrieving file linux... | 6.0 MB 00:00 ...
Retrieving file initrd.gz... | 29 MB 00:00 ...
Creating storage file kvm1.img | 8.0 GB 00:00
WARNING Unable to connect to graphical console: virt-viewer not
installed. Please install the 'virt-viewer' package.
Domain installation still in progress. You can reconnect to
the console to complete the installation process.
root@kvm:~#
```

2. Attach to the console to complete the installation by running the following code:

```
root@kvm:~# virsh console kvm1
Connected to domain kvm1
Escape character is ^]
```

3. Once connected to the console, you should be presented with a screen similar to the one here:

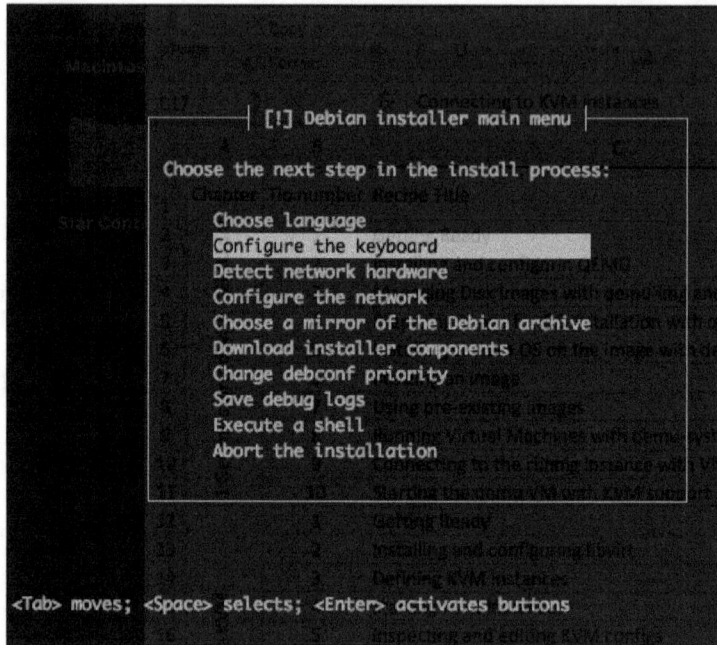

The console output once connected with the virsh console command

4. Complete the installation by following the text menu prompts.
5. Start the newly provisioned VM:

```
root@kvm:~# virsh start kvm1
Domain kvm1 started

root@kvm:~#
```

6. Using your favorite VNC client, connect to the instance, log in with the username and password you created during the installation process in step 3 and enable the serial console access by running the following command:

```
root@debian:~# systemctl enable serial-getty@ttyS0.service
root@debian:~# systemctl start serial-getty@ttyS0.service
root@debian:~#
```

7. Close the VNC session and connect to the virtual instance from the host OS, using `virsh`:

```
root@kvm:~# virsh console kvm1
Connected to domain kvm1
Escape character is ^]

Debian GNU/Linux 8 debian ttyS0

debian login: root
Password:
Last login: Wed Mar 22 16:38:10 CDT 2017 on tty1
Linux debian 3.16.0-4-amd64 #1 SMP Debian 3.16.39-1+deb8u2
(2017-03-07) x86_64

The programs included with the Debian GNU/Linux system are free
software;
the exact distribution terms for each program are described in the
individual files in /usr/share/doc/*/copyright.

Debian GNU/Linux comes with ABSOLUTELY NO WARRANTY, to the extent
permitted by applicable law.
root@debian:~# free -m
 total used free shared buffers cached
Mem: 1000 98 902 4 9 43
-/+ buffers/cache: 44 956
Swap: 382 0 382
root@debian:~#
```

8. Disconnect from the console using the *Ctrl +]* key combination.

9. Examine the `image` file created after the installation:

```
root@kvm:~# qemu-img info /tmp/kvm1.img
image: /tmp/kvm1.img
file format: raw
virtual size: 8.0G (8589934592 bytes)
disk size: 1.9G
root@kvm:~#
```

> If you are not using systemd-based `init` system on the distribution for the KVM machine, in order to allow access to the serial console of the instance, you will need to edit the `/etc/securetty` or the `/etc/inittab` files.

How it works...

A lot happened in this recipe, so lets go through all the steps in more detail.

In step 1, we started the installation process for a new KVM instance using the `virt-install` utility. We specified the serial console to be enabled during the installation process with the `--extra-args` parameter. We also used the `--location` flag to tell `libvirt` the location of the installation files for the latest Debian distribution. We then specified the location and size of the image file that will contain the guest OS filesystem. Since this file did not exist, `virt-install` created it as a raw image, as shown in step 9.

With console access enabled for the installation, we were able to connect to the console in step 2 and complete the installation process in steps 3 and 4.

After the installation completed, the console session was terminated and the new KVM instance ready to be started. We started the instance in step 5.

In order to enable console access on the serial port, we first connected to the running VM using a VNC client and instruct systemd to started the console service in step 6.

With console access enabled, we were able to connect to the serial console using the virsh tool in step 7.

With all this completed, we now have two ways of connecting to a running KVM instance using either VNC or the console.

In the later recipe, we will enable networking in the guest OS and provide a third way to connect using SSH.

Managing CPU and memory resources in KVM

Changing the amount of allocated memory or the number of CPUs can be done either by editing the XML definition for the VM or using the `libvirt` toolset. In this recipe, we are going to look at examples of changing both the memory and the CPU count for a KVM instance.

Getting ready

For this recipe, we are going to need the following:

- A running KVM instance with 1 GB of memory, 1 CPU allocated, and console access
- The `libvirt` package
- A guest OS with at least 4 GB of available memory and minimum of 4 CPUs

How to do it...

To inspect and update the memory and CPU resources assigned to a virtual machine follow the process outlined here:

1. Get memory statistics for the running instance:

```
root@kvm:~# virsh dommemstat kvm1
actual 1048576
swap_in 0
rss 333644

root@kvm:~#
```

2. Update the available memory for the VM to 2 GB:

```
root@kvm:~# virsh setmem kvm1 --size 1049000

root@kvm:~#
```

3. Stop the running instance:

```
root@kvm:~# virsh destroy kvm1
Domain kvm1 destroyed

root@kvm:~#
```

4. Set the maximum usable memory to 2 GB:

```
root@kvm:~# virsh setmaxmem kvm1 --size 2097152

root@kvm:~#
```

5. Start the instance:

```
root@kvm:~# virsh start kvm1
Domain kvm1 started

root@kvm:~#
```

6. Check the current allocated memory:

```
root@kvm:~# virsh dommemstat kvm1
actual 2097152
swap_in 0
rss 214408

root@kvm:~#
```

7. Connect to the KVM instance and check the memory in the guest OS:

```
root@kvm:~# virsh console kvm1
Connected to domain kvm1
Escape character is ^]

Debian GNU/Linux 8 debian ttyS0

debian login: root
Password:
. . .
root@debian:~# free -m
               total used  free  shared  buffers cached
Mem:            2010    93  1917       5        8     40
-/+ buffers/cache:    43 1966
Swap:            382     0  3 82
root@debian:~#
root@kvm:~#
```

8. Check the memory settings in the instance XML definition:

```
root@kvm:~# virsh dumpxml kvm1 | grep memory
  <memory unit='KiB'>2097152</memory>
root@kvm:~#
```

9. Get information about the guest CPUs:

```
root@kvm:~# virsh vcpuinfo kvm1
VCPU: 0
CPU: 29
State: running
CPU time: 9.7s
```

```
CPU Affinity:  yyyyyyyyyyyyyyyyyyyyyyyyyyyyyyyyyyyyyyyyyyyyyy

root@kvm:~#
```

10. List the number of virtual CPUs used by the guest OS:

```
root@kvm:~# virsh vcpucount kvm1
maximum config 1
maximum live 1
current config 1
current live 1

root@kvm:~#
```

11. Change the number of allocated CPUs to 4 for the VM:

```
root@kvm:~# virsh edit kvm1
. . .
<vcpu placement='static'>4</vcpu>
. . .
Domain kvm1 XML configuration edited.

root@kvm:~#
```

12. Ensure that the CPU count update took effect:

```
root@kvm:~# virsh vcpucount kvm1
maximum config 4
maximum live 4
current config 4
current live 4

root@kvm:~# virsh dumpxml kvm1 | grep -i cpu
 <vcpu placement='static'>4</vcpu>
root@kvm:~#
```

How it works...

In step 1, we gathered some memory statistics for the running KVM instance. From the output, we can see that the VM is configured with 1 GB of memory indicated by the actual parameter, and it's currently using 333644 KB of memory.

In step 2, we updated the available memory to 2 GB and then proceeded to update the maximum memory that can be allocated to the instance in step 4. In order to perform that operation, the instance had to be stopped first, as shown in step 3.

In steps 6, 7, and 8, we made sure that the updates took place by first invoking the `dommemstat` subcommand, then connected to the VMs console and finally checked the current configuration by dumping the instance definition.

The `virsh` command provides few subcommands to inspect the CPU state for a running VM. In steps 9 and 10, we listed the allocated virtual CPUs for the `kvm1` instance, in this case, just one and the current state, load, and affinity.

Finally, in steps 11 and 12, we update the XML definition of the instance, allocating four CPUs and listed the new count.

There's more...

In this recipe, we used the `virsh` command with various subcommands in one liners. This is particularly useful if we need to run the commands from a script. The `virsh` command also provides an interactive terminal, which saves some typing, and provides contextual help. To start the virtualization-interactive terminal, run the following code:

```
root@kvm:~# virsh
Welcome to virsh, the virtualization interactive terminal.

Type: 'help' for help with commands
 'quit' to quit

virsh #
```

Typing `help` will list all available subcommands with a short description. To obtain more information for a particular subcommand type:

```
virsh # help vcpucount
  NAME
    vcpucount - domain vcpu counts

  SYNOPSIS
    vcpucount <domain> [--maximum] [--active] [--live] [--config] [--
current] [--guest]

  DESCRIPTION
    Returns the number of virtual CPUs used by the domain.
```

```
OPTIONS
  [--domain] <string> domain name, id or uuid
  --maximum get maximum count of vcpus
  --active get number of currently active vcpus
  --live get value from running domain
  --config get value to be used on next boot
  --current get value according to current domain state
  --guest retrieve vcpu count from the guest instead of the hypervisor

virsh #
```

All the steps we performed in this recipe can be done in the interactive terminal.

Attaching block devices to virtual machines

In this recipe, we are going to examine a few different ways of adding new block devices to a KVM instance. The new block device can then be partitioned, formatted, and used as a regular block device inside the guest OS. We can add disks to live running instances, or we can attach them persistently by creating XML definitions for the individual block devices offline. From the host OS, we can present any type of block device file to the guest, including iSCSI targets, LVM logical volumes, or image files.

Getting ready

For this recipe, we will need:

- A running KVM instance with console access
- The dd utility

How to do it...

To attach a new block device to a KVM guest, run the following:

1. Create a new 1 GB image file:

```
root@kvm:~# dd if=/dev/zero of=/tmp/new_disk.img bs=1M count=1024
1024+0 records in
1024+0 records out
1073741824 bytes (1.1 GB) copied, 0.670831 s, 1.6 GB/s
root@kvm:~#
```

2. Attach the file as a new disk to the KVM instance:

```
root@kvm:~# virsh attach-disk kvm1 /tmp/new_disk.img vda --live
Disk attached successfully

root@kvm:~#
```

3. Connect to the KVM instance via the console:

```
root@kvm:~# virsh console kvm1
Connected to domain kvm1
Escape character is ^]

Debian GNU/Linux 8 debian ttyS0

debian login: root
Password:
...
root@debian:~#
```

4. Print the kernel ring buffer and check for the new block device:

```
root@debian:~# dmesg | grep vda
[ 3664.134978] sd 2:0:2:0: [vda] 2097152 512-byte logical blocks:
(1.07 GB/1.00 GiB)
[ 3664.135248] sd 2:0:2:0: [vda] Write Protect is off
[ 3664.135251] sd 2:0:2:0: [vda] Mode Sense: 63 00 00 08
[ 3664.135340] sd 2:0:2:0: [vda] Write cache: enabled, read cache:
enabled, doesn't support DPO or FUA
[ 3664.138254] vda: unknown partition table
[ 3664.139008] sd 2:0:2:0: [vda] Attached SCSI disk
root@debian:~#
```

5. Examine the new block device:

```
root@debian:~# fdisk -l /dev/vda

Disk /dev/vda: 1 GiB, 1073741824 bytes, 2097152 sectors
Units: sectors of 1 * 512 = 512 bytes
Sector size (logical/physical): 512 bytes / 512 bytes
I/O size (minimum/optimal): 512 bytes / 512 bytes
root@debian:~#
```

6. Dump the instance configuration from the host OS:

```
root@kvm:~# virsh dumpxml kvm1
<domain type='kvm' id='23'>
...
 <devices>
   <emulator>/usr/bin/qemu-system-x86_64</emulator>
   <disk type='file' device='disk'>
     <driver name='qemu' type='raw'/>
     <source file='/tmp/kvm1.img'/>
     <target dev='hda' bus='ide'/>
     <alias name='ide0-0-0'/>
     <address type='drive' controller='0' bus='0' target='0'
unit='0'/>
   </disk>
   <disk type='file' device='disk'>
     <driver name='qemu' type='raw'/>
     <source file='/tmp/new_disk.img'/>
     <target dev='vda' bus='scsi'/>
     <alias name='scsi0-0-2'/>
     <address type='drive' controller='0' bus='0' target='0'
unit='2'/>
   </disk>
 </devices>
</domain>

root@kvm:~#
```

7. Get information about the new disk:

```
root@kvm:~# virsh domblkstat kvm1 vda
vda rd_req 119
vda rd_bytes 487424
vda wr_req 0
vda wr_bytes 0
vda flush_operations 0
vda rd_total_times 29149092
vda wr_total_times 0
vda flush_total_times 0

root@kvm:~#
```

8. Detach the disk:

```
root@kvm:~# virsh detach-disk kvm1 vda --live
Disk detached successfully

root@kvm:~#
```

9. Copy or create a new raw image:

```
root@kvm:~# cp /tmp/new_disk.img /tmp/other_disk.img
root@kvm:~#
```

10. Write the following `config` file:

```
root@kvm:~# cat other_disk.xml
<disk type='file' device='disk'>
 <driver name='qemu' type='raw' cache='none'/>
 <source file='/tmp/other_disk.img'/>
 <target dev='vdb'/>
</disk>
root@kvm:~#
```

11. Attach the new device:

```
root@kvm:~# virsh attach-device kvm1 --live other_disk.xml
Device attached successfully

root@kvm:~#
```

12. Detach the block device:

```
root@kvm:~# virsh detach-device kvm1 other_disk.xml --live
Device detached successfully

root@kvm:~#
```

How it works...

Attaching more disks to running KVM instances can be quite useful, especially when using LVM inside the guest OS, as this allows for extending the logical volumes, thus adding more disk space on the go. Libvirt provides two different methods for this as we saw in the steps outlined earlier. We can use the `virsh attach-disk` command by passing the location of the image file and the name of the new block device for the guest VM as we saw in step 2.

In step 1, we created a new raw image using the `dd` command; however, we could have used the qemu-img tool as we saw in the *Managing Disk images with qemu-img* and dd recipe from `Chapter 1`, *Getting Started with QEMU and KVM*.

After attaching the new disk in step 2, in steps 3, 4, and 5, we connected to VM and verified that a new block device is indeed present. This is also reflected in the XML definition of the instance in step 6.

> To make the new device available after a VM restart and persist the XML definition changes, pass the `--persist` option to the `virsh attach-disk` command.

In step 7, we display some information about the new disk. This data is quite useful in order to monitor the read/write requests for the block device, without having to attach to the virtual instance.

In step 8, we detached the disk from the running KVM instance. If you dump the instance definition at this point, you will note the absence of the extra disk.

An alternative way of attaching a block device is shown in step 10. We first create a new XML file with the definition of the block device we are attaching. Note how similar the definition is to the output in step 6.

In step 11, we detach the new device yet again. Note that we have to specify the same device XML definition file in order to do that.

Once the disk is visible inside the guest OS, we can use it as a regular block device, we can partition it, create a filesystem, and mount it.

Sharing directories between a running VM and the host OS

In the previous recipe, we saw two examples on how to attach disks to a running KVM instance. In this recipe, we are going to share a directory from the host OS and make it available in the virtual machine. We can only perform this action on a stopped instance however. If you've been following along, you should already have a libvirt KVM instance that you can use.

Getting ready

The prerequisites for this recipe are as follows:

- Stopped libvirt KVM instance with console access
- A guest OS with the `9p` and `virtio` kernel modules (available on most Linux distributions by default)

How to do it...

To share a directory from the host OS to the KVM guest, execute the following:

1. Create a new directory on the host OS and add a file to it:

```
root@kvm:~# mkdir /tmp/shared
root@kvm:~# touch /tmp/shared/file
root@kvm:~#
```

2. Add the following definition to the stopped KVM instance:

```
root@kvm:~# virsh edit kvm1
  ...
  <devices>
    ...
    <filesystem type='mount' accessmode='passthrough'>
      <source dir='/tmp/shared'/>
      <target dir='tmp_shared'/>
    </filesystem>
    ...
  </devices>
  ...
Domain kvm1 XML configuration edited.

root@kvm:~#
```

3. Start the VM:

```
root@kvm:~# virsh start kvm1
Domain kvm1 started

root@kvm:~#
```

4. Connect to the console as follows:

```
root@kvm:~# virsh console kvm1
Connected to domain kvm1
Escape character is ^]

Debian GNU/Linux 8 debian ttyS0

debian login: root
Password:
...
root@debian:~#
```

5. Ensure that the 9p and the virtio kernel modules are loaded:

```
root@debian:~# lsmod | grep 9p
9pnet_virtio 17006 0
9pnet 61632 1 9pnet_virtio
virtio_ring 17513 3 virtio_pci,virtio_balloon,9pnet_virtio
virtio 13058 3 virtio_pci,virtio_balloon,9pnet_virtio
root@debian:~#
```

6. Mount the shared directory to /mnt:

```
root@debian:~# mount -t 9p -o trans=virtio tmp_shared /mnt
root@debian:~#
```

7. List the new mount:

```
root@debian:~# mount | grep tmp_shared
tmp_shared on /mnt type 9p (rw,relatime,sync,dirsync,trans=virtio)
root@debian:~#
```

8. Ensure that the shared file is visible in the host OS:

```
root@debian:~# ls -la /mnt/
total 8
drwxr-xr-x 2  root root 4096 Mar 23 11:25 .
drwxr-xr-x 22 root root 4096 Mar 22 16:28 ..
-rw-r--r-- 1  root root 0    Mar 23 11:25 file
root@debian:~#
```

How it works...

Let's get through the steps and see what was accomplished in more details in the previous section.

In step 1, we create a directory and a file that we want to share with the guest OS. Then, on the stopped KVM instance, we added the new `<filesystem>` definition in step 2. We used the mount type because we are mounting a directory and specified the `accessmode`, which specifies the security mode for accessing the shared resource. There are three access modes:

- `passthrough`: This is the default mode, which accesses the shared directory using the permissions of the user inside the guest OS
- `mapped`: In this mode, the shared directory and its files are accessed using the permissions of the QEMU user, inherited from the host
- `squash`: This mode is similar to the passthrough mode; however, the failures of privileged operations such as `chmod` are ignored

With the new definition in place, we start the VM in step 3 and connect to it in step 4.

On the Debian virtual machine we have been using, the required kernel module has been loaded when the VM started. If this is not the case for your VM, load the modules by running:

```
root@debian:~# modprobe 9p virtio
root@debian:~#
```

The main action happens in step 6, where we mount the shared directory and ensure that it has been successfully mounted and the file present in the subsequent steps.

There's more...

In this chapter, we have been starting KVM virtual machines using the `virsh` command, provided by the `libvirt` toolset and libraries. If you check the process tree after starting a guest, you can see that `virsh` command actually calls the `/usr/bin/qemu-system-x86_64` binary. If you recall from the *Running virtual machines with qemu-system-** recipe in `Chapter 1`, *Getting Started with QEMU and KVM;* this is exactly what we used to start QEMU/KVM virtual machines.

Note the process that the `libvirt` daemon started when we ran started the KVM instance in this recipe:

```
root@kvm:~# pgrep -lfa qemu
6233 /usr/bin/qemu-system-x86_64 -name kvm1 -S -machine pc-i440fx-
trusty,accel=kvm,usb=off -m 2048 -realtime mlock=off -smp
2,sockets=2,cores=1,threads=1 -uuid 6ad84d8a-229d-d1f6-ecfc-d29a25fcfa03 -
no-user-config -nodefaults -chardev
socket,id=charmonitor,path=/var/lib/libvirt/qemu/kvm1.monitor,server,nowait
-mon chardev=charmonitor,id=monitor,mode=control -rtc base=utc -no-shutdown
-boot strict=on -device piix3-usb-uhci,id=usb,bus=pci.0,addr=0x1.0x2 -
device lsi,id=scsi0,bus=pci.0,addr=0x5 -drive
file=/tmp/kvm1.img,if=none,id=drive-ide0-0-0,format=raw -device ide-
hd,bus=ide.0,unit=0,drive=drive-ide0-0-0,id=ide0-0-0,bootindex=1 -fsdev
local,security_model=passthrough,id=fsdev-fs0,path=/tmp/shared -device
virtio-9p-pci,id=fs0,fsdev=fsdev-
fs0,mount_tag=tmp_shared,bus=pci.0,addr=0x6 -netdev tap,fd=25,id=hostnet0 -
device
rtl8139,netdev=hostnet0,id=net0,mac=52:54:00:c5:c8:9d,bus=pci.0,addr=0x3 -
chardev pty,id=charserial0 -device isa-
serial,chardev=charserial0,id=serial0 -vnc 146.20.141.158:0 -device cirrus-
vga,id=video0,bus=pci.0,addr=0x2 -device virtio-balloon-
pci,id=balloon0,bus=pci.0,addr=0x4
root@kvm:~#
```

Instead of using libvirt, we can start a new guest OS with the same shared directory we use in this recipe, by just running the following, just make sure to stop the `libvirt` instance we started earlier first:

```
root@kvm:~# qemu-system-x86_64 -name debian -fsdev
local,id=tmp,path=/tmp/shared,security_model=passthrough -device virtio-9p-
pci,fsdev=tmp,mount_tag=tmp_shared -enable-kvm -usbdevice tablet -vnc
146.20.141.158:0 -m 1024 -drive format=raw,file=/tmp/kvm1.img -daemonize
root@kvm:~#
```

You should be able to use your VNC client to connect to the guest and perform the same steps to mount the shared directory, as we did earlier.

Autostarting KVM instances

Once a KVM instance has been defined and started, it will run until the host OS is up. Once the host OS restarts, instances build with libvirt will not automatically start once the host is up and the `libvirt` daemon is running. In this recipe, we are going to change this behavior and ensure virtual instance start when the `libvirt` daemon starts.

Getting ready

For this recipe, we are going to need a single KVM instance build with libvirt.

How to do it...

To configure a KVM guest to automatically start after a server, or `libvirtd` restart, run the following:

1. Enable the VM `autostart`:

   ```
   root@kvm:~# virsh autostart kvm1
   Domain kvm1 marked as autostarted

   root@kvm:~#
   ```

2. Obtain information for the instance:

   ```
   root@kvm:~# virsh dominfo kvm1
   Id: 31
   Name: kvm1
   UUID: 6ad84d8a-229d-d1f6-ecfc-d29a25fcfa03
   OS Type: hvm
   State: running
   CPU(s): 2
   CPU time: 10.9s
   Max memory: 2097152 KiB
   Used memory: 1048576 KiB
   Persistent: yes
   Autostart: enable
   Managed save: no
   Security model: none
   Security DOI: 0

   root@kvm:~#
   ```

3. Stop the running instance and ensure that it is in the `shut off` state:

   ```
   root@kvm:~# virsh destroy kvm1
   Domain kvm1 destroyed

   root@kvm:~# virsh list --all
    Id  Name   State
   ----------------------------------------------------
    -    kvm1   shut off
   ```

```
root@kvm:~#
```

4. Stop the `libvirt` daemon and ensure that it is not running:

```
root@kvm:~# /etc/init.d/libvirt-bin stop
libvirt-bin stop/waiting
root@kvm:~# pgrep -lfa libvirtd
root@kvm:~#
```

5. Start back the `libvirt` daemon:

```
root@kvm:~# /etc/init.d/libvirt-bin start
libvirt-bin start/running, process 6639
root@kvm:~#
```

6. List all running instances:

```
root@kvm:~# virsh list --all
 Id Name State
----------------------------------------------------
 2  kvm1 running

root@kvm:~#
```

7. Disable the `autostart` option:

```
root@kvm:~# virsh autostart kvm1 --disable
Domain kvm1 unmarked as autostarted

root@kvm:~#
```

8. Verify the change:

```
root@kvm:~# virsh dominfo kvm1 | grep -i autostart
Autostart: disable
root@kvm:~#
```

How it works...

In this simple recipe, we enabled the `autostart` feature of a libvirt controlled KVM instance.

In step 1, we enabled `autostart` and verified that it has been enabled in step 2.

Next, to simulate a server restart, we first stop the running instance in step 3 and the `libvirt` daemon in step 4.

In step 5, we started the `libvirt` daemon back and observe that it started the virtual machine as well, as seen in step 6.

Finally, in steps 7 and 8, we disable the `autostart` feature and ensure that it indeed has been disabled.

Working with storage pools

Libvirt provides a centralized way of managing instance volumes (being image files or directories) by defining storage pools. A storage pool is a collection of volumes that then can be assigned to virtual machines and used to host their filesystems or added as additional block devices. The main benefits of using storage pools is the ability for libvirt to present and manage the given storage type to VMs in a centralized way.

As of this writing, the following storage pool backends are available:

- Directory backend
- Local filesystem backend
- Network filesystem backend
- Logical backend
- Disk backend
- iSCSI backend
- SCSI backend
- Multipath backend
- RADOS block device backend
- Sheepdog backend
- Gluster backend
- ZFS backend
- Virtuozzo storage backend

In this recipe, we are going to create a directory-backed storage pool, move an existing image to it, and then provision a new KVM instance using the storage pool and volume.

Getting ready

For this recipe, we are going to need the following:

- The Debian raw image we created in the *Building new KVM instances with virt-install and using the console* recipe
- The `libvirt` package

How to do it...

The following steps demonstrate how to create a new storage pool, inspect it, and assign it to a virtual machine:

1. Copy the raw Debian image file we created in the *Building new KVM instances with virt-install and using the console* recipe earlier in this chapter:

```
root@kvm:~# cp /tmp/kvm1.img /var/lib/libvirt/images/
root@kvm:~#
```

2. Create the following storage pool definition:

```
root@kvm:~# cat file_storage_pool.xml
<pool type="dir">
 <name>file_virtimages</name>
 <target>
   <path>/var/lib/libvirt/images</path>
 </target>
</pool>
root@kvm:~#
```

3. Define the new storage pool:

```
root@kvm:~# virsh pool-define file_storage_pool.xml
Pool file_virtimages defined from file_storage_pool.xml

root@kvm:~#
```

4. List all storage pools:

```
root@kvm:~# virsh pool-list --all
 Name             State    Autostart
-------------------------------------------------
 file_virtimages inactive no

root@kvm:~#
```

5. Start the new storage pool and ensure that it's active:

```
root@kvm:~# virsh pool-start file_virtimages
Pool file_virtimages started

root@kvm:~# virsh pool-list --all
 Name              State   Autostart
-------------------------------------------
 file_virtimages active no

root@kvm:~#
```

6. Enable the `autostart` feature on the storage pool:

```
root@kvm:~# virsh pool-autostart file_virtimages
Pool file_virtimages marked as autostarted

root@kvm:~# virsh pool-list --all
 Name              State   Autostart
-------------------------------------------
 file_virtimages active yes

root@kvm:~#
```

7. Obtain more information about the storage pool:

```
root@kvm:~# virsh pool-info file_virtimages
Name: file_virtimages
UUID: d51d500b-8885-4c26-8000-2ae46ffe9018
State: running
Persistent: yes
Autostart: yes
Capacity: 219.87 GiB
Allocation: 7.99 GiB
Available: 211.88 GiB

root@kvm:~#
```

8. List all volumes that are a part of the storage pool:

```
root@kvm:~# virsh vol-list file_virtimages
 Name     Path
-----------------------------------------------------------
 kvm1.img /var/lib/libvirt/images/kvm1.img

root@kvm:~#
```

9. Obtain information on the volume:

```
root@kvm:~# virsh vol-info /var/lib/libvirt/images/kvm1.img
Name: kvm1.img
Type: file
Capacity: 8.00 GiB
Allocation: 1.87 GiB

root@kvm:~#
```

10. Start new KVM instance using the storage pool and volume, then ensure that it's running:

```
root@kvm:~# virt-install --name kvm1 --ram 1024 --graphics
vnc,listen=146.20.141.158 --hvm --disk vol=file_virtimages/kvm1.img
--import

Starting install...
Creating domain... | 0 B 00:00
Domain creation completed. You can restart your domain by running:
 virsh --connect qemu:///system start kvm1
root@kvm:~#

root@kvm:~# virsh list --all
 Id Name State
----------------------------------------------------------
 3  kvm1 running

root@kvm:~#
```

How it works...

We start this recipe with an image of a Debian OS that we installed earlier in the book; however, you can use an empty, raw, or qcow2 image, add it to the storage pool, and install the virtual machine OS on it with almost no changes to the recipe steps if you don't have that image already.

In step 1, we copy the VM image to the default libvirt storage pool location in /var/lib/libvirt/images/, but you can create your own directory, the location does not matter as long as it's defined in the storage pool configuration file. We do that in step 2.

In step 3, we define the new storage pool, by specifying a name, target directory, and the type of the pool, in this case, a directory backend pool. We then proceed to list the new pool in step 4. Note that, once defined, we still need to start it, just like defining a new KVM instance from an XML file. By default, the `autostart` option is not enabled on a new storage pool.

In step 5, we start the storage pool and ensure that it's active. We then proceed to enable the `autostart` feature so that the volumes can be used in case the host server restarts in step 6.

Although not mandatory, we check the metadata provided for the storage pool and its volumes in step 7. Note that the allocation field shows how much space is used by the volumes in the pool. We currently have a single raw image with that exact size.

In step 8, we list all volumes that are a part of the new storage pool and obtain further information about the single volume in step 9.

Finally in step 10, we start a new KVM instance using the storage pool and volume by passing the storage pool and volume names to the vol disk type.

There's more...

Let's look at a slightly more complicated example of using storage pools by defining an iSCSI-backed pool.

Creating an iSCSI target and logging it on the initiator server is beyond the scope of this recipe, so we assume that you have an iSCSI target ready to be used from a remote server. The new storage pool definition is as follows:

```
<pool type='iscsi'>
 <name>iscsi_virtimages</name>
 <source>
   <host name='iscsi-target.linux-admins.net'/>
   <device path='iqn.2004-04.ubuntu:ubuntu16:iscsi.libvirtkvm'/>
 </source>
 <target>
   <path>/dev/disk/by-path</path>
 </target>
</pool>
```

The file is very similar to the directory-backed storage pool, the main difference are the following attributes:

- The `<host>` attribute specifies the hostname of the iSCSI target server that is exporting the iSCSI LUN
- The `<device>` specifies the name of the iSCSI LUN we are going to log in
- Once a new iSCSI block device has been logged in, it will appear in the location specified in `<path>`, on most Linux distributions in the `/dev/disk/by-path` directory

We define and start the new storage pool the same way we did in steps 3 and 5 earlier in the recipe. Once the storage pool is active, libvirt will log the remote iSCSI target LUNs. We can list the available iSCSI volumes as usual:

```
root@kvm:~# virsh vol-list iscsi_virtimages
Name Path
---------------------------------------------
10.0.0.1 /dev/disk/by-path/ip-10.184.226.106:3260-iscsi-
iqn.2004-04.ubuntu:ubuntu16:iscsi.libvirtkvm-lun-1
root@kvm:~#
```

To start a new installation process using the iSCSI volume as the target for the guest OS filesystem, run the following code:

```
root@kvm:~# virt-install --name kvm1 --ram 1024 --extra-args="text
console=tty0 utf8 console=ttyS0,115200" --graphics
vnc,listen=146.20.141.158 --hvm --
location=http://ftp.us.debian.org/debian/dists/stable/main/installer-amd64/
--disk vol=iscsi_virtimages/10.0.0.1
Starting install...
...
root@kvm:~#
```

> For more information about the XML definition of the other backend types, please refer to `https://libvirt.org/storage.html`.

Managing volumes

In the previous recipe, we saw how to create new storage pools, add a volume to it, and create a new KVM instance using that volume. In this recipe, we are going to focus on manipulating volumes that are a part of an existing storage pool. Strictly speaking, we are not required to use storage pools and volumes in order to build VMs. We can use other tools to manage and manipulate the virtual instance images, such as the qemu-img utility. Using volumes is just a convenience for having a centralized storage repository of various backend types.

Getting ready

The main requirement of this recipe is to have an existing storage pool with the directory backend. If you skipped the previous recipe, now is that time to create a new one, as we'll be using it to manipulate volumes.

How to do it...

To create, inspect and assign volumes to an instance, run the following:

1. List the available storage pools:

```
root@kvm:~# virsh pool-list --all
 Name              State   Autostart
-------------------------------------------------
 file_virtimages  active  yes

root@kvm:~#
```

2. List the available volumes, that are a part of the storage pool:

```
root@kvm:~# virsh vol-list file_virtimages
 Name      Path
---------------------------------------------------------------------------
-
 kvm1.img /var/lib/libvirt/images/kvm1.img

root@kvm:~#
```

3. Create a new volume with the specified size:

```
root@kvm:~# virsh vol-create-as file_virtimages new_volume.img 9G
Vol new_volume.img created

root@kvm:~#
```

4. List the volumes on the filesystem:

```
root@kvm:~# ls -lah /var/lib/libvirt/images/
total 11G
drwx--x--x 2 root root 4.0K Mar 23 20:38 .
drwxr-xr-x 8 root root 4.0K Mar 21 23:16 ..
-rwxr-xr-x 1 libvirt-qemu kvm 8.0G Mar 23 20:23 kvm1.img
-rw------- 1 root root 9.0G Mar 23 20:38 new_volume.img
root@kvm:~#
```

5. Obtain information about the new volume:

```
root@kvm:~# qemu-img info /var/lib/libvirt/images/new_volume.img
image: /var/lib/libvirt/images/new_volume.img
file format: raw
virtual size: 9.0G (9663676416 bytes)
disk size: 9.0G
root@kvm:~#
```

6. Use the `virsh` command to get even more information:

```
root@kvm:~# virsh vol-info new_volume.img --pool file_virtimages
Name: new_volume.img
Type: file
Capacity: 9.00 GiB
Allocation: 9.00 GiB

root@kvm:~#
```

7. Dump the volume configuration:

```
root@kvm:~# virsh vol-dumpxml new_volume.img --pool file_virtimages
<volume type='file'>
  <name>new_volume.img</name>
  <key>/var/lib/libvirt/images/new_volume.img</key>
  <source>
  </source>
  <capacity unit='bytes'>9663676416</capacity>
  <allocation unit='bytes'>9663680512</allocation>
  <target>
    <path>/var/lib/libvirt/images/new_volume.img</path>
```

```
        <format type='raw'/>
        <permissions>
          <mode>0600</mode>
          <owner>0</owner>
          <group>0</group>
        </permissions>
        <timestamps>
          <atime>1490301514.446004048</atime>
          <mtime>1490301483.698003615</mtime>
          <ctime>1490301483.702003615</ctime>
        </timestamps>
     </target>
   </volume>

root@kvm:~#
```

8. Resize the volume and display the new size:

```
root@kvm:~# virsh vol-resize new_volume.img 10G --pool
file_virtimages
Size of volume 'new_volume.img' successfully changed to 10G

root@kvm:~# virsh vol-info new_volume.img --pool file_virtimages
Name: new_volume.img
Type: file
Capacity: 10.00 GiB
Allocation: 9.00 GiB

root@kvm:~#
```

9. Delete the volume and list all available volumes in the storage pool:

```
root@kvm:~# virsh vol-delete new_volume.img --pool file_virtimages
Vol new_volume.img deleted

root@kvm:~# virsh vol-list file_virtimages
 Name       Path
-------------------------------------------------------------------
 kvm1.img /var/lib/libvirt/images/kvm1.img

root@kvm:~#
```

10. Clone the existing volume:

```
root@kvm:~# virsh vol-clone kvm1.img kvm2.img --pool
file_virtimages
Vol kvm2.img cloned from kvm1.img
```

```
root@kvm:~# virsh vol-list file_virtimages
 Name      Path
-------------------------------------------------------------------
-
 kvm1.img /var/lib/libvirt/images/kvm1.img
 kvm2.img /var/lib/libvirt/images/kvm2.img

root@kvm:~#
```

How it works...

We start this recipe with the `file_virtimages` storage pool we created in the previous recipe. We list all storage pools in step 1 to confirm that. In step 2, we see that our storage pool contains a single volume. No surprises here as we created that in the last recipe in this chapter.

In step 3, we create a new volume, by specifying its name, size, and the storage pool we want it to be a part of. Since this is a directory-backed storage pool, we can see the volume as a raw image file in step 4.

In steps 5 and 6, we collect more information about the new volume. We can see that it is a raw, therefore by default a sparse image. Sparse images don't allocate all of the disk space and grow as more data is being written to it.

In step 7, we dump the definition of the volume. We can use that to define a new volume later on with the `virsh vol-create` command.

Libvirt provides a convenient way to resize existing images. This is what we do in step 8-- we resize the image to 10 GB. We can now see that the allocation size is smaller than the capacity; this is because the image is raw.

Finally, in step 9, we delete the image, though we could have used it to install a new virtual machine, as shown in the *Working with storage pools* recipe.

In the last step, we use the existing Debian image and created a clone volume from it. Starting a virtual machine using the cloned volume will result in an identical KVM instance, as the one we cloned the volume from. This combined with a dump of the instance definition is a great way to backup your KVM instances, as long as you store the volume image file and the XML definition file to a remote location. We are going to explore backing up KVM instances in later recipes.

Managing secrets

Libvirt provides an API to create, store, and use secrets. Secrets are objects that contain sensitive information such as passwords, that can be associated with different volume backend types. Recall from the *Working with storage pools* recipe, which we created an iSCSI pool and volume from a remote iSCSI target and used it as the image for a KVM guest. In production environments, more often than not iSCSI targets are presented with CHAP authentication. In this recipe, we are going to create a secret to be used with an iSCSI volume.

Getting ready

For this recipe, we are going to need the following:

- A storage pool with an iSCSI-backed volume
- The `libvirt` package

How to do it...

To define and list secrets with libvirt, perform the steps outlined here:

1. List all available secrets:

```
root@kvm:~# virsh secret-list
 UUID Usage
-------------------------------------------------------------------
root@kvm:~#
```

2. Create the following secrets definition:

```
root@kvm:~# cat volume_secret.xml
<secret ephemeral='no'>
 <description>Passphrase for the iSCSI iscsi-target.linux-
admins.net target server</description>
 <usage type='iscsi'>
   <target>iscsi_secret</target>
 </usage>
</secret>
root@kvm:~#
```

3. Create the secret and ensure that it has been successfully created:

```
root@kvm:~# virsh secret-define volume_secret.xml
Secret 7ad1c208-c2c5-4723-8dc5-e2f4f576101a created

root@kvm:~# virsh secret-list
 UUID                                        Usage
--------------------------------------------------------------------
 7ad1c208-c2c5-4723-8dc5-e2f4f576101a iscsi iscsi_secret

root@kvm:~#
```

4. Set a value for the secret:

```
root@kvm:~# virsh secret-set-value 7ad1c208-c2c5-4723-8dc5-
e2f4f576101a $(echo "some_password" | base64)
Secret value set

root@kvm:~#
```

5. Create a new iSCSI pool definition file:

```
root@kvm:~# cat iscsi.xml
<pool type='iscsi'>
 <name>iscsi_virtimages</name>
 <source>
   <host name='iscsi-target.linux-admins.net'/>
   <device path='iqn.2004-04.ubuntu:ubuntu16:iscsi.libvirtkvm'/>
   <auth type='chap' username='iscsi_user'>
     <secret usage='iscsi_secret'/>
   </auth>
 </source>
 <target>
   <path>/dev/disk/by-path</path>
 </target>
</pool>
root@kvm:~#
```

How it works...

In step 1, we list all available secrets that libvirt knows about. Since we haven't created any, the list is empty.

In step 2, we create the XML definition of the secret. The XML elements that we use to define the secret are:

- The `<secret>` root element, with an optional `ephemeral` attribute, telling `libvirt` that the password should only be stored in memory, if set to yes.
- The `<description>` attribute containing an arbitrary description.
- The `<usage>` element specifies what the secrets is going to be used for and its type. In this example, the `type` attribute is set to iSCSI. The other available types are `volume`, `ceph`, and `tls`. The `type` attribute is mandatory.
- The `<target>` element that specifies an arbitrary name is to be used in the iSCSI pool definition.

With the configuration file in place, we create the secret in step 3. If the operation is successful, libvirt returns an UUID that identifies the secret.

In step 4, we set a value for the secret, by base64 encoding the `some_password` string, which is the password for the iSCSI target we would like to use, as a storage pool volume.

And finally in step 5, we add the `<auth>` attribute under the `<source>` section of the iSCSI pool definition. Note that the secret we would like the iSCSI volume to use is specified in the `<secret usage='iscsi_secret'/>` attribute. Libvirt can now use the `iscsi_secret` name to locate the actual password that it has stored.

3
KVM Networking with libvirt

In this chapter, we are going to cover the following topics:

- The Linux bridge
- The Open vSwitch
- Configuring NAT forwarding network
- Configuring bridged network
- Configuring PCI passthrough network
- Manipulating network interfaces

Introduction

With libvirt, we can define different network types for our KVM guests, using the already familiar XML definition syntax and the `virsh` and `virt-install` userspace tools. In this chapter, we are going to deploy three different network types, explore the network XML format, and see examples on how to define and manipulate virtual interfaces for the KVM instances.

To be able to connect the virtual machines to the host OS or to each other, we are going to use the Linux bridge and the **Open vSwitch** (**OVS**) daemons, userspace tools, and kernel modules. Both software bridging technologies are great at creating **Software-defined Networking** (**SDN**) of various complexity, in a consistent and easy-to-manipulate manner. The Linux bridge and OVS both act as a bridge/switch that the virtual interfaces of the KVM guests can connect to.

With all this in mind, let's start by learning more about the software bridges in Linux.

The Linux bridge

The Linux bridge is a software layer 2 device that provides some of the functionality of a physical bridge device. It can forward frames between KVM guests, the host OS, and virtual machines running on other servers, or networks. The Linux bridge consists of two components--a userspace administration tool that we are going to use in this recipe and a kernel module that performs all the work of connecting multiple Ethernet segments together. Each software bridge we create can have a number of ports attached to it, where network traffic is forwarded to and from. When creating KVM instances, we can attach the virtual interfaces that are associated with them to the bridge, which is similar to plugging a network cable from a physical server's NIC to a bridge/switch device. Being a layer 2 device, the Linux bridge works with MAC addresses and maintains a kernel structure to keep track of ports and associated MAC addresses in the form of a **Content Addressable Memory (CAM)** table.

In this recipe, we are going to create a new Linux bridge and use the `brctl` utility to manipulate it.

Getting ready

For this recipe, we are going to need the following:

- Recent Linux kernel with enabled `802.1d Ethernet` bridging options

  To check whether your kernel is compiled with those features or exposed as kernel modules, run the following command:

  ```
  root@kvm:~# cat /boot/config-`uname -r` | grep -i bridg
  # PC-card bridges
  CONFIG_BRIDGE_NETFILTER=y
  CONFIG_NF_TABLES_BRIDGE=m
  CONFIG_BRIDGE_NF_EBTABLES=m
  CONFIG_BRIDGE_EBT_BROUTE=m
  CONFIG_BRIDGE_EBT_T_FILTER=m
  CONFIG_BRIDGE_EBT_T_NAT=m
  CONFIG_BRIDGE_EBT_802_3=m
  CONFIG_BRIDGE_EBT_AMONG=m
  CONFIG_BRIDGE_EBT_ARP=m
  CONFIG_BRIDGE_EBT_IP=m
  CONFIG_BRIDGE_EBT_IP6=m
  CONFIG_BRIDGE_EBT_LIMIT=m
  CONFIG_BRIDGE_EBT_MARK=m
  CONFIG_BRIDGE_EBT_PKTTYPE=m
  ```

```
CONFIG_BRIDGE_EBT_STP=m
CONFIG_BRIDGE_EBT_VLAN=m
CONFIG_BRIDGE_EBT_ARPREPLY=m
CONFIG_BRIDGE_EBT_DNAT=m
CONFIG_BRIDGE_EBT_MARK_T=m
CONFIG_BRIDGE_EBT_REDIRECT=m
CONFIG_BRIDGE_EBT_SNAT=m
CONFIG_BRIDGE_EBT_LOG=m
# CONFIG_BRIDGE_EBT_ULOG is not set
CONFIG_BRIDGE_EBT_NFLOG=m
CONFIG_BRIDGE=m
CONFIG_BRIDGE_IGMP_SNOOPING=y
CONFIG_BRIDGE_VLAN_FILTERING=y
CONFIG_SSB_B43_PCI_BRIDGE=y
CONFIG_DVB_DDBRIDGE=m
CONFIG_EDAC_SBRIDGE=m
# VME Bridge Drivers
root@kvm:~#
```

- The `bridge` kernel module

  To verify that the module is loaded and to obtain more information about its version and features, execute the following command:

  ```
  root@kvm:~# lsmod | grep bridge
  bridge 110925 0
  stp 12976 2 garp,bridge
  llc 14552 3 stp,garp,bridge
  root@kvm:~#
  root@kvm:~# modinfo bridge
  filename: /lib/modules/3.13.0-107-
  generic/kernel/net/bridge/bridge.ko
  alias: rtnl-link-bridge
  version: 2.3
  license: GPL
  srcversion: 49D4B615F0B11CA696D8623
  depends: stp,llc
  intree: Y
  vermagic: 3.13.0-107-generic SMP mod_unload modversions
  signer: Magrathea: Glacier signing key
  sig_key:
  E1:07:B2:8D:F0:77:39:2F:D6:2D:FD:D7:92:BF:3B:1D:BD:57:0C:D8
  sig_hashalgo: sha512
  root@kvm:~#
  ```

- The `bridge-utils` package that provides the tool to create and manipulate the Linux bridge
- The ability to create new KVM guests using libvirt or the QEMU utilities or an existing KVM instance from the previous chapters

How to do it...

To create, list, and manipulate a new Linux bridge, follow these steps:

1. Install the Linux bridge package, if it is not already present:

```
root@kvm:~# apt install bridge-utils
```

2. Build a new KVM instance using the raw image from the *Installing a custom OS on the image with debootstrap* recipe from `Chapter 1`, *Getting Started with QEMU and KVM*, if you are not reading this book cover to cover:

```
root@kvm:~# virt-install --name kvm1 --ram 1024 --disk
path=/tmp/debian.img,format=raw --graphics
vnc,listen=146.20.141.158 --noautoconsole --hvm --import

Starting install...
Creating domain... | 0 B 00:00
Domain creation completed. You can restart your domain by running:
 virsh --connect qemu:///system start kvm1
root@kvm:~#
```

3. List all the available bridge devices:

```
root@kvm:~# brctl show
bridge name      bridge id           STP enabled      interfaces
virbr0           8000.fe5400559bd6   yes              vnet0
root@kvm:~#
```

4. Bring the virtual bridge down, delete it, and ensure that it's been deleted:

```
root@kvm:~# ifconfig virbr0 down
root@kvm:~# brctl delbr virbr0
root@kvm:~# brctl show
bridge name bridge id STP enabled interfaces
root@kvm:~#
```

5. Create a new bridge and bring it up:

```
root@kvm:~# brctl addbr virbr0
root@kvm:~# brctl show
bridge name     bridge id               STP enabled interfaces
virbr0          8000.000000000000       no
root@kvm:~# ifconfig virbr0 up
root@kvm:~#
```

6. Assign an IP address to bridge:

```
root@kvm:~# ip addr add 192.168.122.1 dev virbr0
root@kvm:~# ip addr show virbr0
39: virbr0: <BROADCAST,MULTICAST,UP,LOWER_UP> mtu 1500 qdisc
noqueue state UNKNOWN group default
 link/ether 32:7d:3f:80:d7:c6 brd ff:ff:ff:ff:ff:ff
 inet 192.168.122.1/32 scope global virbr0
 valid_lft forever preferred_lft forever
 inet6 fe80::307d:3fff:fe80:d7c6/64 scope link
 valid_lft forever preferred_lft forever
root@kvm:~#
```

7. List the virtual interfaces on the host OS:

```
root@kvm:~# ip a s | grep vnet
38: vnet0: <BROADCAST,MULTICAST,UP,LOWER_UP> mtu 1500 qdisc
pfifo_fast state UNKNOWN group default qlen 500
root@kvm:~#
```

8. Add the virtual interface vnet0 to the bridge:

```
root@kvm:~# brctl addif virbr0 vnet0
root@kvm:~# brctl show virbr0
bridge name     bridge id               STP enabled     interfaces
virbr0          8000.fe5400559bd6       no              vnet0
root@kvm:~#
```

9. Enable the **Spanning Tree Protocol** (STP) on bridge and obtain more information:

```
root@kvm:~# brctl stp virbr0 on
root@kvm:~# brctl showstp virbr0
virbr0
 bridge id 8000.fe5400559bd6
 designated root 8000.fe5400559bd6
 root port 0 path cost 0
 max age 20.00 bridge max age 20.00
```

```
hello time 2.00 bridge hello time 2.00
forward delay 15.00 bridge forward delay 15.00
ageing time 300.00
hello timer 0.26 tcn timer 0.00
topology change timer 0.00 gc timer 90.89
flags


vnet0 (1)
 port id 8001 state forwarding
 designated root 8000.fe5400559bd6 path cost 100
 designated bridge 8000.fe5400559bd6 message age timer 0.00
 designated port 8001 forward delay timer 0.00
 designated cost 0 hold timer 0.00
 flags

root@kvm:~#
```

10. From inside the KVM instance, bring the interface up, request an IP address, and test connectivity to the host OS:

```
root@debian:~# ifconfig eth0 up
root@debian:~# dhclient eth0
root@debian:~# ip a s eth0
2: eth0: <BROADCAST,MULTICAST,UP,LOWER_UP> mtu 1500 qdisc
pfifo_fast state UP group default qlen 1000
 link/ether 52:54:00:55:9b:d6 brd ff:ff:ff:ff:ff:ff
 inet 192.168.122.92/24 brd 192.168.122.255 scope global eth0
 valid_lft forever preferred_lft forever
 inet6 fe80::5054:ff:fe55:9bd6/64 scope link
 valid_lft forever preferred_lft forever
root@debian:~#
root@debian:~# ping 192.168.122.1 -c 3
PING 192.168.122.1 (192.168.122.1) 56(84) bytes of data.
64 bytes from 192.168.122.1: icmp_seq=1 ttl=64 time=0.276 ms
64 bytes from 192.168.122.1: icmp_seq=2 ttl=64 time=0.226 ms
64 bytes from 192.168.122.1: icmp_seq=3 ttl=64 time=0.259 ms

--- 192.168.122.1 ping statistics ---
3 packets transmitted, 3 received, 0% packet loss, time 1999ms
rtt min/avg/max/mdev = 0.226/0.253/0.276/0.027 ms
root@debian:~#
```

How it works...

When we first installed and started the `libvirt` daemon, a few things happened
automatically:

- A new Linux bridge was created with the name and IP address defined in
  the `/etc/libvirt/qemu/networks/default.xml` configuration file
- The `dnsmasq` service was started with a configuration specified in
  the `/var/lib/libvirt/dnsmasq/default.conf` file

Let's examine the default `libvirt` bridge configuration:

```
root@kvm:~# cat /etc/libvirt/qemu/networks/default.xml
<network>
 <name>default</name>
 <bridge name="virbr0"/>
 <forward/>
 <ip address="192.168.122.1" netmask="255.255.255.0">
   <dhcp>
     <range start="192.168.122.2" end="192.168.122.254"/>
   </dhcp>
 </ip>
</network>
root@kvm:~#
```

This is the default network that libvirt created for us, specifying the bridge name, IP
address, and the IP range used by the DHCP server that was started. We are going to talk
about libvirt networking in much more detail later in this chapter; however, we've shown
it here to help you understand where all the IP addresses and the bridge name came from.

We can see that a DHCP server is running on the host OS and its configuration file by
running the following command:

```
root@kvm:~# pgrep -lfa dnsmasq
38983 /usr/sbin/dnsmasq --conf-file=/var/lib/libvirt/dnsmasq/default.conf
root@kvm:~# cat /var/lib/libvirt/dnsmasq/default.conf
##WARNING: THIS IS AN AUTO-GENERATED FILE. CHANGES TO IT ARE LIKELY TO BE
##OVERWRITTEN AND LOST. Changes to this configuration should be made using:
## virsh net-edit default
## or other application using the libvirt API.
##
## dnsmasq conf file created by libvirt
strict-order
user=libvirt-dnsmasq
pid-file=/var/run/libvirt/network/default.pid
except-interface=lo
```

```
bind-dynamic
interface=virbr0
dhcp-range=192.168.122.2,192.168.122.254
dhcp-no-override
dhcp-leasefile=/var/lib/libvirt/dnsmasq/default.leases
dhcp-lease-max=253
dhcp-hostsfile=/var/lib/libvirt/dnsmasq/default.hostsfile
addn-hosts=/var/lib/libvirt/dnsmasq/default.addnhosts
root@kvm:~#
```

From the configuration file earlier, note how the IP address range for the DHCP service and the name of the virtual bridge match what is configured in the default libvirt network file that we just saw.

With all this in mind, let's step through all the actions we performed earlier:

In step 1, we installed the userspace tool `brctl` that we use to create, configure, and inspect the Linux bridge configuration in the Linux kernel.

In step 2, we provisioned a new KVM instance using a custom raw image containing the guest OS. This step is not required if you completed the recipes in the previous chapters.

In step 3, we invoked the `bridge` utility to list all available bridge devices. From the output, we can observe that currently there's one bridge, named `virbr0`, which libvirt created automatically. Note that under the interfaces column, we can see the `vnet0` interface. This is the virtual NIC that was exposed to the host OS, when we started the KVM instance. This means that the virtual machine is connected to the host bridge.

In step 4, we first bring the bridge down in order to delete it, then we use the `brctl` command again to remove the bridge and ensure that it's not present on the host OS.

In step 5, we recreated the bridge and brought it back up. We do this to demonstrate the steps required to create a new bridge.

In step 6, we reassigned the same IP address to the bridge and listed it.

In steps 7 and 8, we list all virtual interfaces on the host OS. Because we only have one KVM guest currently running on the server, we only see one virtual interface, that is, `vnet0`. We then proceed to add/connect the virtual NIC to the bridge.

In step 9, we enabled the STP on the bridge. STP is a layer 2 protocol that helps prevent network loops if we have redundant network paths. This is especially useful in larger, more complex network topologies, where multiple bridges are connected together.

Finally, in step 10, we connect to the KVM guest using the console, list its interface configuration, and ensure that we can ping the bridge on the host OS. In order to do that, we need to bring the network interface inside the guest up with `ifconfig eth0 up`, then obtain an IP address with the `dhclient eth0` command from the `dnsmasq` server running on the host.

There's more...

There are few more useful commands we can use on the Linux bridge.

We already know that a bridge forwards frames based on the MAC addresses contained therein. To examine the table of MAC addresses the bridge knows about, run the following command:

```
root@kvm:~# brctl showmacs virbr0
port no   mac addr              is local?     ageing timer
   1      52:54:00:55:9b:d6     no            268.02
   1      fe:54:00:55:9b:d6     yes           0.00
root@kvm:~#
```

From the preceding output, we can see that the bridge has recorded two MAC addresses on its only port. The first record is a nonlocal address, and it belongs to the network interface inside the KVM instances. We can confirm that by connecting to the KVM guest as follows:

```
root@kvm:~# virsh console kvm1
Connected to domain kvm1
Escape character is ^]

root@debian:~# ip a s eth0
2: eth0: <BROADCAST,MULTICAST,UP,LOWER_UP> mtu 1500 qdisc pfifo_fast state
UP group default qlen 1000
 link/ether 52:54:00:55:9b:d6 brd ff:ff:ff:ff:ff:ff
 inet6 fe80::5054:ff:fe55:9bd6/64 scope link
 valid_lft forever preferred_lft forever
root@debian:~#
```

The second MAC address is the address of the bridge itself and the MAC address of the virtual interface, belonging to the KVM virtual machine, exposed to the host OS. To confirm this, run the following command:

```
root@kvm:~# ifconfig | grep "fe:54:00:55:9b:d6"
virbr0 Link encap:Ethernet HWaddr fe:54:00:55:9b:d6
vnet0  Link encap:Ethernet HWaddr fe:54:00:55:9b:d6
root@kvm:~#
```

When the bridge sees a frame on one of its ports, it records the time then after a set amount of time not seeing the same MAC address again, it will remove the record from the its CAM table. We can set the time limit in seconds before the bridge will expire the MAC address entry by executing the following command:

```
root@kvm:~# brctl setageing virbr0 600
root@kvm:~#
```

The `brctl` command is well documented; to list all available subcommands, run it without any parameters:

```
root@kvm:~# brctl
Usage: brctl [commands]
commands:
        addbr <bridge> add bridge
        delbr <bridge> delete bridge
        addif <bridge> <device> add interface to bridge
        delif <bridge> <device> delete interface from bridge
        hairpin <bridge> <port> {on|off} turn hairpin on/off
        setageing <bridge> <time> set ageing time
        setbridgeprio <bridge> <prio> set bridge priority
        setfd <bridge> <time> set bridge forward delay
        sethello <bridge> <time> set hello time
        setmaxage <bridge> <time> set max message age
        setpathcost <bridge> <port> <cost> set path cost
        setportprio <bridge> <port> <prio> set port priority
        show [ <bridge> ] show a list of bridges
        showmacs <bridge> show a list of mac addrs
        showstp <bridge> show bridge stp info
        stp <bridge> {on|off} turn stp on/off
root@kvm:~#
```

Most Linux distributions package the `brctl` utility and this is what we used in this recipe. However, to use the latest version, or if a package is not available for your distribution, we can build the utility from source by cloning the project with `git`, then configure and compile:

```
root@kvm:~# cd /usr/src/
root@kvm:/usr/src# apt-get update && apt-get install build-essential
automake pkg-config git
root@kvm:/usr/src# git clone
git://git.kernel.org/pub/scm/linux/kernel/git/shemminger/bridge-utils.git
Cloning into 'bridge-utils'...
remote: Counting objects: 654, done.
remote: Total 654 (delta 0), reused 0 (delta 0)
Receiving objects: 100% (654/654), 131.72 KiB | 198.00 KiB/s, done.
Resolving deltas: 100% (425/425), done.
```

```
Checking connectivity... done.
root@kvm:/usr/src# cd bridge-utils/
root@kvm:/usr/src/bridge-utils# autoconf
root@kvm:/usr/src/bridge-utils# ./configure && make && make install
root@kvm:/usr/src/bridge-utils# brctl --version
bridge-utils, 1.5
root@kvm:/usr/src/bridge-utils#
```

From the preceding output, we can see that we first cloned the `git` repository for the `bridge-utils` project and then compiled the source code.

On a RedHat/CentOS host, the process is similar:

```
[root@centos ~]# cd /usr/src/
[root@centos src]#
[root@centos src]# yum groupinstall "Development tools"
[root@centos src]# git clone
git://git.kernel.org/pub/scm/linux/kernel/git/shemminger/bridge-utils.git
Cloning into 'bridge-utils'...
remote: Counting objects: 654, done.
remote: Total 654 (delta 0), reused 0 (delta 0)
Receiving objects: 100% (654/654), 131.72 KiB | 198.00 KiB/s, done.
Resolving deltas: 100% (425/425), done.
Checking connectivity... done.
[root@centos src]# cd bridge-utils
[root@centos bridge-utils]# autoconf
[root@centos bridge-utils]# ./configure && make && make install
[root@centos bridge-utils]# brctl --version
bridge-utils, 1.5
[root@centos bridge-utils]#
```

The Open vSwitch

OVS is another software bridging/switching device that can be used to create various virtual network topologies and connect KVM instances to it. OVS can be used instead of the Linux bridge, and it provides an extensive feature set, including policy routing, **Access Control Lists** (**ACLs**), **Quality of Service** (**QoS**) policing, traffic monitoring, flow management, VLAN tagging, GRE tunneling, and much more.

In this recipe, we are going to install, configure, and use the OVS bridge to connect a KVM instance to the host OS, in a similar way to what we did in the previous recipe with the Linux bridge.

Getting ready

In order for this recipe to work, we need to ensure the following:

- The Linux bridge is deleted, if present, and OVS is installed
- We have at least one KVM instance running

How to do it...

To create a new OVS bridge and attach the virtual interface of a KVM guest, follow these steps:

1. Remove the existing Linux bridge, if any:

```
root@kvm:~# brctl show
bridge name       bridge id            STP enabled        interfaces
virbr0            8000.fe5400559bd6    yes                vnet0
root@kvm:~# ifconfig virbr0 down
root@kvm:~# brctl delbr virbr0
root@kvm:~# brctl show
bridge name bridge id STP enabled interfaces
root@kvm:~#
```

> **TIP**
>
> On some Linux distributions, it helps to unload the kernel module for the Linux bridge before using OVS. To do this, execute `root@kvm:/usr/src# modprobe -r bridge`.

2. Install the OVS package on Ubuntu:

```
root@kvm:~# apt-get install openvswitch-switch
...
Setting up openvswitch-common (2.0.2-0ubuntu0.14.04.3) ...
Setting up openvswitch-switch (2.0.2-0ubuntu0.14.04.3) ...
openvswitch-switch start/running
...
root@kvm:~#
```

3. Ensure that the OVS processes are running:

```
root@kvm:~# pgrep -lfa switch
22255 ovsdb-server /etc/openvswitch/conf.db -vconsole:emer -
vsyslog:err -vfile:info --remote=punix:/var/run/openvswitch/db.sock
--private-key=db:Open_vSwitch,SSL,private_key --
```

```
certificate=db:Open_vSwitch,SSL,certificate --bootstrap-ca-
cert=db:Open_vSwitch,SSL,ca_cert --no-chdir --log-
file=/var/log/openvswitch/ovsdb-server.log --
pidfile=/var/run/openvswitch/ovsdb-server.pid --detach --monitor
22264 ovs-vswitchd: monitoring pid 22265 (healthy)
22265 ovs-vswitchd unix:/var/run/openvswitch/db.sock -vconsole:emer
-vsyslog:err -vfile:info --mlockall --no-chdir --log-
file=/var/log/openvswitch/ovs-vswitchd.log --
pidfile=/var/run/openvswitch/ovs-vswitchd.pid --detach --monitor
root@kvm:~#
```

4. Ensure that the OVS kernel module has been loaded:

```
root@kvm:~# lsmod | grep switch
openvswitch         70989   0
gre                 13796   1 openvswitch
vxlan               37611   1 openvswitch
libcrc32c           12644   1 openvswitch
root@kvm:~#
```

5. List the available OVS switches:

```
root@kvm:~# ovs-vsctl show
e5164e3e-7897-4717-b766-eae1918077b0
 ovs_version: "2.0.2"
root@kvm:~#
```

6. Create a new OVS switch:

```
root@kvm:~# ovs-vsctl add-br virbr1
root@kvm:~# ovs-vsctl show
e5164e3e-7897-4717-b766-eae1918077b0
 Bridge "virbr1"
   Port "virbr1"
     Interface "virbr1"
       type: internal
 ovs_version: "2.0.2"
root@kvm:~#
```

7. Add the interface of the running KVM instance to the OVS switch:

```
root@kvm:~# ovs-vsctl add-port virbr1 vnet0
root@kvm:~# ovs-vsctl show
e5164e3e-7897-4717-b766-eae1918077b0
 Bridge "virbr1"
   Port "virbr1"
     Interface "virbr1"
       type: internal
```

```
      Port "vnet0"
         Interface "vnet0"
    ovs_version: "2.0.2"
root@kvm:~#
```

8. Configure an IP address on the OVS switch:

```
root@kvm:~# ip addr add 192.168.122.1/24 dev virbr1
root@kvm:~# ip addr show virbr1
41: virbr1: <BROADCAST,UP,LOWER_UP> mtu 1500 qdisc noqueue state
UNKNOWN group default
 link/ether b2:52:e0:73:89:4e brd ff:ff:ff:ff:ff:ff
 inet 192.168.122.1/24 scope global virbr1
 valid_lft forever preferred_lft forever
 inet6 fe80::b0a8:c2ff:fed4:bb3f/64 scope link
 valid_lft forever preferred_lft forever
root@kvm:~#
```

9. Configure an IP address inside the KVM guest and ensure connectivity to the
    host OS (if the image does not have console access configure, connect to it using
    VNC):

```
root@kvm:~# virsh console kvm1
Connected to domain kvm1
Escape character is ^]

root@debian:~# ifconfig eth0 up && ip addr add 192.168.122.210/24
dev eth0
root@debian:~# ip addr show eth0
2: eth0: <BROADCAST,MULTICAST,UP,LOWER_UP> mtu 1500 qdisc
pfifo_fast state UP group default qlen 1000
 link/ether 52:54:00:55:9b:d6 brd ff:ff:ff:ff:ff:ff
 inet 192.168.122.210/24 scope global eth0
 valid_lft forever preferred_lft forever
 inet6 fe80::5054:ff:fe55:9bd6/64 scope link
 valid_lft forever preferred_lft forever
root@debian:~# ping 192.168.122.1
PING 192.168.122.1 (192.168.122.1) 56(84) bytes of data.
64 bytes from 192.168.122.1: icmp_seq=1 ttl=64 time=0.711 ms
64 bytes from 192.168.122.1: icmp_seq=2 ttl=64 time=0.394 ms
64 bytes from 192.168.122.1: icmp_seq=3 ttl=64 time=0.243 ms
^C
--- 192.168.122.1 ping statistics ---
3 packets transmitted, 3 received, 0% packet loss, time 2001ms
rtt min/avg/max/mdev = 0.243/0.449/0.711/0.195 ms
root@debian:~#
```

How it works...

In order to simplify our setup and avoid conflicts, it's prudent to first remove the Linux bridge before creating a new OVS switch. We delete the bridge in step 1 and optionally unloaded the kernel module.

In step 2, we install the OVS package that also starts the main OVS daemon `ovs-vswitchd` responsible for creating and modifying the bridges/switches on the host OS.

In step 4, we make sure that the OVS kernel module has been loaded, and we list all available OVS switches on the host in step 5.

In steps 6 and 7, we create a new OVS switch and add the KVM virtual interface to the switch.

The `ovsdb`-server process that was also started after installing the package, as seen from the output in step 3, is a database engine that uses JSON **Remote Procedure Calls** (**RPC**) to communicate with the main OVS daemon. The `ovsdb` server process stores information, such as the switch network flows, ports, and `QoS` to name just few. You can query the database by running the following command:

```
root@kvm:~# ovsdb-client list-dbs
Open_vSwitch
root@kvm:~# ovsdb-client list-tables
Table
------------------------
Port
Manager
Bridge
Interface
SSL
IPFIX
Open_vSwitch
Queue
NetFlow
Mirror
QoS
Controller
Flow_Table
sFlow
Flow_Sample_Collector_Set
root@kvm:~# ovsdb-client dump Open_vSwitch
...
Port table
_uuid bond_downdelay bond_fake_iface bond_mode bond_updelay external_ids
fake_bridge interfaces lacp mac name other_config qos statistics status tag
```

```
trunks vlan_mode
----------------------------------------- ---------------- ----------------- --------
-- ------------ ------------ ----------- ----------------------------------
---- ---- --- -------- ------------- --- ---------- ------ --- ------ ------
---
9b4b743d-66b2-4779-9dd8-404b3aa55e18 0 false [] 0 {} false [e7ed4e2b-
a73c-46c7-adeb-a203be56587c] [] [] "virbr1" {} [] {} {} [] [] []
f2a033aa-9072-4be3-808e-6e0fce67ce7b 0 false [] 0 {} false
[86a10eed-698f-4ccc-b3b7-dd20c13e3ee3] [] [] "vnet0" {} [] {} {} [] [] []
...
root@kvm:~#
```

Note from the preceding output that the new switch `virbr1` and port `vnet0` are now displaying, when querying the OVS database.

In steps 8 and 9, we assign IP addresses to the OVS switch and the KVM guest and ensure that we can reach the host bridge from inside the virtual machine.

There's more...

OVS is a rather complex software switch; in this recipe, we only scratched the surface. In the next few recipes, we can use both the Linux bridge and OVS, with minor configuration changes in libvirt, which we are going to point out as we go.

To remove the KVM virtual interface from the OVS switch, execute the following command:

```
root@kvm:~# ovs-vsctl del-port virbr1 vnet0
root@kvm:~#
```

To completely delete the OVS switch, run the following command:

```
root@kvm:~# ovs-vsctl del-br virbr1 && ovs-vsctl show
e5164e3e-7897-4717-b766-eae1918077b0
  ovs_version: "2.0.2"
root@kvm:~#
```

> For more information about the OVS, please visit the projects website, `htt p://openvswitch.org/`.

Configuring NAT forwarding network

When the `libvirt` daemon starts, it creates a default network defined in the `/etc/libvirt/qemu/networks/default.xml` configuration file. When a new KVM guest is build without specifying any networking options, it will use the default network to communicate with the host OS and other guests and networks. The default `libvirt` network is using the **Network Address Translation** (**NAT**) method. NAT provides a mapping from one IP address space to another, by modifying the IP address in the header of the IP datagram packet. This is especially useful when the host OS provides one IP address allowing multiple guests on the same host to use that address to establish outbound connections. The virtual machines IP addresses are essentially translated to appear as the host machine's IP address.

The default NAT forwarding network defines and sets up a Linux bridge, for the guests to connect to. In this recipe, we are going to explore the default NAT network and learn about the XML attributes used to define it. Then, we are going to create a new NAT network and connect our KVM guest to it.

Getting ready

For this recipe, we are going to need the following:

- A Linux host with libvirt installed and the daemon running.
- The `iptables` and `iproute2` packages installed on the host OS. If you installed libvirt from a package, chances are that `iptables` and `iproute2` have been installed, as dependencies of the `libvirt` package. If you've built libvirt from source, you might need to install them manually.
- A running KVM instances.

How to do it...

To configure a new NAT network and connect a KVM instance to it, run the following:

1. List all available networks:

```
root@kvm:~# virsh net-list --all
 Name        State    Autostart    Persistent
----------------------------------------------------------
 default     active   yes          yes
```

```
root@kvm:~#
```

2. Dump the configuration of the default network:

```
root@kvm:~# virsh net-dumpxml default
<network connections='1'>
 <name>default</name>
 <uuid>2ab5d22c-5928-4304-920e-bc43b8731bcf</uuid>
 <forward mode='nat'>
   <nat>
     <port start='1024' end='65535'/>
   </nat>
 </forward>
 <bridge name='virbr0' stp='on' delay='0'/>
 <ip address='192.168.122.1' netmask='255.255.255.0'>
   <dhcp>
     <range start='192.168.122.2' end='192.168.122.254'/>
   </dhcp>
 </ip>
</network>

root@kvm:~#
```

3. Compare that with the XML definition file for the default network:

```
root@kvm:~# cat /etc/libvirt/qemu/networks/default.xml
<network>
 <name>default</name>
 <bridge name="virbr0"/>
 <forward/>
 <ip address="192.168.122.1" netmask="255.255.255.0">
   <dhcp>
     <range start="192.168.122.2" end="192.168.122.254"/>
   </dhcp>
 </ip>
</network>
root@kvm:~#
```

4. List all running instances on the host:

```
root@kvm:~# virsh list --all
 Id    Name     State
----------------------------------------------------
 3     kvm1     running

root@kvm:~#
```

5. Ensure that the KVM instances are connected to the default Linux bridge:

```
root@kvm:~# brctl show
bridge name     bridge id              STP enabled    interfaces
virbr0          8000.fe5400559bd6      yes            vnet0
root@kvm:~#
```

6. Create a new NAT network definition:

```
root@kvm:~# cat nat_net.xml
<network>
 <name>nat_net</name>
 <bridge name="virbr1"/>
 <forward/>
 <ip address="10.10.10.1" netmask="255.255.255.0">
   <dhcp>
      <range start="10.10.10.2" end="10.10.10.254"/>
   </dhcp>
 </ip>
</network>
root@kvm:~#
```

7. Define the new network:

```
root@kvm:~# virsh net-define nat_net.xml
Network nat_net defined from nat_net.xml

root@kvm:~# virsh net-list --all
 Name        State       Autostart    Persistent
----------------------------------------------------------------
 default     active      yes          yes
 nat_net     inactive    no           yes

root@kvm:~#
```

8. Start the new network and enable autostarting:

```
root@kvm:~# virsh net-start nat_net
Network nat_net started

root@kvm:~# virsh net-autostart nat_net
Network nat_net marked as autostarted

root@kvm:~# virsh net-list
 Name        State       Autostart    Persistent
----------------------------------------------------------------
 default     active      yes          yes
 nat_net     active      yes          yes
```

```
root@kvm:~#
```

9. Obtain more information about the new network:

```
root@kvm:~# virsh net-info nat_net
Name: nat_net
UUID: fba2ca2b-8ca7-4dbb-beee-14799ee04bc3
Active: yes
Persistent: yes
Autostart: yes
Bridge: virbr1

root@kvm:~#
```

10. Edit the XML definition of the kvm1 instance and change the name of the source network:

```
root@kvm:~# virsh edit kvm1
...
 <interface type='network'>
   ...
   <source network='nat_net'/>
   ...
 </interface>
...

Domain kvm1 XML configuration edited.

root@kvm:~#
```

11. Restart the KVM guest:

```
root@kvm:~# virsh destroy kvm1
Domain kvm1 destroyed

root@kvm:~# virsh start kvm1
Domain kvm1 started

root@kvm:~#
```

12. List all software bridges on the host:

```
root@kvm:~# brctl show
bridge name     bridge id               STP enabled interfaces
virbr0          8000.000000000000 yes
virbr1          8000.525400ba8e2c yes                virbr1-nic
                                                     vnet0
root@kvm:~#
```

13. Connect to the KVM instances and check the IP address of the `eth0` interface and ensure connectivity to the host bridge (if the image is not configured for console access, use a VNC client instead):

```
root@kvm:~# virsh console kvm1
Connected to domain kvm1
Escape character is ^]

Debian GNU/Linux 8 debian ttyS0

debian login: root
Password:
. . .
root@debian:~# ip a s eth0 | grep inet
  inet 10.10.10.92/24 brd 10.10.10.255 scope global eth0
  inet6 fe80::5054:ff:fe55:9bd6/64 scope link
root@debian:~# ifconfig eth0 up && dhclient eth0
root@debian:~# ping 10.10.10.1 -c 3
PING 10.10.10.1 (10.10.10.1) 56(84) bytes of data.
64 bytes from 10.10.10.1: icmp_seq=1 ttl=64 time=0.313 ms
64 bytes from 10.10.10.1: icmp_seq=2 ttl=64 time=0.136 ms
64 bytes from 10.10.10.1: icmp_seq=3 ttl=64 time=0.253 ms

--- 10.10.10.1 ping statistics ---
3 packets transmitted, 3 received, 0% packet loss, time 2000ms
rtt min/avg/max/mdev = 0.136/0.234/0.313/0.073 ms
root@debian:~#
```

14. On the host OS, examine which DHCP services are running:

```
root@kvm:~# pgrep -lfa dnsmasq
38983 /usr/sbin/dnsmasq --conf-
file=/var/lib/libvirt/dnsmasq/default.conf
40098 /usr/sbin/dnsmasq --conf-
file=/var/lib/libvirt/dnsmasq/nat_net.conf
root@kvm:~#
```

15. Check the IP of the new bridge interface:

```
root@kvm:~# ip a s virbr1
43: virbr1: <BROADCAST,MULTICAST,UP,LOWER_UP> mtu 1500 qdisc
noqueue state UP group default
  link/ether 52:54:00:ba:8e:2c brd ff:ff:ff:ff:ff:ff
  inet 10.10.10.1/24 brd 10.10.10.255 scope global virbr1
    valid_lft forever preferred_lft forever
root@kvm:~#
```

16. List the `iptables` rules for the NAT table:

```
root@kvm:~# iptables -L -n -t nat
Chain PREROUTING (policy ACCEPT)
target prot opt source destination

Chain INPUT (policy ACCEPT)
target prot opt source destination

Chain OUTPUT (policy ACCEPT)
target prot opt source destination

Chain POSTROUTING (policy ACCEPT)
target prot opt source destination
RETURN all -- 10.10.10.0/24 224.0.0.0/24
RETURN all -- 10.10.10.0/24 255.255.255.255
MASQUERADE tcp -- 10.10.10.0/24 !10.10.10.0/24 masq ports:
1024-65535
MASQUERADE udp -- 10.10.10.0/24 !10.10.10.0/24 masq ports:
1024-65535
MASQUERADE all -- 10.10.10.0/24 !10.10.10.0/24
RETURN all -- 192.168.122.0/24 224.0.0.0/24
RETURN all -- 192.168.122.0/24 255.255.255.255
MASQUERADE tcp -- 192.168.122.0/24 !192.168.122.0/24 masq ports:
1024-65535
MASQUERADE udp -- 192.168.122.0/24 !192.168.122.0/24 masq ports:
1024-65535
MASQUERADE all -- 192.168.122.0/24 !192.168.122.0/24
RETURN all -- 192.168.122.0/24 224.0.0.0/24
RETURN all -- 192.168.122.0/24 255.255.255.255
MASQUERADE tcp -- 192.168.122.0/24 !192.168.122.0/24 masq ports:
1024-65535
MASQUERADE udp -- 192.168.122.0/24 !192.168.122.0/24 masq ports:
1024-65535
MASQUERADE all -- 192.168.122.0/24 !192.168.122.0/24
root@kvm:~#
```

How it works...

We start by listing all available networks on the host OS in step 1. As we can see from the output of the `virsh` command, there's only one default network running.

In step 2, we examine the configuration of the default network. The XML definition uses the following attributes:

- The `<network>` attribute is the root element, instructing libvirt that we are defining a network.
- The `<name>` element specifies the name of the network and needs to be unique.
- The `<uuid>` attribute provides a globally unique identifier for the virtual network and if omitted, it will be autogenerated.
- The `<forward>` element and its mode attribute define the network as being connected to the host network stack, using NAT. If this element is missing, libvirt will create an isolated network.
- The `<nat>` subelement further defines the `<port>` range that will be used while the host is preforming NAT.
- The `<bridge>` element specifies the bridge to be created, its name, and STP options.
- The `<ip>` attribute defines the IP range for the DHCP server to assign addresses to the guest VMs.

In step 3, we look at the config file for the default network on this. Note that some of the attributes are missing. Libvirt autogenerates certain attributes and assigns default values where appropriate.

In step 4 and 5, we make sure that we have a running instance connected to the default Linux bridge.

In step 6, we create a new network definition using the default network as a template. We change the name of the network and define new IP range.

With the new network definition file ready, in steps 7 and 8, we define the new network, start it, and make sure that it will automatically start when the `libvirt` daemon starts, in the case of a server reboot.

After obtaining more information about the newly created network in step 9, we proceed to edit the XML definition of the KVM guest in step 10. To make the VM part of the new network, all we need to do is update the `<source network>` element.

After restarting the KVM guest in step 11, we proceed to list all available software bridges on the host OS in step 12. Note that we now have two bridges, with the new bridge having the VMs virtual interface `vnet0` connected to it.

We then connect to the running KVM guest and ensure that its eth0 network interface has obtained an IP address from the DHCP server running on the host and that the IP is part of the address range we configured earlier. We also ensured connectivity to the host bridge using the `ping` command.

Back on the host OS, in steps 14 and 15, we check what DHCP services are running. Note, from the output of the `pgrep` command, that we now have two `dnsmasq` processes running: one for each defined network.

The NAT forwarding is achieved by setting iptables rules as we can see in step 18. Each time we define and start a new NAT network, libvirt creates the required rules in iptables. From the output in step 18, we can observe the presence of two sets of NAT rules, one for each running NAT network.

Configuring bridged network

With full bridging, we can connect the KVM guests directly to the host network, without using NAT. However, this setup requires an IP address, which is part of the host subnet, for each virtual machine. If you cannot allocate that many IP addresses, consider using the NAT network setup, as described in the *Configuring NAT forwarding network* recipe given before. In this networking mode, the virtual machines still use the host OS bridge for connectivity; however, the bridge enslaves the physical interface that is going to be used for the guests.

Getting ready

For this recipe, we are going to need the following:

- A server with at least two physical interfaces
- The ability to provision and start KVM instances with libvirt
- A running KVM instance

How to do it...

To define a new bridged network and attach a guest to it, follow the steps:

1. Take down the interface we are going to bridge:

   ```
   root@kvm:~# ifdown eth1
   root@kvm:~#
   ```

2. Edit the network configuration file on the host and replace the eth1 block with the following, if your host OS is Debian/Ubuntu:

   ```
   root@kvm:~# vim /etc/network/interfaces
   ...
    auto virbr2
    iface virbr2 inet static
         address 192.168.1.2
         netmask 255.255.255.0
         network 192.168.1.0
         broadcast 192.168.1.255
         gateway 192.168.1.1
         bridge_ports eth1
         bridge_stp on
         bridge_maxwait 0
   ...
   root@kvm:~#
   ```

3. If using RedHat/CentOS distributions, edit the following two files instead:

   ```
   root@kvm:~# cat /etc/sysconfig/ifcfg-eth1
   DEVICE=eth1
   NAME=eth1
   NM_CONTROLLED=yes
   ONBOOT=yes
   TYPE=Ethernet
   BRIDGE=virbr2
   root@kvm:~# cat /etc/sysconfig/ifcfg-bridge_net
   DEVICE=virbr2
   NAME=virbr2
   NM_CONTROLLED=yes
   ONBOOT=yes
   TYPE=Bridge
   STP=on
   IPADDR=192.168.1.2
   NETMASK=255.255.255.0
   GATEWAY=192.168.1.1
   root@kvm:~#
   ```

4. Start the new interface up:

```
root@kvm:~# ifup virbr2
root@kvm:~#
```

5. Disable sending packets to `iptables` that originate from the guest VMs:

```
root@kvm:~# sysctl -w net.bridge.bridge-nf-call-iptables=0
net.bridge.bridge-nf-call-iptables = 0
root@kvm:~# sysctl -w net.bridge.bridge-nf-call-iptables=0
net.bridge.bridge-nf-call-iptables = 0
root@kvm:~# sysctl -w net.bridge.bridge-nf-call-arptables=0
net.bridge.bridge-nf-call-arptables = 0
root@kvm:~#
```

6. List all bridges on the host:

```
root@kvm:~# # brctl show
bridge name     bridge id              STP enabled     interfaces
virbr0          8000.000000000000      yes
virbr2          8000.000a0ac60210      yes             eth1
root@kvm:~#
```

7. Edit the XML definition for the KVM instance:

```
root@kvm:~# virsh edit kvm1
...
 <interface type='bridge'>
   <source bridge='virbr2'/>
 </interface>
...

Domain kvm1 XML configuration edited.

root@kvm:~#
```

8. Restart the KVM instance:

```
root@kvm:~# virsh destroy kvm1
Domain kvm1 destroyed

root@kvm:~# virsh start kvm1
Domain kvm1 started

root@kvm:~#
```

How it works...

To set up bridge networking, in steps 1 and 2, we first bring the physical interface (eth1 in this example) down, in order to enslave it (make it a part of the new bridge we are going to create). We then create the network configuration, specifying the new bridge and the physical interface that is going to be a part of that bridge. This in effect maps the subnet that is configured on the physical interface to the bridge. If your server has only one network interface, you can still enslave it. However, you will need an additional way of connecting to the server because once you bring your main interface down, you will loose connectivity and troubleshooting might be impossible over an SSH connection.

Once the new bridge has been configured, we start it in step 3.

In step 4, we instruct the kernel not to apply iptable rules to any traffic originating from the virtual guests connected to the Linux bridge because we are not using any NAT rules.

With the new interface up, we can now see the bridge and the enslaved physical interface attached to it, in step 5.

In step 6, we edit the XML definition of the kvm1 instance, where we specify the type of network we would like to use; for this recipe, it's the bridge network. If you recall from the *Configuring NAT forwarding network* recipe, we used the network type instead of bridge and we specified a libvirt network name, instead of the bridge name.

Finally, after restarting the KVM instance in step 7, the guest OS should now be able to reach other instances that are a part of the same subnet without using NAT.

Configuring PCI passthrough network

The KVM hypervisor supports directly attaching PCI devices from the host OS to the virtual machines. We can use this feature to attach a network interface directly to the guest OS, without the need for using NAT or software bridges.

In this recipe, we are going to attach a **Network Interface Card** (**NIC**) that supports SR-IOV **Single Root I/O Virtualization** (**SR-IOV**) from the host to the KVM guest. SR-IOV is a specification that allows a **Peripheral Component Interconnect Express** (**PCIe**) device to appear as multiple separate physical devices that can be shared between many virtual machines on the same host, bypassing the hypervisor layer, thus achieving native network speeds. Cloud providers such as Amazon AWS expose this feature for its EC2 compute instances through API calls.

Getting ready

In order to complete this recipe, we are going to need the following:

- A physical host with NIC that supports SR-IOV
- A 802.1Qbh capable switch with connection to the physical server
- CPU with either the Intel VT-d or AMD IOMMU extensions
- Linux host with libvirt installed, ready-to-provision KVM instances

How to do it...

To set up a new PCI passthrough network follow the steps:

1. Enumerate all devices on the host OS:

```
root@kvm:~# virsh nodedev-list --tree
computer
 |
 +- net_lo_00_00_00_00_00_00
 +- net_ovs_system_0a_c6_62_34_19_b4
 +- net_virbr1_nic_52_54_00_ba_8e_2c
 +- net_vnet0_fe_54_00_55_9b_d6
 ...
 |
 +- pci_0000_00_03_0
 | |
 | +- pci_0000_03_00_0
 | | |
 | | +- net_eth0_58_20_b1_00_b8_61
 | |
 | +- pci_0000_03_00_1
 | |
 | +- net_eth1_58_20_b1_00_b8_61
 |
 ...
root@kvm:~#
```

2. List all PCI Ethernet adapters:

```
root@kvm:~# lspci | grep Ethernet
03:00.0 Ethernet controller: Intel Corporation 82599ES 10-Gigabit
SFI/SFP+ Network Connection (rev 01)
03:00.1 Ethernet controller: Intel Corporation 82599ES 10-Gigabit
SFI/SFP+ Network Connection (rev 01)
```

```
root@kvm:~#
```

3. Obtain more information about NIC that the eth1 device is using:

```
root@kvm:~# virsh nodedev-dumpxml pci_0000_03_00_1
<device>
 <name>pci_0000_03_00_1</name>
 <path>/sys/devices/pci0000:00/0000:00:03.0/0000:03:00.1</path>
 <parent>pci_0000_00_03_0</parent>
 <driver>
   <name>ixgbe</name>
 </driver>
 <capability type='pci'>
   <domain>0</domain>
   <bus>3</bus>
   <slot>0</slot>
   <function>1</function>
   <product id='0x10fb'>82599ES 10-Gigabit SFI/SFP+ Network
Connection</product>
   <vendor id='0x8086'>Intel Corporation</vendor>
 </capability>
</device>

root@kvm:~#
```

4. Convert the domain, bus, slot, and function values to hexadecimal:

```
root@kvm:~# printf %x 0
0
root@kvm:~# printf %x 3
3
root@kvm:~# printf %x 0
0
root@kvm:~# printf %x 1
1
root@kvm:~#
```

5. Create a new libvirt network definition file:

```
root@kvm:~# cat passthrough_net.xml
<network>
 <name>passthrough_net</name>
 <forward mode='hostdev' managed='yes'>
   <pf dev='eth1'/>
 </forward>
</network>
root@kvm:~#
```

6. Define, start, and enable autostarting on the new `libvirt` network:

```
root@kvm:~# virsh net-define passthrough_net.xml
Network passthrough_net defined from passthrough_net.xml

root@kvm:~# virsh net-start passthrough_net
Network passthrough_nett started

root@kvm:~# virsh net-autostart passthrough_net
Network passthrough_net marked as autostarted

root@kvm:~# virsh net-list
 Name                State      Autostart    Persistent
-----------------------------------------------------------
 default             active     yes          yes
 passthrough_net     active     yes          yes

root@kvm:~#
```

7. Edit the XML definition for the KVM guest:

```
root@kvm:~# virsh edit kvm1
...
 <devices>
 ...
 <interface type='hostdev' managed='yes'>
   <source>
     <address type='pci' domain='0x0' bus='0x00' slot='0x07'
function='0x0'/>
   </source>
   <virtualport type='802.1Qbh' />
 </interface>
 <interface type='network'>
   <source network='passthrough_net'>
 </interface>
 ...
 </devices>
...

Domain kvm1 XML configuration edited.

root@kvm:~#
```

8. Restart the KVM instance:

```
root@kvm:~# virsh destroy kvm1
Domain kvm1 destroyed

root@kvm:~# virsh start kvm1
Domain kvm1 started

root@kvm:~#
```

9. List the **Virtual Functions** (**VFs**) provided by SR-IOV NIC:

```
root@kvm:~# virsh net-dumpxml passthrough_net
<network connections='1'>
   <name>passthrough_net</name>
   <uuid>a4233231-d353-a112-3422-3451ac78623a</uuid>
   <forward mode='hostdev' managed='yes'>
     <pf dev='eth1'/>
     <address type='pci' domain='0x0000' bus='0x02' slot='0x10'
function='0x1'/>
     <address type='pci' domain='0x0000' bus='0x02' slot='0x10'
function='0x3'/>
     <address type='pci' domain='0x0000' bus='0x02' slot='0x10'
function='0x5'/>
     <address type='pci' domain='0x0000' bus='0x02' slot='0x10'
function='0x7'/>
     <address type='pci' domain='0x0000' bus='0x02' slot='0x11'
function='0x1'/>
     <address type='pci' domain='0x0000' bus='0x02' slot='0x11'
function='0x3'/>
     <address type='pci' domain='0x0000' bus='0x02' slot='0x11'
function='0x5'/>
   </forward>
</network>
root@kvm:~#
```

How it works...

In order to directly attach PCI NIC from the host OS to the guest VM, we first need to gather some hardware information about the device, such as domain, bus, slot, and function IDs. In step 1, we collect information about all available devices on the host server. We are interested in using the eth1 network interface for this example; therefore, we note down the unique PCI identification from the output--pci_0000_03_00_1 in this case.

To confirm this is indeed NIC we would like to expose to the guest, we list all PCI devices in step 2. From the output, we can see that the PCI ID is the same `03:00.1`.

Using the PCI ID from step 1, we proceed to collect more information about NIC in step 3. Note that `0000_03_00_1` ID is broken down into domain ID, bus ID, slot ID, and function ID, as shown by the XML attributes. We are going to use those IDs in step 7; however, we need to convert them to hexadecimals first, which we do in step 4.

In steps 5 and 6, we define a new `libvirt` network for our guest, start the network, and enable autostarting in case the host server restarts. If you completed the other recipes in this chapter, you should be already familiar with most of the attributes in the XML definition file for the network we just created. The `hostdev` mode defined in the `<forward>` attribute is what instructs `libvirt` that the new network is going to use PCI passthrough. The `managed=yes` parameter, as specified in the `<forward>` attribute, tells `libvirt` to first detach the PCI device from the host before passing it on to the guest and reattaching it back to the host after the guest terminates. Finally, the `<pf>` subelement specifies the physical interface that will be virtualized and presented to the guest.

> For more information on the available XML attributes, please refer to `http://libvirt.org/formatdomain.html`.

In step 7, we edit the XML definition of the KVM instance, specifying the PCI IDs we obtained in step 3 and defined an interface that will use the new PCI passthrough network we created in steps 5 and 6.

We restart the KVM instance in step 8 and finally verify that the physical PCI NIC device is now part of the new passthrough network we defined earlier. Note the presence of multiple PCI type devices. This is because the PCI passthrough device we are using supports SR-IOV. All KVM guests that will use this network will now be able to directly use the host NIC by assigning one of the listed virtual PCI devices.

Manipulating network interfaces

Libvirt provides a handy way to manage network interfaces on the host through the already familiar XML definition syntax. We can use the `virsh` command to define, provision, and delete Linux bridges and obtain more information about existing network interfaces, as you've already seen in this chapter.

In this recipe, we are going to define a new Linux bridge, create it, and finally remove it using `virsh`. If you recall from earlier recipes, we can manipulate the Linux bridge through utilities such as `brctl`. With libvirt, however, we have a way to control this programmatically by writing the definition file and using the API bindings, as we'll see in `Chapter 7`, *Using Python to Build and Manage KVM Instances*.

Getting ready

For this recipe, we are going to need the following:

- The `libvirt` package installed on the host
- A Linux host with the bridge kernel module

How to do it...

To create a new bridge interface using libvirt, run the following commands:

1. Create a new bridge interface configuration file:

```
root@kvm:~# cat test_bridge.xml
<interface type='bridge' name='test_bridge'>
 <start mode="onboot"/>
   <protocol family='ipv4'>
 <ip address='192.168.1.100' prefix='24'/>
 </protocol>
 <bridge>
   <interface type='ethernet' name='vnet0'>
     <mac address='fe:54:00:55:9b:d6'/>
   </interface>
 </bridge>
</interface>
root@kvm:~#
```

2. Define the new interface:

```
root@kvm:~# virsh iface-define test_bridge.xml
Interface test_bridge defined from test_bridge.xml

root@kvm:~#
```

3. List all interfaces libvirt knows about:

```
root@kvm:~# virsh iface-list --all
 Name               State           MAC Address
--------------------------------------------------------
 bond0              active          58:20:b1:00:b8:61
 bond0.129          active          bc:76:4e:20:10:6b
 bond0.229          active          bc:76:4e:20:17:7e
 eth0               active          58:20:b1:00:b8:61
 eth1               active          58:20:b1:00:b8:61
 lo                 active          00:00:00:00:00:00
 test_bridge        inactive

root@kvm:~#
```

4. Start the new bridge interface:

```
root@kvm:~# virsh iface-start test_bridge
Interface test_bridge started

root@kvm:~# virsh iface-list --all | grep test_bridge
 test_bridge     active     4a:1e:48:e1:e7:de
root@kvm:~#
```

5. List all bridge devices on the host:

```
root@kvm:~# brctl show
bridge name         bridge id               STP enabled     interfaces
test_bridge         8000.000000000000       no
virbr0              8000.000000000000       yes
virbr1              8000.525400ba8e2c       yes             virbr1-nic
                                                            vnet0

root@kvm:~#
```

6. Check the active network configuration of the new bridge:

```
root@kvm:~# ip a s test_bridge
46: test_bridge: <BROADCAST,MULTICAST,UP,LOWER_UP> mtu 1500 qdisc
noqueue state UNKNOWN group default
 link/ether 4a:1e:48:e1:e7:de brd ff:ff:ff:ff:ff:ff
 inet 192.168.1.100/24 brd 192.168.1.255 scope global test_bridge
 valid_lft forever preferred_lft forever
 inet6 fe80::481e:48ff:fee1:e7de/64 scope link
 valid_lft forever preferred_lft forever
root@kvm:~#
```

7. Obtain the MAC address of bridge:

```
root@kvm:~# virsh iface-mac test_bridge
4a:1e:48:e1:e7:de

root@kvm:~#
```

8. Obtain the name of the bridge based by providing its MAC address:

```
root@kvm:~# virsh iface-name 4a:1e:48:e1:e7:de
test_bridge

root@kvm:~#
```

9. Destroy the interface, as follows:

```
root@kvm:~# virsh iface-destroy test_bridge
Interface test_bridge destroyed

root@kvm:~# virsh iface-list --all | grep test_bridge
 test_bridge inactive
root@kvm:~# virsh iface-undefine test_bridge
Interface test_bridge undefined

root@kvm:~# virsh iface-list --all | grep test_bridge
root@kvm:~#
```

How it works...

In step 1, we write the XML definition for the new network interface. We specify bridge as the type, an IP address for the interface, and optionally a MAC address.

In steps 2 and 3, we define the new bridge interface and list it. Defining an interface does not automatically make it active, so we activate it in step 4.

Activating the bridge creates the actual interface on the host, as shown in step 5.

In step 6, we confirm that the IP and MAC address assigned to the bridge are indeed what we specified in step 1.

In steps 7 and 8, we obtain both the name and MAC address using the `virsh` utility and finally, in step 9, we remove the `bridge` interface.

4
Migrating KVM Instances

In this chapter, we are going to demonstrate the following libvirt KVM migration concepts:

- Manual offline migration using an iSCSI storage pool
- Manual offline migration using GlusterFS shared volumes
- Online migration using the virsh command with shared storage
- Offline migration using the virsh command and local image
- Online migration using the virsh command and local image

Introduction

Migrating KVM instances is the process of sending the state of the guest virtual machine's memory, CPU, and virtualized devices attached to it, to a different server. Migrating KVM instances is a somewhat complicated process, depending on what backend storage the VM is using (that is, directory, image file, iSCSI volume, shared storage, or storage pools), the network infrastructure, and the number of block devices attached to the guest. There are following the two types of migrations as far as libvirt is concerned:

- Offline migration involves downtime for the instance. It works by first suspending the guest VM, then copying an image of the guest memory to the destination hypervisor. The KVM machine is then resumed on the target host. If the filesystem of the VM is not on a shared storage, then it needs to be moved to the target server as well.
- Live migration works by moving the instance in its current state with no perceived downtime, preserving the memory and CPU register states.

Broadly speaking, the offline migration involves the following:

- Stopping the instance
- Dumping its XML definition to a file
- Copying the guest filesystem image to the destination server (if not using shared storage)
- Defining the instance on the destination host and starting it

In contrast, the online migration requires shared storage, such as NFS or GlusterFS, removing the need to transfer the guest filesystem to the target server. The speed of the migration depends on how often the memory of the source instance is being updated/written to, the size of the memory, and the available network bandwidth between the source and target hosts.

Live migration follows this process:

- The original VM continues to run while the content of its memory is being transferred to the target host
- Libvirt monitors for any changes in the already transferred memory pages, and if they have been updated, it retransmits them
- Once the memory content has been transferred to the destination host, the original instance is suspended and the new instance on the target host is resumed

In this chapter, we are going to perform offline and live migrations using iSCSI and GlusterFS with the help of storage pools.

Manual offline migration using an iSCSI storage pool

In this recipe, we are going to set up an iSCSI target, configure a storage pool for it, and create a new KVM instance using the attached iSCSI block device as its backend volume. Then, we are going to perform a manual offline migration of the instance to a new host.

Getting ready

For this recipe, we are going to need the following:

- Two servers with `libvirt` and `qemu` installed and configured, named `kvm1` and `kvm2`. The two hosts must be able to connect to each other using SSH keys and short hostname.
- A server with an available block device that will be exported as an iSCSI target and reachable from both `libvirt` servers. If a block device is not available, please refer to the *There's more...* section in this recipe for instructions on how to create one using a regular file. The name of the iSCSI target server in this recipe is `iscsi_target`.
- Connectivity to a Linux repository to install the guest OS.

How to do it...

To perform a manual offline migration of a KVM guest using an iSCSI storage pool, follow these steps:

1. On the iSCSI target host, install the `iscsitarget` package and kernel module package:

   ```
   root@iscsi_target:~# apt-get update && apt-get install iscsitarget
   iscsitarget-dkms
   ```

2. Enable the target functionality:

   ```
   root@iscsi_target:~# sed -i
   's/ISCSITARGET_ENABLE=false/ISCSITARGET_ENABLE=true/g'
   /etc/default/iscsitarget
   root@iscsi_target:~# cat /etc/default/iscsitarget
   ISCSITARGET_ENABLE=true
   ISCSITARGET_MAX_SLEEP=3

   # ietd options
   # See ietd(8) for details
   ISCSITARGET_OPTIONS=""
   root@iscsi_target:~#
   ```

3. Configure the block device to export with iSCSI:

```
root@iscsi_target:~# cat /etc/iet/ietd.conf
Target iqn.2001-04.com.example:kvm
        Lun 0 Path=/dev/loop1,Type=fileio
        Alias kvm_lun

root@iscsi_target:~#
```

Replace the /dev/loop1 device with the block device you are exporting with iSCSI.

4. Restart the iSCSI target service:

```
root@iscsi_target:~# /etc/init.d/iscsitarget restart
 * Removing iSCSI enterprise target devices: [ OK ]
 * Stopping iSCSI enterprise target service: [ OK ]
 * Removing iSCSI enterprise target modules: [ OK ]
 * Starting iSCSI enterprise target service  [ OK ]
root@iscsi_target:~#
```

5. On both libvirt hosts, install the iSCSI initiator:

```
root@kvm1/2:~# apt-get update && apt-get install open-iscsi
```

6. On both libvirt servers, enable the iSCSI initiator service and start it:

```
root@kvm1/2:~# sed -i 's/node.startup = manual/node.startup =
automatic/g' /etc/iscsi/iscsid.conf
root@kvm1/2:~# /etc/init.d/open-iscsi restart
```

7. From both libvirt initiator hosts, list what iSCSI volumes are available by querying the iSCSI target server:

```
root@kvm1/2:~# iscsiadm -m discovery -t sendtargets -p iscsi_target
10.184.226.74:3260,1 iqn.2001-04.com.example:kvm
172.99.88.246:3260,1 iqn.2001-04.com.example:kvm
192.168.122.1:3260,1 iqn.2001-04.com.example:kvm
root@kvm:~#
```

8. On one of the `libvirt` servers, create a new iSCSI storage pool:

```
root@kvm1:~# cat iscsi_pool.xml
<pool type="iscsi">
 <name>iscsi_pool</name>
 <source>
   <host name="iscsi_target.example.com"/>
   <device path="iqn.2001-04.com.example:kvm"/>
 </source>
 <target>
   <path>/dev/disk/by-path</path>
 </target>
</pool>
root@kvm1:~# virsh pool-define iscsi_pool.xml
Pool iscsi_pool defined from iscsi_pool.xml

root@kvm1:~# virsh pool-list --all
 Name          State      Autostart
---------------------------------------------
 iscsi_pool   inactive    no

root@kvm1:~#
```

Make sure to replace the hostname of the iSCSI target server with what is appropriate for your environment. Both a hostname and an IP address can be used when specifying the iSCSI target host.

9. Start the new iSCIS pool:

```
root@kvm1:~# virsh pool-start iscsi_pool
Pool iscsi_pool started

root@kvm1:~# virsh pool-list --all
 Name          State    Autostart
---------------------------------------------
 iscsi_pool   active    no

root@kvm1:~#
```

10. List the available iSCSI volumes from the pool and obtain more information on it:

```
root@kvm1:~# virsh vol-list --pool iscsi_pool
 Name Path
-----------------------------------------------------------------
-----------
 unit:0:0:0 /dev/disk/by-path/ip-10.184.22.74:3260-iscsi-
```

```
iqn.2001-04.com.example:kvm-lun-0

root@kvm1:~# virsh vol-info unit:0:0:0 --pool iscsi_pool
Name:         unit:0:0:0
Type:         block
Capacity:     10.00 GiB
Allocation:   10.00 GiB

root@kvm1:~#
```

11. List the iSCSI session and the associated block devices:

```
root@kvm1:~# iscsiadm -m session
tcp: [5] 10.184.226.74:3260,1 iqn.2001-04.com.example:kvm
root@kvm1:~# ls -la /dev/disk/by-path/
total 0
drwxr-xr-x 2 root root 100 Apr 12 16:24 .
drwxr-xr-x 6 root root 120 Mar 21 22:14 ..
lrwxrwxrwx 1 root root 9 Apr 12 16:24 ip-10.184.22.74:3260-iscsi-
iqn.2001-04.com.example:kvm-lun-0 -> ../../sdf
root@kvm1:~#
```

12. Examine the partition scheme of the iSCSI block device:

```
root@kvm1:~# fdisk -l /dev/disk/by-path/ip-10.184.22.74\:3260-
iscsi-iqn.2001-04.com.example\:kvm-lun-0

Disk /dev/disk/by-path/ip-10.184.22.74:3260-iscsi-
iqn.2001-04.com.example:kvm-lun-0: 10.7 GB, 10737418240 bytes
64 heads, 32 sectors/track, 10240 cylinders, total 20971520 sectors
Units = sectors of 1 * 512 = 512 bytes
Sector size (logical/physical): 512 bytes / 512 bytes
I/O size (minimum/optimal): 512 bytes / 512 bytes
Disk identifier: 0x00000000

Disk /dev/disk/by-path/ip-10.184.22.74:3260-iscsi-
iqn.2001-04.com.example:kvm-lun-0 doesn't contain a valid partition
table
root@kvm1:~#
```

13. Install a new KVM guest using the iSCSI volume and pool:

```
root@kvm1:~# virt-install --name iscsi_kvm --ram 1024 --extra-
args="text console=tty0 utf8 console=ttyS0,115200" --graphics
vnc,listen=0.0.0.0 --hvm --
location=http://ftp.us.debian.org/debian/dists/stable/main/installe
r-amd64/ --disk vol=iscsi_pool/unit:0:0:0
```

```
Starting install...
Retrieving file MANIFEST... | 3.3 kB 00:00 ...
Retrieving file linux...
...
root@kvm1:~# virsh console iscsi_kvm
...
Requesting system reboot
[ 305.315002] reboot: Restarting system
root@kvm1:~#
```

14. Refresh the partition table list and examine the new block devices after the installation:

```
root@kvm1:~# partprobe
root@kvm1:~# ls -la /dev/disk/by-path/
total 0
drwxr-xr-x 2 root root 160 Apr 12 16:36 .
drwxr-xr-x 6 root root 120 Mar 21 22:14 ..
lrwxrwxrwx 1 root root 9 Apr 12 16:36 ip-10.184.22.74:3260-iscsi-
iqn.2001-04.com.example:kvm-lun-0 -> ../../sdf
lrwxrwxrwx 1 root root 10 Apr 12 16:36 ip-10.184.22.74:3260-iscsi-
iqn.2001-04.com.example:kvm-lun-0-part1 -> ../../sdf1
lrwxrwxrwx 1 root root 10 Apr 12 16:36 ip-10.184.22.74:3260-iscsi-
iqn.2001-04.com.example:kvm-lun-0-part2 -> ../../sdf2
lrwxrwxrwx 1 root root 10 Apr 12 16:36 ip-10.184.22.74:3260-iscsi-
iqn.2001-04.com.example:kvm-lun-0-part5 -> ../../sdf5
root@kvm1:~# fdisk -l /dev/sdf

Disk /dev/sdf: 10.7 GB, 10737418240 bytes
255 heads, 63 sectors/track, 1305 cylinders, total 20971520 sectors
Units = sectors of 1 * 512 = 512 bytes
Sector size (logical/physical): 512 bytes / 512 bytes
I/O size (minimum/optimal): 512 bytes / 512 bytes
Disk identifier: 0x37eb1540

 Device Boot Start End Blocks Id System
/dev/sdf1 * 2048 20013055 10005504 83 Linux
/dev/sdf2 20015102 20969471 477185 5 Extended
/dev/sdf5 20015104 20969471 477184 82 Linux swap / Solaris
root@kvm1:~#
```

15. Start the new KVM guest and ensure that it's running, and that you can connect to it using a VNC client:

```
root@kvm1:~# virsh start iscsi_kvm
Domain iscsi_kvm started

root@kvm1:~# virsh list --all
```

```
Id  Name         State
----------------------------------------------------------
19  iscsi_kvm    running

root@kvm1:~#
```

16. To manually migrate the instance to a new host, first stop the VM and the iSCSI pool:

```
root@kvm1:~# virsh destroy iscsi_kvm
Domain iscsi_kvm destroyed

root@kvm1:~# virsh pool-destroy iscsi_pool
Pool iscsi_pool destroyed

root@kvm1:~# iscsiadm -m session
iscsiadm: No active sessions.
root@kvm1:~#
```

17. Dump the XML configuration of the KVM instance to a file and examine it:

```
root@kvm1:~# virsh dumpxml iscsi_kvm > iscsi_kvm.xml
root@kvm1:~# cat iscsi_kvm.xml
<domain type='kvm'>
 <name>iscsi_kvm</name>
 <uuid>306e05ed-e398-ef33-d6e2-3708e90b89a6</uuid>
 <memory unit='KiB'>1048576</memory>
 <currentMemory unit='KiB'>1048576</currentMemory>
 <vcpu placement='static'>1</vcpu>
 <os>
   <type arch='x86_64' machine='pc-i440fx-trusty'>hvm</type>
   <boot dev='hd'/>
 </os>
 <features>
   <acpi/>
   <apic/>
   <pae/>
 </features>
 <clock offset='utc'/>
 <on_poweroff>destroy</on_poweroff>
 <on_reboot>restart</on_reboot>
 <on_crash>restart</on_crash>
 <devices>
   <emulator>/usr/bin/qemu-system-x86_64</emulator>
   <disk type='block' device='disk'>
     <driver name='qemu' type='raw'/>
     <source dev='/dev/disk/by-path/ip-10.184.22.74:3260-iscsi-
iqn.2001-04.com.example:kvm-lun-0'/>
```

```
      <target dev='hda' bus='ide'/>
      <address type='drive' controller='0' bus='0' target='0'
unit='0'/>
   </disk>
   <controller type='usb' index='0'>
      <address type='pci' domain='0x0000' bus='0x00' slot='0x01'
function='0x2'/>
   </controller>
   <controller type='pci' index='0' model='pci-root'/>
   <controller type='ide' index='0'>
      <address type='pci' domain='0x0000' bus='0x00' slot='0x01'
function='0x1'/>
   </controller>
   <interface type='network'>
      <mac address='52:54:00:8b:b8:e3'/>
      <source network='default'/>
      <model type='rtl8139'/>
      <address type='pci' domain='0x0000' bus='0x00' slot='0x03'
function='0x0'/>
   </interface>
   <serial type='pty'>
      <target port='0'/>
   </serial>
   <console type='pty'>
      <target type='serial' port='0'/>
   </console>
   <input type='mouse' bus='ps2'/>
   <input type='keyboard' bus='ps2'/>
   <graphics type='vnc' port='-1' autoport='yes' listen='0.0.0.0'>
      <listen type='address' address='0.0.0.0'/>
   </graphics>
   <video>
      <model type='cirrus' vram='9216' heads='1'/>
      <address type='pci' domain='0x0000' bus='0x00' slot='0x02'
function='0x0'/>
   </video>
   <memballoon model='virtio'>
      <address type='pci' domain='0x0000' bus='0x00' slot='0x04'
function='0x0'/>
   </memballoon>
 </devices>
</domain>

root@kvm1:~#
```

18. Remotely create the iSCSI storage pool from the `kvm1` host to the `kvm2` host:

```
root@kvm1:~# virsh --connect qemu+ssh://kvm2/system pool-define
iscsi_pool.xml
Pool iscsi_pool defined from iscsi_pool.xml

root@kvm1:~#
```

> If you are not using keys for the SSH connection between both the KVM hosts, you will be asked to provide a password before the `libvirt` command can proceed. We recommend that you use SSH keys on the `libvirt` hosts you are migrating between.

19. Remotely start the iSCSI pool on the `kvm2` server and ensure that it's running:

```
root@kvm1:~# virsh --connect qemu+ssh://kvm2/system pool-start
iscsi_pool
Pool iscsi_pool started

root@kvm1:~# virsh --connect qemu+ssh://kvm2/system pool-list --all
 Name           State    Autostart
------------------------------------------------
 iscsi_pool   active   no

root@kvm1:~#
```

> You can also SSH to the `kvm2` server and perform all of the pool and volume operations locally. We do it remotely to demonstrate the concept.

20. Remotely list the available iSCSI volumes on the `kvm2` node from the source host:

```
root@kvm1:~# virsh --connect qemu+ssh://kvm2/system vol-list --pool
iscsi_pool
 Name Path
-----------------------------------------------------------------
-
 unit:0:0:0 /dev/disk/by-path/ip-10.184.22.74:3260-iscsi-
iqn.2001-04.com.example:kvm-lun-0

root@kvm1:~#
```

21. SSH to the second KVM server and ensure that the iSCSI block devices are now available on the host OS:

```
root@kvm2:~# iscsiadm -m session
tcp: [3] 10.184.226.74:3260,1 iqn.2001-04.com.example:kvm
root@kvm2:~# ls -la /dev/disk/by-path/
total 0
drwxr-xr-x 2 root root 120 Apr 12 17:44 .
drwxr-xr-x 6 root root 120 Apr 12 17:44 ..
lrwxrwxrwx 1 root root 9 Apr 12 17:44 ip-10.184.22.74:3260-iscsi-
iqn.2001-04.com.example:kvm-lun-0 -> ../../sdc
lrwxrwxrwx 1 root root 10 Apr 12 17:44 ip-10.184.22.74:3260-iscsi-
iqn.2001-04.com.example:kvm-lun-0-part1 -> ../../sdc1
lrwxrwxrwx 1 root root 10 Apr 12 17:44 ip-10.184.22.74:3260-iscsi-
iqn.2001-04.com.example:kvm-lun-0-part2 -> ../../sdc2
lrwxrwxrwx 1 root root 10 Apr 12 17:44 ip-10.184.22.74:3260-iscsi-
iqn.2001-04.com.example:kvm-lun-0-part5 -> ../../sdc5
root@kvm2:~#
```

22. Complete the migration by remotely defining the KVM instance and starting it on the target host:

```
root@kvm1:~# virsh --connect qemu+ssh://kvm2/system define
iscsi_kvm.xml
Domain iscsi_kvm defined from iscsi_kvm.xml

root@kvm1:~# virsh --connect qemu+ssh://kvm2/system list --all
 Id    Name         State
----------------------------------------------------------
 -     iscsi_kvm    shut off

root@kvm:~# virsh --connect qemu+ssh://kvm2/system start iscsi_kvm
Domain iscsi_kvm started

root@kvm:~# virsh --connect qemu+ssh://kvm2/system list --all
 Id    Name         State
----------------------------------------------------------
 3     iscsi_kvm    running

root@kvm1:~#
```

How it works...

In this recipe, we demonstrated how to manually perform an offline migration of a KVM instance from one host to another, using an iSCSI pool. In the *Online migration using the virsh command* recipe later in this chapter, we are going to perform a live migration using the same iSCSI pool and instance we created in this recipe, using the `virsh` command, thus avoiding downtime for the instance.

Let's step through the process and explore in more detail how the manual offline migration was accomplished.

We start with the server that is going to be presenting the iSCSI target by first installing the required iSCSI target server packages in step 1.
In step 2, we enable the iSCSI target functionality, enabling the server to export block devices via the iSCSI protocol.
In step 3, we specify an identified (iSCSI qualified name) `iqn.2001-04.com.example:kvm` for the iSCSI target device that the initiators are going to use. We are using the `/dev/loop1` block device for this example. The iSCSI-qualified name has the format **iqn.yyyy-mm.naming-authority:unique name** where:

- **iqn**: This is the iSCSI-qualified name identifier
- **yyyy-mm**: This is the year and month when the naming authority was established
- **naming-authority:** This is usually reverse syntax of the Internet domain name of the naming authority or the domain name of the server
- **Unique name**: This is any name you would like to use

> For more information about iSCSI and the naming scheme it uses, please refer to `https://en.wikipedia.org/wiki/ISCSI`.

With the target definition in place, in step 4, we restart the iSCSI service on the server.

In steps 5 and 6, we install and configure the iSCSI initiator service on both KVM nodes, and in step 7, we request all available iSCSI targets. In steps 8 and 9, we define and start a new iSCSI-based storage pool. The syntax of the storage pool definition should look familiar if you've completed the *Working with storage pools* recipe from `Chapter 2`, *Using libvirt to Manage KVM*.

After creating the iSCSI storage pool, we proceeded to list the volumes part of that pool in step 10. Note that when we started the pool, it logged the iSCSI target in, resulting in a new block device present in the `/dev/disk/by-path/` directory, as we can further see in step 11. We can now use this block device locally to install a new Linux OS. In step 12, we can see that the iSCSI block device presented to the host OS does not yet contain any partitions.

With the new block device present, we proceed to build a new KVM instance in step 13, specifying the storage pool and volume as the target for the installation. After the guest OS installation completes, we can now see that there are multiple partitions on the iSCSI block device in step 14. We then proceed to start the new guest in step 15.

Now that we have a running KVM instance using an iSCSI block device, we can proceed with the offline manual migration from the `kvm1` hosts to the `kvm2` hosts.

We start the migration process by first stopping the running KVM instance and the associated storage pool in step 16. We then dump the XML configuration of the KVM guest to a file in step 17. We are going to use it to define the guest on the target server. We have a few options for this: we can copy the file over to the target server and define the instance there or we can do that remotely from the original host.

In steps 18 and 19, we create the iSCSI storage pool remotely from the original host to the target host. We could have logged in to the target host and performed the same operations locally as well with the same result. The point here is that we can use the `qemu+ssh` connection string to remotely connect to other qemu instances over SSH. In steps 20 and 21, we ensure that the same iSCSI volume has been successfully logged in to the target host.

Finally, in step 22, we define the instance on the target host using the XML configuration we dumped in step 17 and then start it. Because we are using the same XML definition file and the same iSCSI block device containing the guest OS filesystem, we now have exactly the same instance created on the new server, thus completing the offline migration.

There's more...

If the iSCSI target server does not have any available block devices to export, we can create a new block device using a regular file by following the steps outlined here:

1. Create a new image file of a given size:

```
root@iscsi_target:~# truncate --size 10G xvdb.img
root@iscsi_target:~# file -s xvdb.img
xvdb.img: data
root@kvmiscsi_target:~# qemu-img info xvdb.img
image: xvdb.img
```

```
file format: raw
virtual size: 10G (10737418240 bytes)
disk size: 0
root@iscsi_target:~#
```

2. Ensure that the loop kernel module is compiled in (or load it with `modprobe loop`) and find the first available loop device to use:

    ```
    root@iscsi_target:~# grep 'loop' /lib/modules/`uname -
    r`/modules.builtin
    kernel/drivers/block/loop.ko
    root@iscsi_target:~# losetup --find
    /dev/loop0
    root@iscsi_target:~#
    ```

3. Associate the raw file image with the first available loop device:

    ```
    root@iscsi_target:~# losetup /dev/loop0 xvdb.img
    root@iscsi_target:~# losetup --all
    /dev/loop0: [10300]:263347 (/root/xvdb.img)
    root@iscsi_target:~#
    ```

In step 1, we create a new image file using the `truncate` command.

In step 2, we list the first available block device to use and in step 3, we associate it with the raw image file we created in step 1. The result is a new block device available as `/dev/loop0` that we can use to export in iSCSI.

Manual offline migration using GlusterFS shared volumes

In the *Manual offline migration using an iSCSI storage pool* recipe, we created an iSCSI storage pool and used it while performing manual offline migration. With storage pools, we can delegate the operation of a shared storage to libvirt rather than manually having to log in/log out iSCSI targets, for example. This is especially useful when we perform live migrations with the `virsh` command, as we are going to see in the next recipe. Even though the use of storage pools is not required, it simplifies and centralizes the management of backend volumes.

In this recipe, we are going to use the GlusterFS network filesystem to demonstrate an alternative way of manually migrating a KVM instance, this time not using storage pools.

GlusterFS has the following two components:

- **Server component**: This runs the `GlusterFS` daemon and exports local block devices named **bricks** as volumes that can be mounted by the client component
- **Client component**: This connects to the GlusterFS cluster over TCP/IP and can mount the exported volumes

There are the following three types of volumes:

- **Distributed**: These are volumes that distribute files throughout the cluster
- **Replicated**: These are volumes that replicate data across two or more nodes in the storage cluster
- **Striped**: These are stripe files across multiple storage nodes

For high availability, we are going to use two GFS nodes using the replicated volumes (two bricks containing the same data).

Getting ready

To complete this recipe, we are going to use the following:

- Two servers that will host the GlusterFS shared filesystem.
- Two hosts running `libvirt` and `qemu` that will be used to migrate the KVM guest.
- All servers should be able to communicate with each other using hostnames.
- Both servers hosting the shared volumes should have one block device available for use as GlusterFS bricks. If a block device is not available, please refer to the *There's more...* section of the *Manual offline migration using an iSCSI storage pool* recipe in this chapter on how to create one using a regular file.
- Connectivity to a Linux repository to install the guest OS.

How to do it...

To migrate a KVM guest using a shared GlusterFS backend store, run the following:

1. On both servers that will host the shared volumes, install GlusterFS:

```
root@glusterfs1/2:~# apt-get update && apt-get install glusterfs-
server
```

2. From one of the GlusterFS nodes, probe the other in order to form a cluster:

```
root@glusterfs1:~# gluster peer status
peer status: No peers present
root@glusterfs1:~# gluster peer probe glusterfs2
peer probe: success
root@glusterfs1:~#
```

3. Verify that the GlusterFS nodes are aware of each other:

```
root@glusterfs1:~# gluster peer status
Number of Peers: 1

Hostname: glusterfs2
Port: 24007
Uuid: 923d152d-df3b-4dfd-9def-18dbebf2b76a
State: Peer in Cluster (Connected)
root@glusterfs1:~#
```

4. On both GlusterFS hosts, create a filesystem on the block devices that will be used as GlusterFS bricks and mount them:

```
root@glusterfs1/2:~# mkfs.ext4 /dev/loop5
. . .
Allocating group tables: done
Writing inode tables: done
Creating journal (32768 blocks): done
Writing superblocks and filesystem accounting information: done
root@glusterfs1/2:~# mount /dev/loop5 /mnt/
root@glusterfs1/2:~# mkdir /mnt/bricks
root@glusterfs1/2:~#
```

Make sure to replace the block device name with what is appropriate on your system.

5. From one of the GlusterFS nodes, create the replicated storage volume, using the bricks from both servers and then list it:

```
root@glusterfs1:~# gluster volume create kvm_gfs replica 2
transport tcp glusterfs1:/mnt/bricks/gfs1
glusterfs2:/mnt/bricks/gfs2
volume create: kvm_gfs: success: please start the volume to access
data
root@glusterfs1:~# gluster volume list
kvm_gfs
```

```
root@glusterfs1:~#
```

6. From one of the GlusterFS hosts, start the new volume and obtain more information on it:

```
root@glusterfs1:~# gluster volume start kvm_gfs
volume start: kvm_gfs: success
root@glusterfs1:~# gluster volume info

Volume Name: kvm_gfs
Type: Replicate
Volume ID: 69823a48-8b1b-469f-b06a-14ef6f33a6f5
Status: Started
Number of Bricks: 1 x 2 = 2
Transport-type: tcp
Bricks:
Brick1: glusterfs1:/mnt/bricks/gfs1
Brick2: glusterfs2:/mnt/bricks/gfs2
root@glusterfs1:~#
```

7. On both `libvirt` nodes, install the GlusterFS client and mount the GlusterFS volume that will be used to host the KVM image:

```
root@kvm1/2:~# apt-get update && apt-get install glusterfs-client
root@kvm1/2:~# mkdir /tmp/kvm_gfs
root@kvm1/2:~# mount -t glusterfs glusterfs1:/kvm_gfs /tmp/kvm_gfs
root@kvm1/2:~#
```

> When mounting the GlusterFS volume, you can specify either one of the cluster nodes. In the preceding example, we are mounting from the `glusterfs1` node.

8. On one of the `libvirt` nodes, build a new KVM instance, using the mounted GlusterFS volume:

```
root@kvm1:~# virt-install --name kvm_gfs --ram 1024 --extra-
args="text console=tty0 utf8 console=ttyS0,115200" --graphics
vnc,listen=0.0.0.0 --hvm --
location=http://ftp.us.debian.org/debian/dists/stable/main/installe
r-amd64/ --disk /tmp/kvm_gfs/gluster_kvm.img,size=5
...
root@kvm1:~#
```

9. Ensure that both `libvirt` nodes can see the guest image:

```
root@kvm1/2:~# ls -al /tmp/kvm_gfs/
total 1820300
drwxr-xr-x 3 root root 4096 Apr 13 14:48 .
drwxrwxrwt 6 root root 4096 Apr 13 15:00 ..
-rwxr-xr-x 1 root root 5368709120 Apr 13 14:59 gluster_kvm.img
root@kvm1/2:~#
```

10. To manually migrate the KVM instance from one `libvirt` node to the other, first stop the instance and dump its XML definition:

```
root@kvm1:~# virsh destroy kvm_gfs
Domain kvm_gfs destroyed

root@kvm1:~# virsh dumpxml kvm_gfs > kvm_gfs.xml
root@kvm1:~#
```

11. From the source `libvirt` node, define the instance on the target host:

```
root@kvm1:~# virsh --connect qemu+ssh://kvm2/system define
kvm_gfs.xml
Domain kvm_gfs defined from kvm_gfs.xml

root@kvm1:~# virsh --connect qemu+ssh://kvm2/system list --all
 Id    Name        State
-----------------------------------------------------------
 -     kvm_gfs     shut off

root@kvm1:~#
```

12. Start the KVM instance on the target host to complete the migration:

```
root@kvm2:~# virsh start kvm_gfs
Domain kvm_gfs started

root@kvm2:~#
```

We can also start the KVM instance on the destination host from the source host using the qemu+ssh connection as follows:
```
root@kvm1:~# virsh --connect qemu+ssh://kvm2/system start
kvm_gfs
```

How it works...

We begin by installing the GlusterFS server-side package on both servers in step 1. Then, in step 2, we proceed to form a cluster by sending a probe from the first GlusterFS node. If the probe was successful, we further obtain information about the cluster in step 3. In step 4, we prepare the block devices on both GlusterFS servers for use by creating a filesystem on them, then mounting them. The block device once mounted will contain the bricks that will form a virtual replicated volume for GlusterFS to export.

In step 5, we create the new replicated volume on one of the nodes (this will affect the entire cluster and only needs to be run from one GlusterFS node). We specify that the type is going to be replicated, using the TCP protocol and the location of the bricks we are going to use. Once the volume is created, we start it in step 6 and get more information about it. Note that from the output of the volume information, we can see the number of bricks in use and their location in the cluster.

In step 7, we install the GlusterFS client component on both `libvirt` servers and mount the GFS volume. Both KVM hosts now share the same replicated storage that is physically hosted on the GlusterFS nodes. We are going to use that shared storage to host the new KVM image file.

In step 8, we proceed with the installation of a new KVM instance, using the GlusterFS volume that we mounted in the previous step. Once the installation is complete, we verify that both `libvirt` servers can see the new KVM image, in step 9.

We start the manual migration in step 10 by first stopping the running KVM instance, then saving its configuration to the disk. In step 11, we remotely define the KVM guest using the XML dump and verify that it has been successfully defined on the target host. Finally, we start the KVM instance on the target server, completing the migration.

Online migration using the virsh command with shared storage

The `virsh` command provides a migrate parameter that we can use to migrate KVM instances between hosts. In the previous two recipes, we saw how to migrate instances manually with downtime. In this recipe, we are going to perform a live migration on an instance that uses either the iSCSI storage pool or the GlusterFS shared volumes that we used earlier in this chapter.

If you recall, live migration only works when the guest filesystem resides on some sort of shared media, such as NFS, iSCSI, GlusterFS, or if we first copy the image file to all nodes and use the `--copy-storage-all` option with `virsh migrate`, as we'll see later in this chapter.

Getting ready

In order to complete this recipe, we are going to need the following:

- Two `libvirt` hosts with a shared storage between them. If you've completed the earlier recipes in this chapter, you can either use the iSCSI storage pool we created and the KVM instance that is using it or the GFS shared storage with the KVM guest.
- Both `libvirt` hosts should be able to communicate with each other using short hostnames.

How to do it...

To perform a live migration using the shared storage, perform the operations listed here:

1. Ensure that the iSCSI KVM instance we built earlier is running on the source host:

```
root@kvm1:~# virsh list --all
 Id   Name          State
----------------------------------------------------------
 26   iscsi_kvm     running

root@kvm1:~#
```

2. Live migrate the instance to the second `libvirt` server (the target node should already have the iSCSI pool configured). If this operation errors out, please consult the *There's more...* section of this recipe for troubleshooting tips:

```
root@kvm1:~# virsh migrate --live iscsi_kvm qemu+ssh://kvm2/system

root@kvm1:~#
```

3. Ensure that the KVM instance has been stopped on the source host and started on the target server:

```
root@kvm1:~# virsh list --all
 Id    Name         State
----------------------------------------------------------
 -     iscsi_kvm    shut off

root@kvm1:~# virsh --connect qemu+ssh://kvm2/system list --all
 Id    Name        State
----------------------------------------------------------
 10    iscsi_kvm   running

root@kvm1:~#
```

4. To migrate the instance back, from the kvm2 node, run the following:

```
root@kvm2:~# virsh migrate --live iscsi_kvm qemu+ssh://kvm1/system

root@kvm2:~# virsh list --all
 Id Name State
----------------------------------------------------------

root@kvm2:~# virsh --connect qemu+ssh://kvm1/system list --all
 Id    Name         State
----------------------------------------------------------
 28    iscsi_kvm    running

root@kvm2:~#
```

How it works...

When migrating a KVM instance that is using a shared storage, such as the iSCSI storage pool in this example, once we initiate the migration with the migrate --live parameter, libvirt takes care of logging out the iSCSI session from the original host and logging it in to the target server, thus making the block device containing the guest filesystem present on the destination server without the need to copy all the data. You might have noted that the migration took only a few seconds because the only data that was migrated was the memory pages of the running VM on the source host.

There's more...

Depending on your Linux distribution and the server type (on-metal or a cloud instance) you are running this recipe on, you might encounter a few common errors when trying to migrate the instance.

Error: error: Unsafe migration: Migration may lead to data corruption if disks use cache != none.

Solution: Edit the XML definition of the instance you are trying to migrate and update the driver section of the block device to contain the `cache=none` attribute:

```
root@kvm1:~# virsh edit iscsi_kvm
...
<devices>
 ...
 <disk type='block' device='disk'>
   <driver name='qemu' type='raw' cache='none'/>
   <source dev='/dev/disk/by-path/ip-10.184.22.74:3260-iscsi-
iqn.2001-04.com.example:kvm-lun-0'/>
   <target dev='hda' bus='ide'/>
   <address type='drive' controller='0' bus='0' target='0' unit='0'/>
 </disk>
 ...
</devices>
```

Error: error: Internal error: Attempt to migrate guest to the same host `02000100-0300-0400-0005-000600070008`.

Solution: Some servers, usually virtualized, may return the same system UUID, which causes the migration to fail. To see if this is the case, run the following on both the source and target machines:

```
root@kvm1/2:~# virsh sysinfo | grep -B5 -A3 uuid
 <system>
   <entry name='manufacturer'>FOXCONN</entry>
   <entry name='product'>CL7100</entry>
   <entry name='version'>PVT1-X05</entry>
   <entry name='serial'>2M2542Z069</entry>
   <entry name='uuid'>02000100-0300-0400-0005-000600070008</entry>
   <entry name='sku'>NULL</entry>
   <entry name='family'>Intel Grantley EP</entry>
 </system>
root@kvm1/2:~#
```

If the UUID is the same on both servers, edit the `libvirt` configuration file and assign a unique UUID, then restart `libvirt`:

```
root@kvm2:~# vim /etc/libvirt/libvirtd.conf
...
host_uuid = "02000100-0300-0400-0006-000600070008"
...
root@kvm2:~# /etc/init.d/libvirt-bin restart
libvirt-bin stop/waiting
libvirt-bin start/running, process 12167
root@kvm2:~#
```

Error: error: Unable to resolve address kvm2.localdomain service 49152: Name or service is not known.

Solution: This indicates that `libvirt` is unable to resolve the hostname of the instances. Make sure that the hostname does not resolve to localhost and that you can ping, or SSH between the source and target servers using the hostname instead of the IP address of the server. An example of a working host file for both `libvirt` nodes is as follows:

```
root@kvm1:~# cat /etc/hosts
127.0.0.1 localhost

10.184.226.106 kvm1.example.com kvm1
10.184.226.74  kvm2.example.com kvm2
root@kvm1:~#

root@kvm2:~# cat /etc/hosts
127.0.0.1 localhost

10.184.226.106 kvm1.example.com kvm1
10.184.226.74  kvm2.example.com kvm2
root@kvm2:~#
```

You can find more information about the operation of an instance by examining the following logs:

```
root@kvm1:~# cat /var/log/libvirt/libvirtd.log
...
2017-04-12 19:26:02.297+0000: 33149: error : virCommandWait:2399 : internal
error: Child process (/usr/bin/iscsiadm --mode session) unexpected exit
status 21
...
root@kvm1:~# cat /var/log/libvirt/qemu/iscsi_kvm.log
...
2017-04-13 17:59:48.040+0000: starting up
LC_ALL=C PATH=/usr/local/sbin:/usr/local/bin:/usr/bin:/usr/sbin:/sbin:/bin
QEMU_AUDIO_DRV=none /usr/bin/qemu-system-x86_64 -name iscsi_kvm -S -machine
```

```
pc-i440fx-trusty,accel=kvm,usb=off -m 1024 -realtime mlock=off -smp
1,sockets=1,cores=1,threads=1 -uuid 306e05ed-e398-ef33-d6e2-3708e90b89a6 -
no-user-config -nodefaults -chardev
socket,id=charmonitor,path=/var/lib/libvirt/qemu/iscsi_kvm.monitor,server,n
owait -mon chardev=charmonitor,id=monitor,mode=control -rtc base=utc -no-
shutdown -boot strict=on -device piix3-usb-
uhci,id=usb,bus=pci.0,addr=0x1.0x2 -drive file=/dev/disk/by-
path/ip-10.184.226.74:3260-iscsi-iqn.2001-04.com.example:kvm-
lun-0,if=none,id=drive-ide0-0-0,format=raw,cache=none -device ide-
hd,bus=ide.0,unit=0,drive=drive-ide0-0-0,id=ide0-0-0,bootindex=1 -netdev
tap,fd=24,id=hostnet0 -device
rtl8139,netdev=hostnet0,id=net0,mac=52:54:00:8b:b8:e3,bus=pci.0,addr=0x3 -
chardev pty,id=charserial0 -device isa-
serial,chardev=charserial0,id=serial0 -vnc 0.0.0.0:0 -device cirrus-
vga,id=video0,bus=pci.0,addr=0x2 -incoming tcp:[::]:49153 -device virtio-
balloon-pci,id=balloon0,bus=pci.0,addr=0x4
char device redirected to /dev/pts/0 (label charserial0)
qemu: terminating on signal 15 from pid 33148
2017-04-13 18:34:49.684+0000: shutting down
...
root@kvm1:~#
```

Offline migration using the virsh command and local image

Performing offline migration with virsh does not require a shared storage; however, we are responsible for providing the guest filesystem to the new host (by coping the image file and so on). The offline migration transfers the instance definition without starting the guest on the destination host and without stopping it on the source host. In this recipe, we are going to perform an offline migration using the virsh command on a running KVM guest using an image file for its filesystem.

Getting ready

For this simple recipe, we are going to need the following:

- Two libvirt hosts and a running KVM instance. If one is not present on your host, you can install and start a new guest VM using a local image file:

    ```
    root@kvm:~# virt-install --name kvm_no_sharedfs --ram 1024 --extra-
    args="text console=tty0 utf8 console=ttyS0,115200" --graphics
    vnc,listen=0.0.0.0 --hvm --
    ```

```
location=http://ftp.us.debian.org/debian/dists/stable/main/installe
r-amd64/ --disk /tmp/kvm_no_sharedfs.img,size=5
```

- Both hosts should be able to communicate with each other using hostnames.

How to do it...

To perform an offline migration using the `virsh` command, run the following:

1. Make sure that we have a running KVM instance:

```
root@kvm1:~# virsh list --all
 Id   Name              State
----------------------------------------------------
 26   kvm_no_sharedfs   running

root@kvm1:~#
```

2. Migrate the instance using the offline mode. If this operation errors out, please consult the *There's more...* section of the *Online migration using the virsh command* recipe for troubleshooting tips:

```
root@kvm1:~# virsh migrate --offline --persistent kvm_no_sharedfs
qemu+ssh://kvm2/system

root@kvm1:~#
```

3. Unlike the live migration, the source instance is still running, and the destination instance is stopped:

```
root@kvm1:~# virsh list --all
 Id     Name              State
----------------------------------------------------
 29     kvm_no_sharedfs   running

root@kvm1:~# virsh --connect qemu+ssh://kvm2/system list --all
 Id     Name              State
----------------------------------------------------
 -      kvm_no_sharedfs   shut off

root@kvm1:~#
```

How it works...

Offline migrations are quite simple; the `virsh` command transfers the definition file from the target host to the destination and defines the instance. The original KVM guest is left running. In order to start the migrated instance, its image file needs to be transferred to the destination first and be present on the exact same location as the one on the source server. The main difference when performing an offline migration as compared with just dumping the XML file and defining it on the destination host is that `libvirt` makes updates to the destination XML file, such as assigning new UUIDs.

In the earlier-mentioned example, the only two new flags were the offline and persistent flags. The prior specifies an offline type migration, and the latter leaves the domain persistent on the destination host.

Online migration using the virsh command and local image

In this recipe, we are going to live migrate a running instance, without shared storage.

Getting ready

For this recipe, we are going to need the following:

- Two `libvirt` servers with a running KVM instance using a local image file. We are going to use the KVM guest we built in the previous recipe, *Offline migration using the virsh command and local image*.
- Both servers must be able to communicate with each other using their hostnames.

How to do it...

To migrate an instance without shared storage, use the following steps:

1. Ensure that the KVM guest is running:

   ```
   root@kvm1:~# virsh list --all
    Id    Name              State
   ----------------------------------------------------
    33    kvm_no_sharedfs   running

   root@kvm1:~#
   ```

2. Find the location of the image file:

   ```
   root@kvm1:~# virsh dumpxml kvm_no_sharedfs | grep "source file"
    <source file='/tmp/kvm_no_sharedfs.img'/>
   root@kvm1:~#
   ```

3. Transfer the image file to the destination host:

   ```
   root@kvm1:~# scp /tmp/kvm_no_sharedfs.img kvm2:/tmp/
   kvm_no_sharedfs.img 100% 5120MB 243.8MB/s 00:21
   root@kvm1:~#
   ```

4. Migrate the instance and ensure that it's running on the destination host:

   ```
   root@kvm1:~# virsh migrate --live --persistent --verbose --copy-
   storage-all kvm_no_sharedfs qemu+ssh://kvm2/system
   Migration: [100 %]
   root@kvm1:~# virsh list --all
    Id    Name              State
   ----------------------------------------------------
    -     kvm_no_sharedfs   shut off

   root@kvm1:~# virsh --connect qemu+ssh://kvm2/system list --all
    Id    Name              State
   ----------------------------------------------------
    17    kvm_no_sharedfs   running

   root@kvm1:~#
   ```

5. From the destination host, migrate the instance back, using the incremental image transfer:

```
root@kvm2:~# virsh migrate --live --persistent --verbose --copy-
storage-inc kvm_no_sharedfs qemu+ssh://kvm/system
Migration: [100 %]
root@kvm2:~#
```

How it works...

After we ensure that the source instance is in a running state in step 1, we transfer the image file to the destination file, in the exact same location as the source in step 3. With the image file in place, we can now perform a live migration, which we do in step 4 and then back in step 5.

The two new parameters we haven't used so far are --copy-storage-all and copy-storage-inc. The first one instructs libvirt to transfer the entire image file to the destination, whereas the second performs an incremental transfer, copying only the data that has changed, reducing the transfer time.

5
Monitoring and Backup of KVM Virtual Machines

In this chapter, we are going to cover the following topics:

- Resource usage collection with libvirt
- Monitoring KVM instances with Sensu
- Simple KVM backups with tar and rsync
- Creating snapshots
- Listing snapshots
- Inspecting snapshots
- Editing snapshots
- Reverting snapshots
- Deleting snapshots

Introduction

It goes without saying that monitoring and backing up of production KVM instances is important in order to meet uptime **Service-Level Agreements** (**SLAs**) and to satisfy high-availability and performance requirements. Monitoring and backing up of virtual machines is not very different from monitoring and backing up of physical servers. In some cases, it's even more convenient to back up a single image file for VM or create a snapshot, rather than the filesystem of an OS running on a physical server.

In this chapter, we are going to see examples on how to gather resource usage metrics for live KVM instances and how to monitor the resource usage and alert on predefined thresholds with tools such as Sensu. Following this, we are going to focus on different ways of backing up KVM guests using tools such as `rsync`, and creating and managing snapshots with the help of the `virsh` command.

Resource usage collection with libvirt

The first step in monitoring virtual machines is to get familiar with the tools to collect metrics on the subsystems we would like to later alert on. In this recipe, we are going to focus on CPU, memory, and block device utilization of the KVM guests. We are also going to learn how to use the QEMU monitoring socket and the QEMU guest agent.

Libvirt exposes a set of calls that the `virsh` command leverages to gather resource usage information on the specified guest/domain. We are going to monitor and alert on the information collected here in the *Monitoring KVM instances with Sensu* recipe later in this chapter.

Getting ready

For this recipe, we are going to need the following:

- A server with libvirt installed and configured
- A running KVM instance

How to do it...

To collect various resource usage information for a running instance or the hypervisor host, perform the following:

1. Obtain information on the hypervisor CPU utilization:

```
root@kvm:~# virsh nodecpustats --percent
usage: 0.0%
user: 0.0%
system: 0.0%
idle: 100.0%
iowait: 0.0%

root@kvm:~#
```

2. Collect information on the hypervisor memory utilization:

```
root@kvm:~# virsh nodememstats
total : 131918328 KiB
free : 103633700 KiB
buffers: 195532 KiB
cached : 25874840 KiB

root@kvm:~#
```

3. Check the state of a KVM instance:

```
root@kvm:~# virsh domstate kvm1
running

root@kvm:~#
```

4. Get a number of assigned virtual CPUs (vCPU) for a KVM instance:

```
root@kvm:~# virsh vcpucount --current kvm1 --live
1

root@kvm:~#
```

5. Collect detailed information about the virtual CPU for a guest:

```
root@kvm:~# virsh vcpuinfo kvm1
VCPU: 0
CPU: 29
State: running
CPU time: 118.8s
CPU Affinity: yyyyyyyyyyyyyyyyyyyyyyyyyyyyyyyyyyyyyyyyyyyyyy

root@kvm:~#
```

6. Gather information about the vCPU timers for the guest VM:

```
root@kvm:~# virsh cpu-stats --total kvm1
Total:
cpu_time 175.003045493 seconds
user_time 2.610000000 seconds
system_time 7.510000000 seconds

root@kvm:~#
```

7. Collect general information about the VM:

```
root@kvm:~# virsh dominfo kvm1
Id: 30
Name: kvm1
UUID: bd167199-c1c4-de7e-4996-43a7f197e565
OS Type: hvm
State: running
CPU(s): 1
CPU time: 175.6s
Max memory: 1048576 KiB
Used memory: 1048576 KiB
Persistent: yes
Autostart: disable
Managed save: no
Security model: none
Security DOI: 0

root@kvm:~#
```

8. Collect the memory utilization for the VM:

```
root@kvm:~# virsh dommemstat --live kvm1
actual 1048576
swap_in 0
rss 252684

root@kvm:~#
```

9. Get information about the block devices associated with the KVM instance:

```
root@kvm:~# virsh domblklist kvm1
Target Source
------------------------------------------------
hda /var/lib/libvirt/images/kvm1.img

root@kvm:~#
```

10. Obtain size information on the block device for the VM:

```
root@kvm:~# virsh domblkinfo --device hda kvm1
Capacity: 8589934592
Allocation: 2012381184
Physical: 2012381184

root@kvm:~#
```

11. Get any block device errors for the KVM instance:

```
root@kvm:~# virsh domblkerror kvm1
No errors found

root@kvm:~#
```

12. Print block device statistic for a KVM guest:

```
root@kvm:~# virsh domblkstat --device hda --human kvm1
Device: hda
number of read operations: 42053
number of bytes read: 106145280
number of write operations: 10648
number of bytes written: 96768000
number of flush operations: 4044
total duration of reads (ns): 833974071
total duration of writes (ns): 1180545967
total duration of flushes (ns): 3458623200

root@kvm:~#
```

How it works...

In this recipe, we collect various hypervisor and guest resource utilization information from the host OS. In later recipes, we will use that information in a monitoring system to alert and trigger actions based on set criteria and thresholds. Let's go through the steps we performed earlier in more detail.

We start by collecting information about the CPU utilization on the hypervisor/host OS in step 1. We then proceed to gather the memory utilization on the physical host in step 2. Note that we can also use other Linux commands to do this instead of `virsh`, but it helps demonstrate the concept.

Monitoring the state of a KVM instance is important in case the VM terminates unexpectedly or does not start automatically after a server reboot. In step 3, we obtain the current state of the virtual machine.

In steps 4, 5, and 6, we collect information about the virtual CPU of the guest. We can see the number of assigned CPUs along with other useful information, such as the time the CPU spends running kernel and userspace code.

In step 7, we collect more general information about the virtual machine; of notable interest is the total and used amount of memory that we can set alerting thresholds on.

In step 8, we get information about the memory utilization of the KVM instance. We can see the total, swap, and resident memory usage in the output.

In step 9, we list the block devices attached to the virtual machine, and we use that in step 10 to get information about its capacity. If there are any errors associated with the block device, the output of the command in step 11 will show that, which we can use to trigger monitoring alerts.

Monitoring the performance of a block device attached to a KVM instance can be done using the output of the command in step 12.

There's more...

When we create a virtual machine with libvirt, the QEMU process that is started exposes a monitoring socket that we can connect to and collect information about the guest.

Let's see how that looks for the KVM instance we've been using:

1. Get the process information for the guest instance:

```
root@kvm:~# pgrep -lfa kvm1
32332 /usr/bin/qemu-system-x86_64 -name kvm1 -S -machine pc-
i440fx-trusty,accel=kvm,usb=off -m 1024 -realtime mlock=off -smp
1,sockets=1,cores=1,threads=1 -uuid bd167199-c1c4-
de7e-4996-43a7f197e565 -no-user-config -nodefaults -chardev
socket,id=charmonitor,path=/var/lib/libvirt/qemu/kvm1.monitor,serve
r,nowait -mon chardev=charmonitor,id=monitor,mode=control -rtc
base=utc -no-shutdown -boot strict=on -device piix3-usb-
uhci,id=usb,bus=pci.0,addr=0x1.0x2 -drive
file=/var/lib/libvirt/images/kvm1.img,if=none,id=drive-
ide0-0-0,format=raw -device ide-hd,bus=ide.0,unit=0,drive=drive-
ide0-0-0,id=ide0-0-0,bootindex=1 -netdev tap,fd=24,id=hostnet0 -
device
rtl8139,netdev=hostnet0,id=net0,mac=52:54:00:55:9b:d6,bus=pci.0,add
r=0x3 -chardev pty,id=charserial0 -device isa-
serial,chardev=charserial0,id=serial0 -vnc 146.20.141.158:0 -device
cirrus-vga,id=video0,bus=pci.0,addr=0x2 -device virtio-balloon-
pci,id=balloon0,bus=pci.0,addr=0x4
root@kvm:~#
```

Notice from the preceding output the `-chardev`
`socket,id=charmonitor,path=/var/lib/libvirt/qemu/kvm1.monito`
`r` and the `-mon`
`chardev=charmonitor,id=monitor,mode=control` parameters passed to
the QEMU process.

2. We can access this socket in two ways, either by connecting to it using tools such
   as `nc` and `socat` or with the `virsh` command, as follows:

```
root@kvm:~# virsh qemu-monitor-command kvm1 --hmp "info"
info balloon -- show balloon information
info block [-v] [device] -- show info of one block device or all
block devices (and details of images with -v option)
info block-jobs -- show progress of ongoing block device operations
info blockstats -- show block device statistics
info capture -- show capture information
info chardev -- show the character devices
info cpus -- show infos for each CPU
info cpustats -- show CPU statistics
info history -- show the command line history
info irq -- show the interrupts statistics (if available)
info jit -- show dynamic compiler info
info kvm -- show KVM information
info mem -- show the active virtual memory mappings
info mice -- show which guest mouse is receiving events
info migrate -- show migration status
info migrate_cache_size -- show current migration xbzrle cache size
info migrate_capabilities -- show current migration capabilities
info mtree -- show memory tree
info name -- show the current VM name
info network -- show the network state
info numa -- show NUMA information
info pci -- show PCI info
info pcmcia -- show guest PCMCIA status
info pic -- show i8259 (PIC) state
info profile -- show profiling information
info qdm -- show qdev device model list
info qtree -- show device tree
info registers -- show the cpu registers
info roms -- show roms
info snapshots -- show the currently saved VM snapshots
info spice -- show the spice server status
info status -- show the current VM status (running|paused)
info tlb -- show virtual to physical memory mappings
info tpm -- show the TPM device
info trace-events -- show available trace-events & their state
info usb -- show guest USB devices
```

```
info usbhost -- show host USB devices
info usernet -- show user network stack connection states
info uuid -- show the current VM UUID
info version -- show the version of QEMU
info vnc -- show the vnc server status

root@kvm:~#
```

3. To obtain information about the network interface of the KVM instance, we can run the following code:

```
root@kvm:~# virsh qemu-monitor-command kvm1 --hmp "info network"
net0: index=0,type=nic,model=rtl8139,macaddr=52:54:00:55:9b:d6
 \ hostnet0: index=0,type=tap,fd=24

root@kvm:~#
```

QEMU provides a guest agent daemon that can be started inside the KVM instance and then can be connected to from the host OS. We can collect additional data or update certain settings for the virtual machine directly from the host.

Let's see an example of installing and using the QEMU guest agent:

1. Create the required directory that will contain the communication socket between libvirt on the host and the guest agent running inside the KVM guest:

```
root@kvm:~# mkdir -p /var/lib/libvirt/qemu/channel/target
root@kvm:~# chown libvirt-qemu:kvm
/var/lib/libvirt/qemu/channel/ -R
root@kvm:~#
```

2. Edit the configuration for the running VM and add the following definition under the `<devices>` section:

```
root@kvm:~# virsh edit kvm1
...
 <devices>
    ...
   <channel type='unix'>
     <source mode='bind'
path='/var/lib/libvirt/qemu/channel/target/kvm1.org.qemu.gu
est_agent.0'/>
     <target type='virtio' name='org.qemu.guest_agent.0'/>
     <alias name='channel0'/>
     <address type='virtio-serial' controller='0' bus='0'
port='1'/>
```

```
        </channel>
        ...
      </devices>
    ...

    Domain kvm1 XML configuration edited.
    root@kvm:~#
```

3. Restart the KVM instance:

```
root@kvm:~# virsh destroy kvm1
Domain kvm1 destroyed

root@kvm:~# virsh start kvm1
Domain kvm1 started

root@kvm:~#
```

4. Connect to the VM and install and start the QEMU guest agent, as follows:

```
root@kvm:~# virsh console kvm1
Connected to domain kvm1
Escape character is ^]

root@debian:~# apt update && apt install qemu-guest-agent
...
root@debian:~# service qemu-guest-agent start
root@debian:~# service qemu-guest-agent status
● qemu-guest-agent.service - LSB: QEMU Guest Agent startup
script
 Loaded: loaded (/etc/init.d/qemu-guest-agent)
 Active: active (running) since Wed 2017-04-19 14:44:08
CDT; 33min ago
 Process: 397 ExecStart=/etc/init.d/qemu-guest-agent start
(code=exited, status=0/SUCCESS)
 CGroup: /system.slice/qemu-guest-agent.service
   └─425 /usr/sbin/qemu-ga --daemonize -m virtio-serial -p
/dev/virti...

Apr 19 14:44:08 debian systemd[1]: Starting LSB: QEMU Guest
Agent startup s.....
Apr 19 14:44:08 debian systemd[1]: Started LSB: QEMU Guest
Agent startup script.
Hint: Some lines were ellipsized, use -l to show in full.
root@debian:~#
```

5. Back on the host, we can see the new socket file:

```
root@kvm:~# ls -la /var/lib/libvirt/qemu/channel/target/
total 8
drwxr-xr-x 2 libvirt-qemu kvm 4096 Apr 19 19:43 .
drwxr-xr-x 3 libvirt-qemu kvm 4096 Apr 19 19:43 ..
srwxr-xr-x 1 libvirt-qemu kvm 0 Apr 19 19:43
kvm1.org.qemu.guest_agent.0
root@kvm:~#
```

6. Let's connect to the guest agent from the host and list the available commands that the guest agent accepts:

```
root@kvm:~# virsh qemu-agent-command kvm1 --pretty --cmd
'{"execute": "guest-info"}'
{
  "return": {
    "version": "2.1.2",
    "supported_commands": [
      {
        "enabled": true,
        "name": "guest-set-vcpus",
        "success-response": true
      },
      {
        "enabled": true,
        "name": "guest-get-vcpus",
        "success-response": true
      },
      {
        "enabled": true,
        "name": "guest-network-get-interfaces",
        "success-response": true
      },
      ...
    ]
  }
}

root@kvm:~#
```

7. Get information about the guest vCPU by running the following code:

```
root@kvm:~# virsh qemu-agent-command kvm1 --pretty --cmd
'{"execute": "guest-get-vcpus"}'
{
  "return": [
    {
```

```
        "online": true,
        "can-offline": false,
        "logical-id": 0
    }
 ]
}

root@kvm:~#
```

Using the monitoring and guest agent sockets provides an additional way of collecting more information about the running virtual machines on the libvirt host that we can later add as monitoring checks.

Monitoring KVM instances with Sensu

Sensu is a complete monitoring solution that uses the client-server model; the server publishes checks in a message queue provided by the Rabbitmq service. The clients/agents subscribe to topics in the queue and execute the specified checks on the host they run on. State and historical data is stored in a Redis server.

In this recipe, we are going to install the Sensu server, Rabbitmq message queue, and the Redis server on one host, write a simple monitoring check using the information we obtained from the *Resource usage collection with libvirt* recipe earlier, and install the Sensu agent inside the KVM guest.

Getting ready

For this recipe, we are going to need the following:

- A Linux host with libvirt installed and running
- A KVM instance running on the libvirt host
- Network connectivity between the KVM instance and the libvirt host

How to do it...

To set up a new Sensu deployment and define various monitoring checks, perform the following steps:

1. Install the Redis server and ensure that it is responding to requests:

```
root@kvm:~# apt-get install -y redis-server
...
root@kvm:~# redis-cli ping
PONG
root@kvm:~#
```

2. Install the Rabbitmq server:

```
root@kvm:~# apt-get install -y rabbitmq-server
...
root@kvm:~#
```

3. Create the virtual host the Sensu agents will subscribe to and the credentials and permissions for the Rabbitmq clients:

```
root@kvm:~# rabbitmqctl add_vhost /sensu
Creating vhost "/sensu" ...
...done.
root@kvm:~# rabbitmqctl add_user sensu secret
Creating user "sensu" ...
...done.
root@kvm:~# rabbitmqctl set_permissions -p /sensu sensu ".*" ".*"
".*"
Setting permissions for user "sensu" in vhost "/sensu" ...
...done.
root@kvm:~#
```

4. Add the Sensu upstream repository and its key and then install the Sensu package:

```
root@kvm:~# wget -q
https://sensu.global.ssl.fastly.net/apt/pubkey.gpg -O- | apt-key
add -
OK
root@kvm:~# echo "deb https://sensu.global.ssl.fastly.net/apt sensu
main" | tee /etc/apt/sources.list.d/sensu.list
deb https://sensu.global.ssl.fastly.net/apt sensu main
root@kvm:~# apt-get update
...
root@kvm:~# apt-get install -y sensu
```

```
. . .
root@kvm:~#
```

5. Sensu uses JSON-based configuration files for its configuration. Create the Sensu API configuration file:

```
root@kvm:/etc/sensu/conf.d# cat api.json
{
  "api": {
    "host": "localhost",
    "bind": "0.0.0.0",
    "port": 4567
  }
}
root@kvm:/etc/sensu/conf.d#
```

6. Configure the transport type for Sensu; we are using Rabbitmq for this deployment:

```
root@kvm:/etc/sensu/conf.d# cat transport.json
{
  "transport": {
    "name": "rabbitmq",
    "reconnect_on_error": true
  }
}
root@kvm:/etc/sensu/conf.d#
```

7. Configure where the Rabbitmq service is accepting connections, the virtual host, and credentials:

```
root@kvm:/etc/sensu/conf.d# cat rabbitmq.json
{
  "rabbitmq": {
    "host": "0.0.0.0",
    "port": 5672,
    "vhost": "/sensu",
    "user": "sensu",
    "password": "secret"
  }
}
root@kvm:/etc/sensu/conf.d#
```

8. Specify the host and port the Redis service is listening on:

```
root@kvm:/etc/sensu/conf.d# cat redis.json
{
 "redis": {
   "host": "localhost",
   "port": 6379
 }
}
root@kvm:/etc/sensu/conf.d#
```

9. Configure the Sensu client:

```
root@kvm:/etc/sensu/conf.d# cat client.json
{
 "client": {
   "name": "ubuntu",
   "address": "127.0.0.1",
   "subscriptions": [
     "base"
   ],
   "socket": {
     "bind": "127.0.0.1",
     "port": 3030
   }
 }
}

root@kvm:/etc/sensu/conf.d#
```

For more information on Sensu, please refer to https://sensuapp.org/docs/.

10. Install the web frontend for Sensu, named **Uchiwa**:

```
root@kvm:/etc/sensu/conf.d# apt-get install -y uchiwa
...
root@kvm:/etc/sensu/conf.d
```

11. Configure the Uchiwa frontend:

```
root@kvm:/etc/sensu/conf.d# cat /etc/sensu/uchiwa.json
{
  "sensu": [
    {
```

```
        "name": "KVM guests",
        "host": "localhost",
        "ssl": false,
        "port": 4567,
        "path": "",
        "timeout": 5000
      }
    ],
  "uchiwa": {
    "port": 3000,
    "stats": 10,
    "refresh": 10000
  }
}

root@kvm:/etc/sensu/conf.d#
```

12. Start the Sensu server, API, client, and frontend components:

```
root@kvm:/etc/sensu/conf.d# /etc/init.d/sensu-server start
 * Starting sensu-server [ OK ]
root@kvm:/etc/sensu/conf.d# /etc/init.d/sensu-api start
 * Starting sensu-api [ OK ]
root@kvm:/etc/sensu/conf.d# /etc/init.d/sensu-client start
 * Starting sensu-client [ OK ]
root@kvm:/etc/sensu/conf.d# /etc/init.d/uchiwa restart
uchiwa started.
root@kvm:/etc/sensu/conf.d#
```

13. Connect to the KVM instance console; install and configure the Sensu client:

```
root@kvm:/etc/sensu/conf.d# virsh console kvm1
Connected to domain kvm1
Escape character is ^]

root@debian:~# wget -q
https://sensu.global.ssl.fastly.net/apt/pubkey.gpg -O- | apt-key
add -
OK
root@debian:~# echo "deb https://sensu.global.ssl.fastly.net/apt
sensu main" | tee /etc/apt/sources.list.d/sensu.list
deb https://sensu.global.ssl.fastly.net/apt sensu main
root@debian:~# apt install apt-transport-https
root@debian:~# apt update && apt install sensu
...
root@debian:~# cd /etc/sensu/conf.d/
root@debian:/etc/sensu/conf.d# cat client.json
{
```

```
  "client": {
    "name": "monitor_kvm",
    "address": "10.10.10.92",
    "subscriptions": ["base"]
  }
}

root@debian:/etc/sensu/conf.d# cat rabbitmq.json
{
  "rabbitmq": {
    "host": "10.10.10.1",
    "port": 5672,
    "vhost": "/sensu",
    "user": "sensu",
    "password": "secret"
  }
}

root@debian:/etc/sensu/conf.d# cat transport.json
{
  "transport": {
    "name": "rabbitmq",
    "reconnect_on_error": true
  }
}

root@debian:/etc/sensu/conf.d#
```

Replace the IP address of the client with the IP address configured inside the KVM instance. Update the IP address of the Rabbitmq server with the IP address configured on the host bridge. Ensure that the KVM guest can ping the bridge IP on the host OS.

14. Start the Sensu client:

```
root@debian:/etc/sensu/conf.d# /etc/init.d/sensu-client start
Starting sensu-client:.
root@debian:/etc/sensu/conf.d#
```

15. Connect to the Uchiwa interface and ensure that the host Sensu client and the KVM guest Sensu client are listed in the **CLIENTS** section:

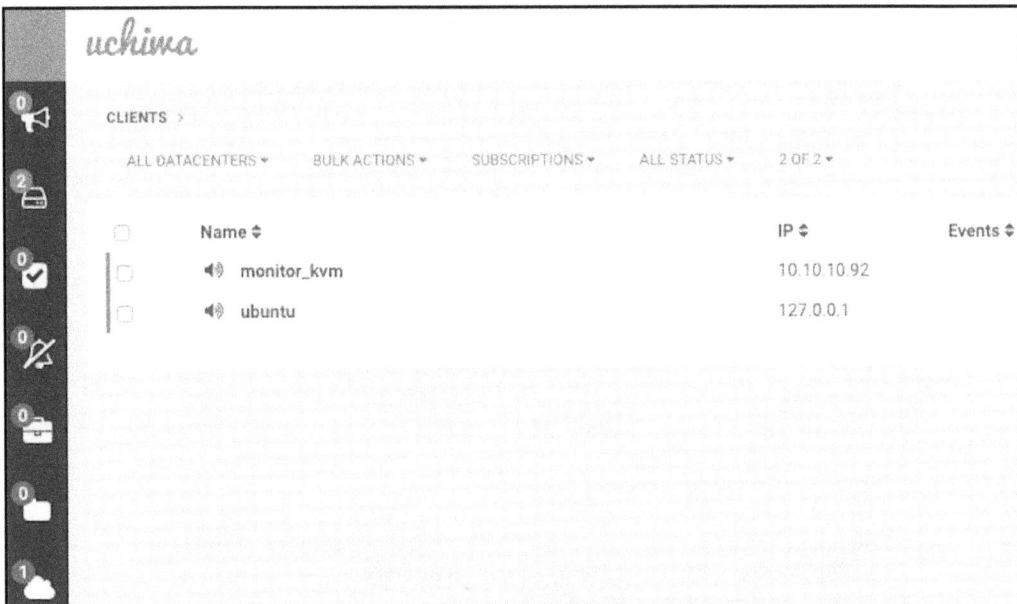

The Uchiwa frontend showing the connected clients

16. While still connected to the KVM guest, install a memory check from the gem repository and test it:

```
root@debian:/etc/sensu/conf.d# apt install rubygems
. . .
root@debian:/etc/sensu/conf.d# gem search sensu | grep plugins |
grep memory
sensu-plugins-memory (0.0.2)
sensu-plugins-memory-checks (2.1.0)
root@debian:/etc/sensu/conf.d#
root@debian:/etc/sensu/conf.d# gem install sensu-plugins-memory-
checks
. . .
root@debian:/etc/sensu/conf.d# /etc/init.d/sensu-client restart
configuration is valid
Stopping sensu-client:.
Starting sensu-client:.
oot@debian:/etc/sensu/conf.d# /usr/local/bin/check-memory-
percent.rb -w 80 -c 9
MEM OK - system memory usage: 11%
root@debian:/etc/sensu/conf.d#
```

17. Back on the host OS, define the new memory check for the KVM guest:

```
root@kvm:/etc/sensu/conf.d# cat check_memory.json
{
  "checks": {
    "memory_check": {
      "command": "/usr/local/bin/check-memory-percent.rb -w 80 -c
90",
      "subscribers": ["base"],
      "handlers": ["default"],
      "interval": 300
    }
  }
}
root@kvm:/etc/sensu/conf.d#
```

18. Restart the Sensu components:

```
root@kvm:/etc/sensu/conf.d# /etc/init.d/uchiwa restart
Killing uchiwa (pid 15350) with SIGTERM
Waiting uchiwa (pid 15350) to die...
Waiting uchiwa (pid 15350) to die...
uchiwa stopped.
uchiwa started.
root@kvm:/etc/sensu/conf.d# /etc/init.d/sensu-server restart
configuration is valid
 * Stopping sensu-server [ OK ]
 * Starting sensu-server [ OK ]
root@kvm:/etc/sensu/conf.d# /etc/init.d/sensu-api restart
configuration is valid
 * Stopping sensu-api [ OK ]
 * Starting sensu-api [ OK ]
root@kvm:/etc/sensu/conf.d#
```

19. The **memory_check** for the KVM instance is now showing in the Uchiwa dashboard:

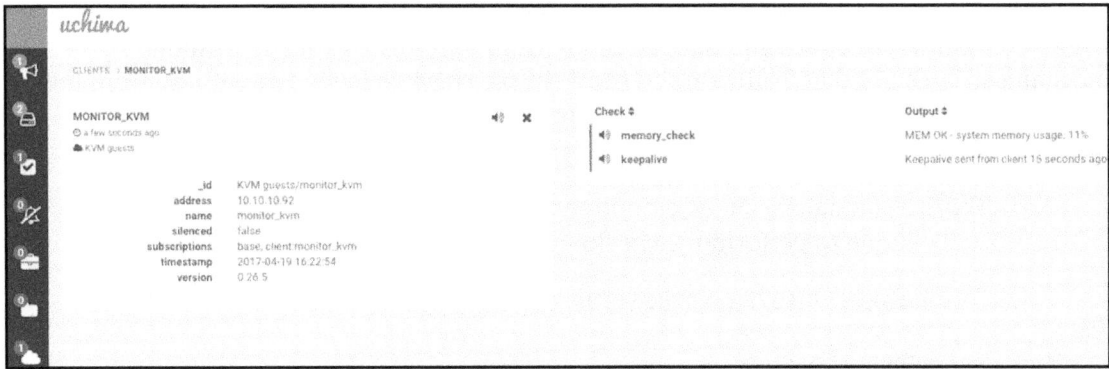

The Uchiwa frontend showing the memory check for the KVM guest

How it works...

In the previous section, we installed a Sensu server and all the required infrastructure components for it to run on the hypervisor host. Then we installed the client inside a KVM instance, installed the memory ruby check, and defined it on the host. Let's examine all the steps in more detail.

In step 1, we install the Redis server and ensure that it is accepting connections. Redis is a key-value store service that Sensu uses to store the historical information about the checks, current state, and connected clients.

With the Redis server in place, we proceed to install and configure Rabbitmq in steps 2 through 9. Rabbitmq is a message bus conforming to the **Advanced Message Queuing Protocol** (**AMQP**) standard. The Sensu server and clients produce and consume messages from the queue to trigger monitoring actions.

Although not required, in steps 10 and 11, we install and configure a web frontend for the Sensu server named Uchiwa. We can use the web interface to check on the status of different checks for the KVM guests we monitor.

In step 13, we install the Sensu client inside the KVM guest instance and proceed to install a memory monitoring script from a gem in step 16. A monitoring script can be written in any language (RUBY in this case) as long as it returns the expected error codes that Sensu expects. In the next section, we are going to write a new check from scratch using Bash.

There's more...

In the previous section, we saw an example of how to use a ruby check inside the KVM instance and monitor the memory utilization. Sensu provides standalone checks that can be triggered from the Sensu client, independently from the Sensu server scheduling mechanism. Let's use that feature and write a simple check in Bash that will run from the host OS, instead of the KVM guest, and use the `virsh` command to check the status of a KVM instance:

1. Write a standalone check definition with the custom script that `sensu-client` will execute to perform the check:

```
root@kvm:/etc/sensu/conf.d# cat check_kvm_instance_status.json
{
  "checks": {
    "check_kvm_instance_status": {
      "command": "check_kvm_instance_status.sh -n kvm1",
      "standalone": true,
      "subscribers": ["base"],
      "interval": 60
    }
  }
}
root@kvm:/etc/sensu/conf.d#
```

2. In the Sensu `plugins` directory, write this simple Bash script:

```
root@kvm:/etc/sensu/conf.d# cd ../plugins/
root@kvm:/etc/sensu/plugins# cat check_kvm_instance_status.sh
#!/bin/bash
# Checks if a KVM instance is running

usage()
{
 echo "Usage: `basename $0` -n|--name kvm1"
 exit 2
}

sanity_check()
{
 if [ "$INSTANCE_NAME" == "" ]
 then
   usage
 fi
}
```

```
report_result()
{
 if [ "$INSTANCE_STATE" == "shut off" ]
 then
   echo "CRITICAL - KVM instance $INSTANCE_NAME is not running"
   exit 2
 else
   echo "OK - KVM instance $INSTANCE_NAME is running"
   exit 0
 fi
}

check_instance_state()
{
 declare -g INSTANCE_STATE="shut off"

 INSTANCE_STATE=$(sudo /usr/bin/virsh domstate $INSTANCE_NAME)
}

main()
{
 sanity_check
 check_instance_state
 report_result
}

while [[ $# > 1 ]]
do
 key=$1

 case $key in
   -n|--name)
     INSTANCE_NAME=$2
     shift
   ;;
   *)
     usage
   ;;
 esac
 shift
done

main

root@kvm:/etc/sensu/plugins#
```

3. Make the script executable, add the Sensu user in a `sudoers` file, and test the check by executing it:

```
root@kvm:/etc/sensu/plugins# chmod u+x check_kvm_instance_status.sh
root@kvm:/etc/sensu/plugins# chown sensu:sensu
check_kvm_instance_status.sh
root@kvm:/etc/sensu/plugins# echo "sensu ALL=(ALL) NOPASSWD:ALL" >
/etc/sudoers.d/sensu
root@kvm:/etc/sensu/plugins# sudo -u sensu
./check_kvm_instance_status.sh --name kvm1
OK - KVM instance kvm1 is running
root@kvm:/etc/sensu/plugins# virsh destroy kvm1
Domain kvm1 destroyed

root@kvm:/etc/sensu/plugins# sudo -u sensu
./check_kvm_instance_status.sh --name kvm1
CRITICAL - KVM instance kvm1 is not running
root@kvm:/etc/sensu/plugins# virsh start kvm1
Domain kvm1 started

root@kvm:/etc/sensu/plugins#
```

4. Restart the Sensu client on the host; check the logs and the Uchiwa dashboard for the new standalone check:

```
root@kvm:/etc/sensu/conf.d# /etc/init.d/sensu-client restart
configuration is valid
 * Stopping sensu-client [ OK ]
 * Starting sensu-client [ OK ]
root@kvm:/etc/sensu/conf.d# cat /var/log/sensu/sensu-client.log |
grep check_kvm_instance_status
{"timestamp":"2017-04-20T17:37:48.409805+0000","level":"warn","mess
age":"loading config
file","file":"/etc/sensu/conf.d/check_kvm_instance_status.json"}
{"timestamp":"2017-04-20T17:38:16.746861+0000","level":"info","mess
age":"publishing check
result","payload":{"client":"ubuntu","check":{"command":"check_kvm_
instance_status.sh -n
kvm1","standalone":true,"subscribers":["base"],"interval":60,"name"
:"check_kvm_instance_status","issued":1492709896,"executed":1492709
896,"duration":0.016,"output":"OK - KVM instance kvm1 is
running\n","status":0}}}
root@kvm:/etc/sensu/conf.d#
```

◀))	check_kvm_instance_status	OK - KVM instance kvm1 is running
◀))	keepalive	Keepalive sent from client 1 seconds ago

The Uchiwa frontend showing the standalone instance check

Using the examples from the *Resource usage collection with libvirt* recipe, you should now be able to write a variety of Sensu monitoring checks executed from the hypervisor or inside the KVM guests.

> For more information on how Sensu can execute scripts when an alert is triggered, please refer to the *handlers* section of the official documentation at `https://sensuapp.org/docs/latest/reference/handlers.html`.

Simple KVM backups with tar and rsync

In this recipe, we are going to create a backup of a KVM instance using `tar` and `rsync` and store it on a remote server. This is the easiest way to backup a KVM instance. In the next few recipes, we are going to create snapshots and use them as a cold backup.

Getting ready

For this extremely simple recipe, we are going to need:

- A libvirt host with a running KVM instance, using an image file as its backing store
- The `tar` and `rsync` Linux utilities
- A remote server to transfer the backup

How to do it...

To back up a virtual machine using `tar` and `rsync`, perform the following steps:

1. Create the backup directory and change to it:

```
root@kvm:~# mkdir backup_kvm1 && cd backup_kvm1
root@kvm:~/backup_kvm1#
```

2. Find the location of the image file of the KVM guest:

```
root@kvm:~/backup_kvm1# virsh dumpxml kvm1 | grep "source file"
 <source file='/var/lib/libvirt/images/kvm1.img'/>
root@kvm:~/backup_kvm1#
```

3. Save the current instance configuration to disk:

```
root@kvm:~/backup_kvm1# virsh dumpxml kvm1 > kvm1.xml
root@kvm:~/backup_kvm1#
```

4. Stop the KVM guest and copy the image file to the backup directory:

```
root@kvm:~/backup_kvm1# virsh destroy kvm1
Domain kvm1 destroyed

root@kvm:~/backup_kvm1# cp /var/lib/libvirt/images/kvm1.img .
root@kvm:~/backup_kvm1# ls -lah
total 2.4G
drwxr-xr-x 2 root root 4.0K Apr 20 18:37 .
drwx------ 7 root root 4.0K Apr 20 18:36 ..
-rwxr-xr-x 1 root root 8.0G Apr 20 18:37 kvm1.img
-rw-r--r-- 1 root root 3.0K Apr 20 18:36 kvm1.xml
root@kvm:~/backup_kvm1#
```

5. Create a single archive for the VM's configuration and image files:

```
root@kvm:~/backup_kvm1# tar jcvf kvm1_backup.tar.bz .
./
./kvm1.img
./kvm1.xml
root@kvm:~/backup_kvm1# rm kvm1.img kvm1.xml
root@kvm:~/backup_kvm1#
```

6. Transfer the backup archive to a remote server:

```
root@kvm:~/backup_kvm1# rsync -vaz kvm1_backup.tar.bz kvm2:/tmp
sending incremental file list
kvm1_backup.tar.bz

sent 842,977,610 bytes received 35 bytes 26,761,195.08 bytes/sec
total size is 845,671,214 speedup is 1.00
root@kvm:~/backup_kvm1#
```

7. To restore from the backup, log in to the remote server and extract the archive:

```
root@kvm2:~# cd /tmp/
root@kvm2:/tmp# tar jxfv kvm1_backup.tar.bz
./
./kvm1.img
./kvm1.xml
root@kvm2:/tmp#
```

8. Copy the image file to the configured location and define the instance:

```
root@kvm2:/tmp# cp kvm1.img /var/lib/libvirt/images/
root@kvm2:/tmp# virsh define kvm1.xml
Domain kvm1 defined from kvm1.xml

root@kvm2:/tmp# virsh list --all | grep kvm1
 - kvm1 shut off
root@kvm2:/tmp#
```

How it works...

After creating the backup directory in step 1, we save the current guest definition to disk in step 3. In step 4, after stopping the virtual machine, we copy its image file to the backup directory. In step 5, we create a bzip2 compressed data file which we transfer to a remote server in step 6.

On the remote server, we extract the archive in step 7 and copy the raw image file to where the XML definition of the instance is expecting it, then define the instance in step 8.

Note that in order to preserve the consistency and integrity of the data while copying the image file to the backup directory, we had to first stop the KVM guest.

Creating snapshots

A virtual machine snapshot preserves the current state of a running or stopped instance at a specific point in time. It can later be used to restore the instance from that point. Snapshots can be used as backups or as templates for building new virtual machines that will be copies of the original instance.

To take advantage of snapshots, the backing store must first support it. If you recall from the *Managing Disk images with qemu-img* recipe in `Chapter 1`, *Getting Started with QEMU and KVM*, we created a raw image type for the KVM guest. In this recipe, we are going to use the **QEMU Copy-On-Write (QCOW2)** image format as the backing store for the KVM instance, because the raw image format does not support snapshots.

Using the QCOW2 image format, we can create a base image containing the guest OS and everything else we need for the virtual machine, and then create several copy-on-write overlay disk images on top of the original base image. These new overlay images can be used in new virtual machines right away, by creating new XML definition files pointing to the new image.

Let's see an example of using QEMU to create image overlays before we proceed with making libvirt snapshots:

1. To collect information about a QCOW2 image, we can use the `qemu-img` utility:

   ```
   root@kvm:~# qemu-img info kvm1.qcow2
   image: kvm1.qcow2
   file format: qcow2
   virtual size: 8.0G (8589934592 bytes)
   disk size: 2.4G
   cluster_size: 65536
   Format specific information:
    compat: 1.1
    lazy refcounts: false
   root@kvm:~#
   ```

   To convert an existing raw image to QCOW2, run:
   ```
   root@kvm:~# qemu-img convert -f raw -O qcow2
   /var/lib/libvirt/images/kvm1.img
   /var/lib/libvirt/images/kvm1.qcow2
   ```

2. Let's create a new overlay image based on the qcow2 preceding image:

   ```
   root@kvm:~# qemu-img create -f qcow2 -b
   /var/lib/libvirt/images/kvm1_copy.qcow2
   /var/lib/libvirt/images/kvm1_copy_2.qcow2
   ```

```
Formatting '/var/lib/libvirt/images/kvm1_copy_2.qcow2', fmt=qcow2
size=8589934592
backing_file='/var/lib/libvirt/images/kvm1_copy.qcow2'
encryption=off cluster_size=65536 lazy_refcounts=off
root@kvm:~#
```

3. Getting information about the new overlay image now shows the backing file it's based on:

```
root@kvm:~# qemu-img info kvm1_copy.qcow2
image: kvm1_copy.qcow2
file format: qcow2
virtual size: 8.0G (8589934592 bytes)
disk size: 196K
cluster_size: 65536
backing file: /var/lib/libvirt/images/kvm1.qcow2
Format specific information:
 compat: 1.1
 lazy refcounts: false
root@kvm:~#
```

4. We can create a new overlay file from the previous overlay file:

```
root@kvm:~# qemu-img create -f qcow2 -b
/var/lib/libvirt/images/kvm1_copy.qcow2
/var/lib/libvirt/images/kvm1_copy_2.qcow2
Formatting '/var/lib/libvirt/images/kvm1_copy_2.qcow2', fmt=qcow2
size=8589934592
backing_file='/var/lib/libvirt/images/kvm1_copy.qcow2'
encryption=off cluster_size=65536 lazy_refcounts=off
root@kvm:~# qemu-img info /var/lib/libvirt/images/kvm1_copy_2.qcow2
image: /var/lib/libvirt/images/kvm1_copy_2.qcow2
file format: qcow2
virtual size: 8.0G (8589934592 bytes)
disk size: 196K
cluster_size: 65536
backing file: /var/lib/libvirt/images/kvm1_copy.qcow2
Format specific information:
 compat: 1.1
 lazy refcounts: false
root@kvm:~#
```

5. Let's list the entire image chain for the last overlay file:

```
root@kvm:~# qemu-img info --backing-chain
/var/lib/libvirt/images/kvm1_copy_2.qcow2
image: /var/lib/libvirt/images/kvm1_copy_2.qcow2
file format: qcow2
```

```
    virtual size: 8.0G (8589934592 bytes)
    disk size: 196K
    cluster_size: 65536
    backing file: /var/lib/libvirt/images/kvm1_copy.qcow2
    Format specific information:
     compat: 1.1
     lazy refcounts: false

    image: /var/lib/libvirt/images/kvm1_copy.qcow2
    file format: qcow2
    virtual size: 8.0G (8589934592 bytes)
    disk size: 196K
    cluster_size: 65536
    backing file: /var/lib/libvirt/images/kvm1.qcow2
    Format specific information:
     compat: 1.1
     lazy refcounts: false

    image: /var/lib/libvirt/images/kvm1.qcow2
    file format: qcow2
    virtual size: 8.0G (8589934592 bytes)
    disk size: 2.4G
    cluster_size: 65536
    Format specific information:
     compat: 1.1
     lazy refcounts: false
    root@kvm:~#
```

Libvirt uses the ability of the QCOW2 image format to create a chain of overlay snapshots that can be used as backups or as templates for new virtual machines. Once an overlay is created, the original base image is treated as read-only. Modifications to the base images (in this example, kvm1.qcow2 and kvm1_copy.qcow2 because both are base images for the kvm1_copy_2.qcow2 image) are not recommended. Here's a diagrammatic representation of the chain of overlay image files we created earlier:

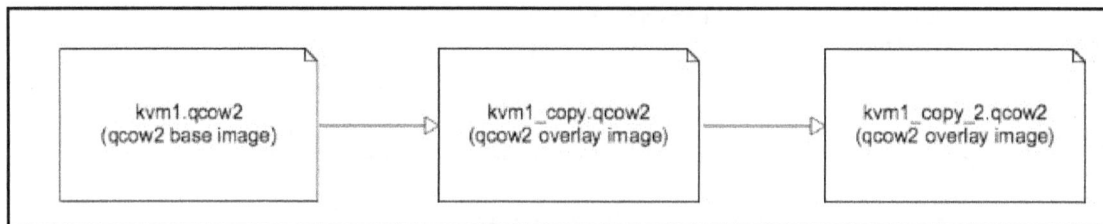

The chain of overlay QCOW2 images, each one serving as a base image for the next

Getting ready

For this recipe, we are going to need the following:

- A libvirt host with an existing QCOW2 image, with no snapshots attached
- A running KVM instance
- The QEMU toolset

How to do it...

To create a new KVM snapshot, follow these steps:

1. Create an internal snapshot of the running instance:

```
root@kvm:~# virsh snapshot-create kvm1
Domain snapshot 1492797458 created
root@kvm:~#
```

2. Examine the location of the new snapshot configuration:

```
root@kvm:~# ls -la /var/lib/libvirt/qemu/snapshot/
total 12
drwxr-xr-x 3 libvirt-qemu kvm 4096 Apr 21 14:05 .
drwxr-x--- 6 libvirt-qemu kvm 4096 Apr 21 14:04 ..
drwxr-xr-x 2 root root 4096 Apr 21 17:57 kvm1
root@kvm:~# ls -la /var/lib/libvirt/qemu/snapshot/kvm1/
total 12
drwxr-xr-x 2 root root 4096 Apr 21 17:57 .
drwxr-xr-x 3 libvirt-qemu kvm 4096 Apr 21 14:05 ..
-rw------- 1 root root 3089 Apr 21 17:57 1492797458.xml
root@kvm:~#
```

3. Examine the snapshot XML definition:

```
root@kvm:~# cat /var/lib/libvirt/qemu/snapshot/kvm1/1492797458.xml
<!--
WARNING: THIS IS AN AUTO-GENERATED FILE. CHANGES TO IT ARE LIKELY
TO BE
OVERWRITTEN AND LOST. Changes to this xml configuration should be
made using:
 virsh snapshot-edit
or other application using the libvirt API.
-->

<domainsnapshot>
```

```
  <name>1492797458</name>
  <state>running</state>
  <creationTime>1492797458</creationTime>
  <memory snapshot='internal'/>
  <disks>
    <disk name='hda' snapshot='internal'/>
  </disks>
  <domain type='kvm'>
    <name>kvm1</name>
    ...
  </domain>
  <active>1</active>
</domainsnapshot>
root@kvm:~#
```

4. Collect information about the base image:

```
root@kvm:~# qemu-img info /var/lib/libvirt/images/kvm1.qcow2
image: /var/lib/libvirt/images/kvm1.qcow2
file format: qcow2
virtual size: 8.0G (8589934592 bytes)
disk size: 2.4G
cluster_size: 65536
Snapshot list:
ID TAG          VM SIZE    DATE                   VM CLOCK
1  1492797458   155M       2017-04-21 17:57:38    03:41:16.790
Format specific information:
 compat: 1.1
 lazy refcounts: false
root@kvm:~#
```

5. Obtain information about the disk device on the virtual machine:

```
root@kvm:~# virsh domblklist kvm1
Target   Source
------------------------------------------------------
hda      /var/lib/libvirt/images/kvm1.qcow2

root@kvm:~#
```

6. Create an external, disk-only snapshot:

```
root@kvm:~# virsh snapshot-create-as kvm1 kvm1_ext_snapshot "Disk
only external snapshot for kvm1" --disk-only --diskspec
hda,snapshot=external,file=/var/lib/libvirt/images/kvm1_disk_extern
al.qcow2
Domain snapshot kvm1_ext_snapshot created
root@kvm:~#
```

7. Get information about the external snapshot:

```
root@kvm:~# qemu-img info
/var/lib/libvirt/images/kvm1_disk_external.qcow2
image: /var/lib/libvirt/images/kvm1_disk_external.qcow2
file format: qcow2
virtual size: 8.0G (8589934592 bytes)
disk size: 196K
cluster_size: 65536
backing file: /var/lib/libvirt/images/kvm1.qcow2
backing file format: qcow2
Format specific information:
 compat: 1.1
 lazy refcounts: false
root@kvm:~#
```

How it works...

There are two main types of snapshot:

- **An internal snapshot**: The base image file itself contains the saved state and all subsequent changes to the virtual machine
- **An external snapshot**: The base image will contain the saved state of the virtual machine thus becoming a read-only base image, and a new overlay image is created to track any future changes

Both types of snapshots can be performed on just the disk or the memory of the virtual machine, either on a live or stopped instance.

In the preceding step 1, we create an internal snapshot of the virtual machine. After the snapshot, there's only one image file: the original image, now containing the snapshot. We can see that the image is a snapshot in step 4, under the *Snapshot list* section of the output.

In step 6, we perform an external, disk-only snapshot, by specifying the virtual machine disk, name, and location for the snapshot. Note that after the snapshot, a new image file has been created to track any further changes. We examine that file in step 7. Note how the backing file is the original qcow2 image.

To perform the disk snapshots, libvirt leverages the QEMU functionality, like the qemu-img command we saw earlier when creating the overlay images.

We can now save the snapshots as backups or use them to start new virtual machines. In the following recipes, we are going to see examples on how to use and manipulate the snapshots.

Listing snapshots

In the previous recipe, we create two snapshots of the same KVM instance: one internal and one disk-only, external snapshot. In this recipe, we are going to learn how to list existing snapshots.

Getting ready

For this recipe, we are going to need:

- A libvirt host with the QEMU toolset
- A running KVM instance
- The snapshots we created in the *Creating snapshots* recipe

How to do it...

To list all existing snapshots, follow the next steps:

1. List all snapshots for the specified KVM instance:

```
root@kvm:~# virsh snapshot-list kvm1
 Name                 Creation Time               State
------------------------------------------------------------
 1492797458           2017-04-21 17:57:38 +0000   running
 kvm1_ext_snapshot    2017-04-21 18:08:49 +0000   disk-snapshot

root@kvm:~#
```

2. List only the disk-based snapshots:

```
root@kvm:~# virsh snapshot-list --disk-only kvm1
 Name                 Creation Time               State
------------------------------------------------------------
 kvm1_ext_snapshot    2017-04-21 18:08:49 +0000   disk-snapshot

root@kvm:~#
```

3. List only the internal snapshots:

```
root@kvm:~# virsh snapshot-list --internal kvm1
 Name            Creation Time                State
--------------------------------------------------------------
 1492797458     2017-04-21 17:57:38 +0000   running

root@kvm:~#
```

4. List the external snapshots only:

```
root@kvm:~# virsh snapshot-list --external kvm1
 Name Creation Time State
--------------------------------------------------------------
 kvm1_ext_snapshot 2017-04-21 18:08:49 +0000 disk-snapshot

root@kvm:~#
```

5. List all images in a hierarchical tree format:

```
root@kvm:~# virsh snapshot-list --tree kvm1
1492797458
 |
 +- kvm1_ext_snapshot

root@kvm:~#
```

How it works...

We used the versatile `virsh snapshot-list` command to list all internal and external snapshots for the specified virtual machine. Note how we can get similar information using the `qemu-img` command directly on the image files, as we saw earlier in this chapter. However, the API calls that libvirt provides for listing snapshots are much more convenient. In the next chapter, we are going to see examples on how to use the libvirt Python bindings to manipulate KVM instances and their snapshots.

Inspecting snapshots

In this short recipe, we are going to see examples on how to obtain more information on existing virtual machine snapshots.

Getting ready

For this recipe, we are going to need the following:

- A libvirt host with the QEMU toolset
- The snapshots we created in the *Creating snapshots* recipe

How to do it...

To inspect a snapshot, run the following commands:

1. List all available snapshots for the specified KVM instance:

    ```
    root@kvm:~# virsh snapshot-list kvm1
     Name                 Creation Time              State
    ------------------------------------------------------------
     1492797458          2017-04-21 17:57:38 +0000  running
     kvm1_ext_snapshot   2017-04-21 18:08:49 +0000  disk-snapshot

    root@kvm:~#
    ```

2. Get information about the running snapshot:

    ```
    root@kvm:~# virsh snapshot-info kvm1 --snapshotname 1492797458
    Name: 1492797458
    Domain: kvm1
    Current: no
    State: running
    Location: internal
    Parent: -
    Children: 1
    Descendants: 1
    Metadata: yes

    root@kvm:~#
    ```

3. Get information about the disk snapshot:

    ```
    root@kvm:~# virsh snapshot-info kvm1 --snapshotname
    kvm1_ext_snapshot
    Name: kvm1_ext_snapshot
    Domain: kvm1
    Current: yes
    State: disk-snapshot
    Location: external
    ```

```
       Parent: 1492797458
       Children: 0
       Descendants: 0
       Metadata: yes

       root@kvm:~#
```

4. Dump the XML configuration for the disk snapshot:

```
root@kvm:~# virsh snapshot-dumpxml kvm1 --snapshotname
kvm1_ext_snapshot --security-info
<domainsnapshot>
 <name>kvm1_ext_snapshot</name>
 <description>Disk only external snapshot for kvm1</description>
 <state>disk-snapshot</state>
 <parent>
    <name>1492797458</name>
 </parent>
 <creationTime>1492798129</creationTime>
 <memory snapshot='no'/>
 <disks>
    <disk name='hda' snapshot='external' type='file'>
      <driver type='qcow2'/>
      <source
file='/var/lib/libvirt/images/kvm1_disk_external.qcow2'/>
    </disk>
 </disks>
 <domain type='kvm'>
    <name>kvm1</name>
    ...
    <devices>
      <emulator>/usr/bin/qemu-system-x86_64</emulator>
      <disk type='file' device='disk'>
        <driver name='qemu' type='qcow2'/>
        <source file='/var/lib/libvirt/images/kvm1.qcow2'/>
        <target dev='hda' bus='ide'/>
        <address type='drive' controller='0' bus='0' target='0'
unit='0'/>
      </disk>
      ...
    </devices>
 <seclabel type='none'/>
 </domain>
</domainsnapshot>
```

How it works...

In step 1, we list all the available snapshots for the kvm1 virtual machine. In steps 2 and 3, we obtain information about the snapshots. Of particular interest is the `Parent` and `Children` fields, showing us the hierarchy of the snapshots.

In step 4, we examine the XML definition of the KVM guest and the disk-only, external snapshot. We can observe the `snapshot='external'` type and the base image location specified with the `<source file='/var/lib/libvirt/images/kvm1_disk_external.qcow2'/>` stanza.

Editing snapshots

In this recipe, we are going to edit the XML definition of an existing snapshot and examine the changes.

Getting ready

For this recipe, we are going to need the following:

- A libvirt host with the QEMU toolset
- The snapshots we created in the *Creating snapshots* recipe

How to do it...

To edit a snapshot, run the following:

1. List all available snapshots for the specified KVM instance:

```
root@kvm:~# virsh snapshot-list kvm1
 Name                Creation Time               State
------------------------------------------------------------
 1492797458          2017-04-21 17:57:38 +0000   running
 kvm1_ext_snapshot   2017-04-21 18:08:49 +0000   disk-snapshot

root@kvm:~#
```

2. Edit the disk snapshot and change its name and description:

```
root@kvm:~# virsh snapshot-edit kvm1 --snapshotname
kvm1_ext_snapshot --rename
<domainsnapshot>
 <name>kvm1_ext_snapshot_renamed</name>
 <description>Disk only external snapshot for kvm1</description>
 . . .
root@kvm:~#
```

3. List the snapshots after the update:

```
root@kvm:~# virsh snapshot-list kvm1
 Name                        Creation Time               State
------------------------------------------------------------------
 1492797458                  2017-04-21 17:57:38 +0000 running
 kvm1_ext_snapshot_renamed   2017-04-21 18:08:49 +0000 disk-snapshot

root@kvm:~#
```

How it works...

Libvirt provides a way to edit the snapshot definition for a virtual machine. We can change various XML attributes, such as the snapshot name, description, or the location of the backing image file. In step 1, we list all available snapshots for the specified KVM instance, then proceed to update the name and description of the disk image. Finally, in step 3, we can see the changed name for the external snapshot.

Reverting snapshots

In this recipe, we are going to create an internal snapshot of a running instance, introduce a change, then restore back to the original instance state using the snapshot.

Getting ready

For this recipe, we are going to need the following:

- A libvirt host with an existing QCOW2 image
- A running KVM instance, using the QCOW2 image
- The QEMU toolset

How to do it...

To revert the state of a KVM instance to an older state, from an existing snapshot, run the following:

1. Connect to the KVM instance and create a new file:

    ```
    root@kvm:~# virsh console kvm1
    Connected to domain kvm1
    Escape character is ^]

    root@debian:~# touch SNAPSHOT
    root@debian:~#
    root@kvm:~#
    ```

2. Create an internal snapshot of the virtual machine:

    ```
    root@kvm:~# virsh snapshot-create kvm1
    Domain snapshot 1492802417 created
    root@kvm:~#
    ```

3. Get information about the snapshot:

    ```
    root@kvm:~# virsh snapshot-info kvm1 --snapshotname 1492802417
    Name: 1492802417
    Domain: kvm1
    Current: yes
    State: running
    Location: internal
    Parent: 1492797458
    Children: 0
    Descendants: 0
    Metadata: yes

    root@kvm:~#
    ```

4. Connect back to the virtual machine and delete the file we created in step 1:

    ```
    root@kvm:~# virsh console kvm1
    Connected to domain kvm1
    Escape character is ^]

    root@debian:~# rm -f SNAPSHOT
    root@debian:~#
    root@kvm:~#
    ```

5. Restore the instance from the latest snapshot:

```
root@kvm:~# virsh snapshot-revert kvm1 --snapshotname 1492802417

root@kvm:~#
```

6. Connect to the virtual machine and confirm that file we deleted in the previous step exists again:

```
root@kvm:~# virsh console kvm1
Connected to domain kvm1
Escape character is ^]

root@debian:~# ls -la SNAPSHOT
-rw-r--r-- 1 root root 0 Apr 21 14:08 SNAPSHOT
root@debian:~#
root@kvm:~#
```

How it works...

In step 1, we connect to the KVM instance using the console and create an empty file. We are going to use the file to track changes on the virtual machine. In step 2, we create an internal snapshot and obtain more information about it in step 3. In step 4, we connect to the KVM guest again and delete the file. In step 5, we restore from the snapshot, confirming that the state of the instance has been indeed reverted to before the snapshot, as shown by the presence of the original file we created earlier.

Deleting snapshots

In this quick recipe, we are going to delete the snapshots we created earlier in the *Creating snapshots* recipe, using libvirt.

Getting ready

For this recipe, we are only going to need the following:

- A libvirt host with the QEMU toolset
- The snapshots we created in the *Creating snapshots* recipe

How to do it...

To delete a snapshot, follow these steps:

1. List all snapshots present on the host:

```
root@kvm:~# virsh snapshot-list kvm1
Name                        Creation Time            State
--------------------------------------------------------------
 1492797458                 2017-04-21 17:57:38 +0000 running
 1492802417                 2017-04-21 19:20:17 +0000 running
 kvm1_ext_snapshot_renamed 2017-04-21 18:08:49 +0000 disk-snapshot

root@kvm:~#
```

2. Delete the latest snapshot based on the creation time:

```
root@kvm:~# virsh snapshot-delete kvm1 --snapshotname 1492802417
Domain snapshot 1492802417 deleted

root@kvm:~#
```

3. List the remaining snapshots:

```
root@kvm:~# virsh snapshot-list kvm1
Name                        Creation Time            State
--------------------------------------------------------------
 1492797458                 2017-04-21 17:57:38 +0000 running
 kvm1_ext_snapshot_renamed  2017-04-21 18:08:49 +0000 disk-snapshot

root@kvm:~#
```

4. Delete the latest snapshot:

```
root@kvm:~# virsh snapshot-delete kvm1 --current
Domain snapshot 1492797458 deleted

root@kvm:~#
```

How it works...

In step 1, we list all snapshots on the host OS. We then delete the latest snapshot, specifying its name, in step 2. In step 3, we verify that the snapshot has been indeed deleted. Finally, in step 4, we delete the latest image by specifying the --current flag.

> Please note that in order to delete or restore an external snapshot a libvirt version newer than 1.2.2 is required. If your Linux distribution does not provide a newer version in its repositories, you will have to compile libvirt from source.

6
Deploying KVM Instances with OpenStack

In this chapter, we are going to cover the following topics:

- Preparing the host for the OpenStack deployment
- Installing and configuring the OpenStack Keystone identity service
- Installing and configuring the OpenStack Glance image service
- Installing and configuring the OpenStack Nova compute service
- Installing and configuring the OpenStack Neutron networking service
- Building and inspecting KVM instances with OpenStack
- Stopping KVM instances with OpenStack
- Terminating KVM instances with OpenStack

Introduction

OpenStack is a cloud operating system that simplifies the deployment and management of virtual machines or containers in a scalable and highly available way. It operates on pools of compute resources (physical or virtual servers) and provides an intelligent scheduling mechanism to select appropriate hosts, and to build or migrate VMs.

OpenStack allows an easier management of virtual images and provides a centralized way of creating and managing software-defined networks. It integrates well with a variety of external and internal projects in order to deliver user and service authentication. OpenStack modular design allows adding and removing services as needed where a minimal production deployment may consist of as few as two projects an image and compute service.

The following diagram shows the ever-growing list of OpenStack projects and the interaction between them:

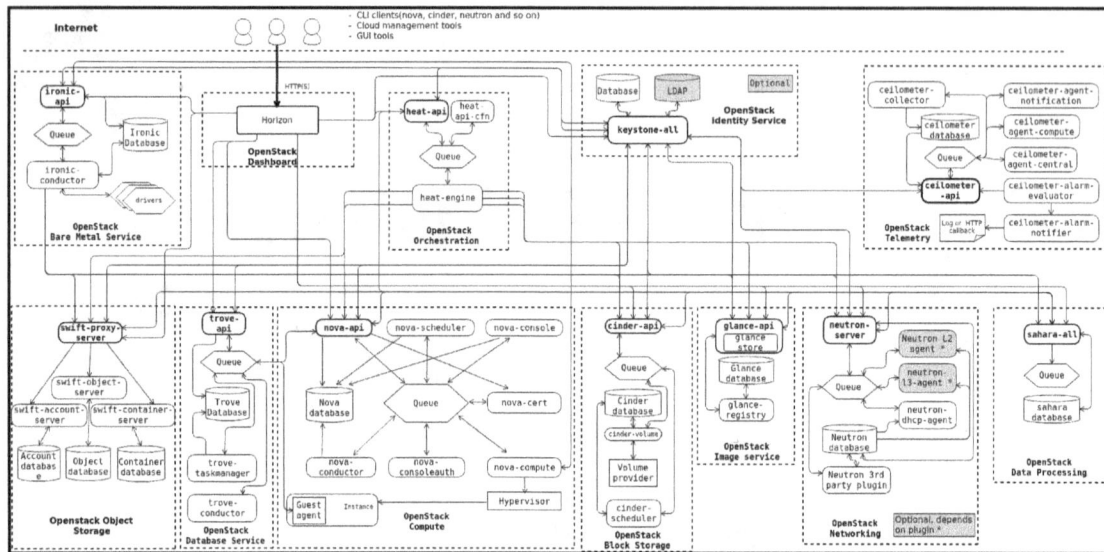

The OpenStack components and how they interact with each other

In this chapter, we are going to create a simple OpenStack deployment on two compute nodes using the Keystone, Glance, Nova, and Neutron projects from the Newton release of OpenStack, on an Ubuntu Xenial 16.04 server.

> For more information on the OpenStack project, please visit https://www.openstack.org/software/.

Preparing the host for the OpenStack deployment

In this recipe, we are going to install the infrastructure components that OpenStack depends on, such as the database server, the message queue, and the caching service. The projects that we are going to use throughout this chapter depend on these services for communication and persistent storage.

Getting ready

For this recipe, we are going to need the following components:

- An Ubuntu server with great virtualization capabilities
- Access to the internet for package installation

How to do it...

In order to keep the deployment simple and focus on the provisioning aspect of OpenStack, we are going to use a single physical server to host all services. In production environments, it is a common approach to separate each service onto their own set of servers, for scalability and high availability. By following the steps outlined in this chapter, you should be able to deploy all services on multiple hosts, by replacing the IP addresses and hostnames in the configuration files, as needed.

1. Update the host and install the package repository for the Newton release:

```
root@controller:~# apt install software-properties-common
root@controller:~# add-apt-repository cloud-archive:newton
root@controller:~# apt update && apt dist-upgrade
root@controller:~# reboot
root@controller:~# apt install python-openstackclient
```

2. Install the MariaDB database server:

```
root@controller:~# apt install mariadb-server python-pymysql
root@controller:~# cat /etc/mysql/mariadb.conf.d/99-openstack.cnf
[mysqld]
bind-address = 10.208.130.36
default-storage-engine = innodb
innodb_file_per_table
max_connections = 4096
collation-server = utf8_general_ci
character-set-server = utf8
root@controller:~#
```

Replace the IP address of the network interface the database server binds to, as per your host.

3. Restart the service and secure the installation:

```
root@controller:~# service mysql restart
root@controller:~# mysql_secure_installation
```

For simplicity, we are going to use `lxcpassword` as a password for all services throughout the chapter.

4. Install the RabbitMQ messaging service, create a new user, password, and set permissions:

```
root@controller:~# apt install rabbitmq-server
root@controller:~# rabbitmqctl add_user openstack lxcpassword
Creating user "openstack" ...
root@controller:~# rabbitmqctl set_permissions openstack ".*" ".*"
".*"
Setting permissions for user "openstack" in vhost "/" ...
root@controller:~#
```

5. Install and configure the `memcached` service:

```
root@controller:~# apt install memcached python-memcache
root@controller:~# sed -i 's/127.0.0.1/10.208.130.36/g'
/etc/memcached.conf
root@controller:~# cat /etc/memcached.conf | grep -vi "#" | sed
'/^$/d'
-d
logfile /var/log/memcached.log
-m 64
-p 11211
-u memcache
-l 10.208.130.36
root@controller:~# service memcached restart
root@controller:~#
```

How it works...

OpenStack uses a SQL database, such as Mysql/MariaDB/Percona, to store information about its services. In the following recipes, we are going to create databases for the Keystone, Glance, Nova, and Neutron projects. We install and configure MariaDB in steps 1 through 3.

The messaging queue we install and configure in step 4 provides a centralized way for the services to communicate with each other by producing and consuming messages. OpenStack supports a few different message bus implementations, such as RabbitMQ, Qpid, and ZeroMQ.

The identity service Keystone caches authentication tokens using the memcached daemon. We install and configure it in step 5.

Installing and configuring the OpenStack Keystone identity service

The identity service provided by the Keystone project is a centralized point in order to manage authentication and authorization, used by other OpenStack components, such as Nova compute and the image service Glance. Keystone also keeps a catalog of services and the endpoints they provide that the user can locate by sending queries to it.

In this recipe, we are going to install and configure Keystone, create two projects (a unit of ownership) for our services and assign users and roles to those projects.

Getting ready

For this recipe, we are going to need the following:

- An Ubuntu Server with Great virtualization capabilities
- Access to the Internet for package installation
- A database server, a message queue, and memcached installed and configured, as described in the *Preparing the host for the OpenStack deployment* recipe

How to do it...

To install, configure, create new projects, user roles, and credentials, perform the following steps in the order presented here:

1. Create the keystone database and grant permissions to the keystone user:

```
root@controller:~# mysql -u root -plxcpassword
MariaDB [(none)]> CREATE DATABASE keystone;
Query OK, 1 row affected (0.01 sec)
```

```
MariaDB [(none)]> GRANT ALL PRIVILEGES ON keystone.* TO
'keystone'@'localhost' IDENTIFIED BY 'lxcpassword';
Query OK, 0 rows affected (0.00 sec)
MariaDB [(none)]> GRANT ALL PRIVILEGES ON keystone.* TO
'keystone'@'%' IDENTIFIED BY 'lxcpassword';
Query OK, 0 rows affected (0.01 sec)
MariaDB [(none)]> exit
Bye
root@controller:~#
```

2. Install the identity service Keystone from the repository we configured earlier:

```
root@controller:~# apt install keystone
```

3. Create the following minimal Keystone configuration:

```
root@controller:~# cat /etc/keystone/keystone.conf
[DEFAULT]
log_dir = /var/log/keystone

[assignment]
[auth]
[cache]
[catalog]
[cors]
[cors.subdomain]
[credential]
[database]
connection =
mysql+pymysql://keystone:lxcpassword@controller/keystone

[domain_config]
[endpoint_filter]
[endpoint_policy]
[eventlet_server]
[federation]
[fernet_tokens]
[identity]
[identity_mapping]
[kvs]
[ldap]
[matchmaker_redis]
[memcache]
[oauth1]
[os_inherit]
[oslo_messaging_amqp]
[oslo_messaging_notifications]
[oslo_messaging_rabbit]
```

```
[oslo_messaging_zmq]
[oslo_middleware]
[oslo_policy]
[paste_deploy]
[policy]
[profiler]
[resource]
[revoke]
[role]
[saml]
[security_compliance]
[shadow_users]
[signing]
[token]
provider = fernet
[tokenless_auth]
[trust]
[extra_headers]
Distribution = Ubuntu
root@controller:~#
```

4. Populate the Keystone database:

```
root@controller:~# su -s /bin/sh -c "keystone-manage db_sync"
keystone
...
root@controller:~#
```

5. Initialize the Fernet key repositories:

```
root@controller:~# keystone-manage fernet_setup --keystone-user
keystone --keystone-group keystone
root@controller:~# keystone-manage credential_setup --keystone-user
keystone --keystone-group keystone
root@controller:~#
```

6. Bootstrap the Keystone service:

```
root@controller:~# keystone-manage bootstrap --bootstrap-password
lxcpassword --bootstrap-admin-url http://controller:35357/v3/ --
bootstrap-internal-url http://controller:35357/v3/ --bootstrap-
public-url http://controller:5000/v3/ --bootstrap region-id
RegionOne
root@controller:~#
```

7. Add the following stanza in Apache and restart the service:

```
root@controller:~# cat /etc/apache2/apache2.conf
...
ServerName controller
...
root@controller:~# service apache2 restart
```

8. Delete the default SQLite database that Keystone is packaged with:

```
root@controller:~# rm -f /var/lib/keystone/keystone.db
```

9. Create an administrative account by defining the following environment variables:

```
root@controller:~# export OS_USERNAME=admin
root@controller:~# export OS_PASSWORD=lxcpassword
root@controller:~# export OS_PROJECT_NAME=admin
root@controller:~# export OS_USER_DOMAIN_NAME=default
root@controller:~# export OS_PROJECT_DOMAIN_NAME=default
root@controller:~# export OS_AUTH_URL=http://controller:35357/v3
root@controller:~# export OS_IDENTITY_API_VERSION=3
root@controller:~#
```

10. Create a project in Keystone for the services to use and list it:

```
root@controller:~# openstack project create --domain default --
description "KVM Project" service
+-------------+----------------------------------+
| Field       | Value                            |
+-------------+----------------------------------+
| description | KVM Project                      |
| domain_id   | default                          |
| enabled     | True                             |
| id          | 9a1a863fe41b42b2955b313f2cca0ef0 |
| is_domain   | False                            |
| name        | service                          |
| parent_id   | default                          |
+-------------+----------------------------------+
root@controller:~# openstack project list
+----------------------------------+---------+
| ID                               | Name    |
+----------------------------------+---------+
| 06f4e2d7e384474781803395b24b3af2 | admin   |
| 9a1a863fe41b42b2955b313f2cca0ef0 | service |
+----------------------------------+---------+
root@controller:~#
```

11. Create an unprivileged project and a user that will be used by regular clients instead of the OpenStack services:

```
root@controller:~# openstack project create --domain default --
description "KVM User Project" kvm
+-------------+----------------------------------+
| Field       | Value                            |
+-------------+----------------------------------+
| description | KVM User Project                 |
| domain_id   | default                          |
| enabled     | True                             |
| id          | eb9cdc2c2b4e4f098f2d104752970d52 |
| is_domain   | False                            |
| name        | kvm                              |
| parent_id   | default                          |
+-------------+----------------------------------+
root@controller:~#
root@controller:~# openstack user create --domain default --
password-prompt kvm
User Password:
Repeat User Password:
+---------------------+----------------------------------+
| Field               | Value                            |
+---------------------+----------------------------------+
| domain_id           | default                          |
| enabled             | True                             |
| id                  | 1e83e0c8ca194f2e9d8161eb61d21030 |
| name                | kvm                              |
| password_expires_at | None                             |
+---------------------+----------------------------------+
root@controller:~#
```

12. Create a user role and associate it with the KVM project and user:

```
root@controller:~# openstack role create user
+-----------+----------------------------------+
| Field     | Value                            |
+-----------+----------------------------------+
| domain_id | None                             |
| id        | 331c0b61e9784112874627264f03a058 |
| name      | user                             |
+-----------+----------------------------------+
root@controller:~# openstack role add --project kvm --user kvm user
root@controller:~#
```

13. Configure the **Web Service Gateway Interface** (**WSGI**) middleware pipeline for Keystone:

```
root@controller:~# cat /etc/keystone/keystone-paste.ini
# Keystone PasteDeploy configuration file.
[filter:debug]
use = egg:oslo.middleware#debug
[filter:request_id]
use = egg:oslo.middleware#request_id
[filter:build_auth_context]
use = egg:keystone#build_auth_context
[filter:token_auth]
use = egg:keystone#token_auth
[filter:admin_token_auth]
use = egg:keystone#admin_token_auth
[filter:json_body]
use = egg:keystone#json_body
[filter:cors]
use = egg:oslo.middleware#cors
oslo_config_project = keystone
[filter:http_proxy_to_wsgi]
use = egg:oslo.middleware#http_proxy_to_wsgi
[filter:ec2_extension]
use = egg:keystone#ec2_extension
[filter:ec2_extension_v3]
use = egg:keystone#ec2_extension_v3
[filter:s3_extension]
use = egg:keystone#s3_extension
[filter:url_normalize]
use = egg:keystone#url_normalize
[filter:sizelimit]
use = egg:oslo.middleware#sizelimit
[filter:osprofiler]
use = egg:osprofiler#osprofiler
[app:public_service]
use = egg:keystone#public_service
[app:service_v3]
use = egg:keystone#service_v3
[app:admin_service]
use = egg:keystone#admin_service
[pipeline:public_api]
pipeline = cors sizelimit http_proxy_to_wsgi osprofiler
url_normalize request_id build_auth_context token_auth json_body
ec2_extension public_service
[pipeline:admin_api]
pipeline = cors sizelimit http_proxy_to_wsgi osprofiler
url_normalize request_id build_auth_context token_auth json_body
ec2_extension s3_extension admin_service
```

```
[pipeline:api_v3]
pipeline = cors sizelimit http_proxy_to_wsgi osprofiler
url_normalize request_id build_auth_context token_auth json_body
ec2_extension_v3 s3_extension service_v3
[app:public_version_service]
use = egg:keystone#public_version_service
[app:admin_version_service]
use = egg:keystone#admin_version_service
[pipeline:public_version_api]
pipeline = cors sizelimit osprofiler url_normalize
public_version_service
[pipeline:admin_version_api]
pipeline = cors sizelimit osprofiler url_normalize
admin_version_service
[composite:main]
use = egg:Paste#urlmap
/v2.0 = public_api
/v3 = api_v3
/ = public_version_api
[composite:admin]
use = egg:Paste#urlmap
/v2.0 = admin_api
/v3 = api_v3
/ = admin_version_api
root@controller:~#
```

14. Request a token for the admin and KVM users:

```
root@controller:~# openstack --os-auth-url
http://controller:35357/v3 --os-project-domain-name default --os-
user-domain-name default --os-project-name admin --os-username
admin token issue
+------------+------------------------------------+
| Field      | Value                              |
+------------+------------------------------------+
| expires    | 2017-04-26 18:29:03+00:00          |
| id         | gAAAAABZMIdwefsdfB8e4rFk5IALgM4U   |
| project_id | 123c1e6f33584dd1876c0a34249a6e11   |
| user_id    | cc14c5dbbd654c438e52d38efaf4f1a6   |
+------------+------------------------------------+
root@controller:~# openstack --os-auth-url
http://controller:5000/v3 --os-project-domain-name default  --os-
user-domain-name default --os-project-name kvm --os-username kvm
token issue
+------------+------------------------------------+
| Field      | Value                              |
+------------+------------------------------------+
| expires    | 2017-04-26 18:29:52+00:00          |
```

```
| id         | gAAAAABZANkQmInUif16Up_PzdH_9OHd |
| project_id | 10a92eccbad9439d9e56c4edda6b211f |
| user_id    | a186b226ed1e4717b25bb978f2bc9958 |
+------------+----------------------------------+
root@controller:~#
```

15. Create the files that will contain the admin and user credentials:

```
root@controller:~# cat rc.admin
export OS_PROJECT_DOMAIN_NAME=default
export OS_USER_DOMAIN_NAME=default
export OS_PROJECT_NAME=admin
export OS_USERNAME=admin
export OS_PASSWORD=lxcpassword
export OS_AUTH_URL=http://controller:35357/v3
export OS_IDENTITY_API_VERSION=3
export OS_IMAGE_API_VERSION=2
root@controller:~#
root@controller:~# cat rc.kvm
export OS_PROJECT_DOMAIN_NAME=default
export OS_USER_DOMAIN_NAME=default
export OS_PROJECT_NAME=kvm
export OS_USERNAME=kvm
export OS_PASSWORD=lxcpassword
export OS_AUTH_URL=http://controller:5000/v3
export OS_IDENTITY_API_VERSION=3
export OS_IMAGE_API_VERSION=2
root@controller:~#
```

16. Source the admin credentials file:

```
root @ controller: ~ #. rc.admin
root @ controller: ~ #
```

17. Request an authentication token for the admin user:

```
root@controller:~# openstack token issue
```

```
+------------+----------------------------------+
| Field      | Value                            |
+------------+----------------------------------+
| expires    | 2017-04-26 18:30:41+00:00        |
| id         | gAAAAABZANlBdsu-DTmz6ME2Z8JFKjJM |
| project_id | 123c1e6f33584dd1876c0a34249a6e11 |
| user_id    | cc14c5dbbd654c438e52d38efaf4f1a6 |
+------------+----------------------------------+
root@controller:~#
```

How it works...

We start by creating the Keystone database in MariaDB with the necessary user permissions in step 1. In step 2, we install the Keystone package.

In step 3, we create the configuration file for the service. As you can see from the output, most of the options have been omitted, and default ones are assumed.

In step 4, we run a script that populates the Keystone database by creating the database schema.

Keystone uses tokens to authenticate and authorize users and services. There are different token formats available for use, such as UUID, PKI, and Fernet tokens. For this deployment, we are going to use the Fernet tokens. The Fernet tokens do not need to be persisted in a backend store. In step 5, we initialize the Fernet key repository.

> For more information on the available identity tokens, refer to `http://doc`
> `s.openstack.org/admin-guide/identity-tokens.html`.

In step 6, we bootstrap Keystone and update the Apache configuration in step 7 and perform some cleanup in step 8.

In step 9, we export a list of environment variables containing the Keystone user, password, and endpoint.

In step 10, we create our first project in Keystone that will be used by the rest of the services. Projects represent a unit of ownership, where all resources are owned by a project. In steps 11 and 12, we create an unprivileged project and associated user.

In step 13, we configure the WSGI middleware pipeline for Keystone.

In step 14, we request and obtain tokens for the admin and KVM users, and in step 15, we create two environment variable files that we can source when we need to switch between users.

In steps 16 and 17, we source the admin credentials and project endpoint and obtain an authorization token.

Installing and configuring the OpenStack Glance image service

The Glance image service provides an API that we can use to discover, register, and obtain images for virtual machines. When we later use Nova compute to build a new KVM instance, the Nova service will send a request to Glance to obtain the requested image type.

In this recipe, we are going to install Glance and register a new Ubuntu image.

Getting ready

For this recipe, we are going to need the following things:

- An Ubuntu server with great virtualization capabilities
- Access to the internet for package installation
- A database server, a message queue, and memcached installed and configured, as described in the *Preparing the host for the OpenStack deployment* recipe
- The Keystone service we deployed in the *Installing and configuring the OpenStack Keystone identity service* recipe

How to do it...

To install, configure, and register an image with Glance, follow the steps outlined here:

1. Create the Glance database and user:

```
root@controller:~# mysql -u root -plxcpassword
MariaDB [(none)]> CREATE DATABASE glance;
Query OK, 1 row affected (0.00 sec)
MariaDB [(none)]> GRANT ALL PRIVILEGES ON glance.* TO
'glance'@'localhost' IDENTIFIED BY 'lxcpassword';
Query OK, 0 rows affected (0.00 sec)
MariaDB [(none)]> GRANT ALL PRIVILEGES ON glance.* TO 'glance'@'%'
IDENTIFIED BY 'lxcpassword';
Query OK, 0 rows affected (0.00 sec)
MariaDB [(none)]> exit
Bye
root@controller:~#
```

2. Create the Glance user and add it to the admin role:

```
root@controller:~# openstack user create --domain default --
password-prompt glance
User Password:
Repeat User Password:
+--------------------+----------------------------------+
| Field              | Value                            |
+--------------------+----------------------------------+
| domain_id          | default                          |
| enabled            | True                             |
| id                 | e566c6e2012148daa374cd68077b38df |
| name               | glance                           |
| password_expires_at | None                            |
+--------------------+----------------------------------+
root@controller:~# openstack role add --project service --user
glance admin
root@controller:~#
```

3. Create the Glance service definition:

```
root@controller:~# openstack service create --name glance --
description "OpenStack Image" image
+-------------+----------------------------------+
| Field       | Value                            |
+-------------+----------------------------------+
| description | OpenStack Image                  |
| enabled     | True                             |
| id          | d4d42a586551461c8b445b927f2144e1 |
| name        | glance                           |
| type        | image                            |
+-------------+----------------------------------+
root@controller:~#
```

4. Create the Glance API endpoints in Keystone:

```
root@controller:~# openstack endpoint create --region RegionOne
image public http://controller:9292
+--------------+----------------------------------+
| Field        | Value                            |
+--------------+----------------------------------+
| enabled      | True                             |
| id           | 618af0c845194f508752f230364d6e0e |
| interface    | public                           |
| region       | RegionOne                        |
| region_id    | RegionOne                        |
| service_id   | d4d42a586551461c8b445b927f2144e1 |
| service_name | glance                           |
```

```
| service_type | image                                |
| url          | http://controller:9292               |
+--------------+--------------------------------------+
root@controller:~# openstack endpoint create --region RegionOne
image internal http://controller:9292
+--------------+--------------------------------------+
| Field        | Value                                |
+--------------+--------------------------------------+
| enabled      | True                                 |
| id           | 991a1b03f7194139b98bafe19acf3518     |
| interface    | internal                             |
| region       | RegionOne                            |
| region_id    | RegionOne                            |
| service_id   | d4d42a586551461c8b445b927f2144e1     |
| service_name | glance                               |
| service_type | image                                |
| url          | http://controller:9292               |
+--------------+--------------------------------------+
root@controller:~# openstack endpoint create --region RegionOne
image admin http://controller:9292
+--------------+--------------------------------------+
| Field        | Value                                |
+--------------+--------------------------------------+
| enabled      | True                                 |
| id           | 991a1b03f7194139b98bafe19acf3322     |
| interface    | admin                                |
| region       | RegionOne                            |
| region_id    | RegionOne                            |
| service_id   | d4d42a586551461c8b445b927f2144e1     |
| service_name | glance                               |
| service_type | image                                |
| url          | http://controller:9292               |
+--------------+--------------------------------------+
root@controller:~#
```

5. Install the Glance service:

```
root@controller:~# apt install glance
```

6. Configure the service:

```
root@controller:~# cat /etc/glance/glance-api.conf
[DEFAULT]
[cors]
[cors.subdomain]

[database]
connection = mysql+pymysql://glance:lxcpassword@controller/glance
```

```
[glance_store]
stores = file,http
default_store = file
filesystem_store_datadir = /var/lib/glance/images/

[image_format]
disk_formats = ami,ari,aki,vhd,vhdx,vmdk,raw,qcow2,vdi,iso,root-tar

[keystone_authtoken]
auth_uri = http://controller:5000
auth_url = http://controller:35357
memcached_servers = controller:11211
auth_type = password
project_domain_name = default
user_domain_name = default
project_name = service
username = glance
password = lxcpassword

[matchmaker_redis]
[oslo_concurrency]
[oslo_messaging_amqp]
[oslo_messaging_notifications]
[oslo_messaging_rabbit]
[oslo_messaging_zmq]
[oslo_middleware]
[oslo_policy]
[paste_deploy]
flavor = keystone

[profiler]
[store_type_location_strategy]
[task]
[taskflow_executor]
root@controller:~#
root@controller:~# cat /etc/glance/glance-registry.conf
[DEFAULT]

[database]
connection = mysql+pymysql://glance:lxcpassword@controller/glance

[keystone_authtoken]
auth_uri = http://controller:5000
auth_url = http://controller:35357
memcached_servers = controller:11211
auth_type = password
project_domain_name = default
user_domain_name = default
```

```
                project_name = service
                username = glance
                password = lxcpassword

                [matchmaker_redis]
                [oslo_messaging_amqp]
                [oslo_messaging_notifications]
                [oslo_messaging_rabbit]
                [oslo_messaging_zmq]
                [oslo_policy]
                [paste_deploy]
                flavor = keystone

                [profiler]
                root@controller:~#
```

7. Populate the Glance database:

```
        root@controller:~# su -s /bin/sh -c "glance-manage db_sync" glance
        ...
        root@controller:~#
```

8. Start the Glance service daemons:

```
        root@controller:~# service glance-registry restart
        root@controller:~# service glance-api restart
        root@controller:~#
```

9. Download a QCOW2 image for the Ubuntu distribution:

```
        root@controller:~# wget
        https://uec-images.ubuntu.com/releases/16.04/release-20170330/ubunt
        u-16.04-server-cloudimg-amd64-disk1.img
        Saving to: 'ubuntu-16.04-server-cloudimg-amd64-disk1.img'
        ubuntu-16.04-server-cloudimg-amd64-disk1.img
        100%[=====================================================>] 309.75M
        31.1MB/s in 13s

        2017-04-26 17:40:21 (24.5 MB/s) - 'ubuntu-16.04-server-cloudimg-
        amd64-disk1.img' saved [324796416/324796416]
        root@controller:~#
```

10. Add the image to the Glance service:

```
        root@controller:~# openstack image create "ubuntu_16.04" --file
        ubuntu-16.04-server-cloudimg-amd64-disk1.img --disk-format qcow2 --
        container-format bare --public
        +------------------+----------------------------------------------
```

```
-------+
| Field                  | Value
|
+-----------------+---------------------------------------------
-------+
| checksum               | 87b0b7a4b03dd0bb2177d5cc02c80720
|
| container_format       | bare
|
| created_at             | 2017-04-26T17:41:44Z
|
| disk_format            | qcow2
|
| file                   | /v2/images/abce08d2-2f9f-4545-
a414-32019d41c0cd/file |
| id                     | abce08d2-2f9f-4545-a414-32019d41c0cd
|
| min_disk               | 0
|
| min_ram                | 0
|
| name                   | ubuntu_16.04
|
| owner                  | 123c1e6f33584dd1876c0a34249a6e11
|
| protected              | False
|
| schema                 | /v2/schemas/image
|
| size                   | 324796416
|
| status                 | active
|
| tags                   |
|
| updated_at             | 2017-04-26T17:41:45Z
|
| virtual_size           | None
|
| visibility             | public
|
+-----------------+---------------------------------------------
-------+
root@controller:~#
```

11. List the available images and their location on the filesystem:

```
root@controller:~# openstack image list
+--------------------------------------+--------------+--------+
| ID                                   | Name         | Status |
+--------------------------------------+--------------+--------+
| abce08d2-2f9f-4545-a414-32019d41c0cd | ubuntu_16.04 | active |
+--------------------------------------+--------------+--------+
root@controller:~# ls -lah /var/lib/glance/images/
drwxr-xr-x 2 glance glance 4.0K Apr 26 17:51 .
drwxr-xr-x 4 glance glance 4.0K Apr 26 17:32 ..
-rw-r----- 1 glance glance 310M Apr 26 17:41 abce08d2-2f9f-4545-
a414-32019d41c0cd
root@controller:~# qemu-img info
/var/lib/glance/images/abce08d2-2f9f-4545-a414-32019d41c0cd
image: /var/lib/glance/images/abce08d2-2f9f-4545-a414-32019d41c0cd
file format: qcow2
virtual size: 2.2G (2361393152 bytes)
disk size: 310M
cluster_size: 65536
Format specific information:
 compat: 0.10
 refcount bits: 16
root@controller:~#
```

How it works...

We start by creating the Glance database in MariaDB in step 1.

In steps 2 and 3, we create the user, role, and service for the Glance project. In step 4, we define the Glance API service endpoints in Keystone. The Nova service and the OpenStack tool can use these endpoints to query Glance for available images.

In step 5, we install the Glance package and create a minimal configuration file in step 6.

We then create the database schemas in step 7, by executing the `glance-manage` Python script and restart the Glance service in step 8.

In step 9, we download a QCOW2 Ubuntu image and add it to the glance registry in step 10.

Finally, in step 11, we list the newly added image and examine it on the host filesystem.

Installing and configuring the OpenStack Nova compute service

The OpenStack Compute service, code named Nova, manages a pool of compute resources and the virtual machines running on them. Nova is a suite of services to create and manage the lifecycle of virtual machines. We will use Nova to create, examine, stop, delete, and migrate KVM instances.

> For more information on the various Nova services, refer to: `http://docs .openstack.org/developer/nova/`.

In this recipe, we are going to install and configure the following Nova components:

- `nova-api`: This is the service that accepts and responds to user requests through a RESTful API. We will use it when creating, running, stopping, and migrating KVM instances.
- `nova-scheduler`: This is the service that makes decisions on where to provision instance, based on filters, such as available memory, disk, and CPU resources.
- `nova-compute`: This is the service that runs on the compute hosts and is responsible for managing the lifecycle of the KVM instance, from provisioning to deletion.
- `nova-conductor`: This is the service that sits between the Nova database we created earlier and the `nova-compute` service.
- `nova-consoleauth`: This is the service that authorizes tokens for users that want to use various consoles to connect to the virtual machines.
- `nova-novncproxy`: This is the service that grants access to instances running VNC.

Getting ready

For this recipe, we are going to need:

- An Ubuntu server with great virtualization capabilities
- Access to the internet for package installation
- A database server, a message queue, and `memcached` installed and configured, as described in the *Preparing the host for the OpenStack deployment* recipe

- The Keystone service we deployed in the *Installing and configuring the OpenStack Keystone identity service* recipe
- The Glance service we deployed in the *Installing and configuring the OpenStack Glance image service* recipe

How to do it...

To install and configure the Nova services outlined earlier, perform the following steps:

1. Create the Nova database and user in MariaDB:

```
root@controller:~# mysql -u root -plxcpassword
MariaDB [(none)]> CREATE DATABASE nova_api;
Query OK, 1 row affected (0.00 sec)
MariaDB [(none)]> CREATE DATABASE nova;
Query OK, 1 row affected (0.00 sec)
MariaDB [(none)]> GRANT ALL PRIVILEGES ON nova_api.* TO
'nova'@'localhost' IDENTIFIED BY 'lxcpassword';
Query OK, 0 rows affected (0.03 sec)
MariaDB [(none)]> GRANT ALL PRIVILEGES ON nova_api.* TO 'nova'@'%'
IDENTIFIED BY 'lxcpassword';
Query OK, 0 rows affected (0.00 sec)
MariaDB [(none)]> GRANT ALL PRIVILEGES ON nova.* TO
'nova'@'localhost' IDENTIFIED BY 'lxcpassword';
Query OK, 0 rows affected (0.00 sec)
MariaDB [(none)]> GRANT ALL PRIVILEGES ON nova.* TO 'nova'@'%'
IDENTIFIED BY 'lxcpassword';
Query OK, 0 rows affected (0.00 sec)
MariaDB [(none)]> exit
Bye
root@controller:~#
```

2. Create the Nova user and add it to the admin role in the Identity service:

```
root@controller:~# openstack user create --domain default --
password-prompt nova
User Password:
Repeat User Password:
+--------------------+----------------------------------+
| Field              | Value                            |
+--------------------+----------------------------------+
| domain_id          | default                          |
| enabled            | True                             |
| id                 | 038aa8840aca449dbd3e653c5d2c5a08 |
| name               | nova                             |
```

```
| password_expires_at | None                                      |
+---------------------+-------------------------------------------+
root@controller:~# openstack role add --project service --user nova
admin
root@controller:~#
```

3. Create the Nova service and endpoints:

```
root@controller:~# openstack service create --name nova --
description "OpenStack Compute" compute
+-------------+----------------------------------+
| Field       | Value                            |
+-------------+----------------------------------+
| description | OpenStack Compute                |
| enabled     | True                             |
| id          | 04132edd7f654f56ba0cc23ac182c9aa |
| name        | nova                             |
| type        | compute                          |
+-------------+----------------------------------+
root@controller:~# openstack endpoint create --region RegionOne
compute public http://controller:8774/v2.1/%(tenant_id)s
+--------------+-------------------------------------------+
| Field        | Value                                     |
+--------------+-------------------------------------------+
| enabled      | True                                      |
| id           | 5fc54236c324412db135dff88807e820          |
| interface    | public                                    |
| region       | RegionOne                                 |
| region_id    | RegionOne                                 |
| service_id   | 04132edd7f654f56ba0cc23ac182c9aa          |
| service_name | nova                                      |
| service_type | compute                                   |
| url          | http://controller:8774/v2.1/%(tenant_id)s |
+--------------+-------------------------------------------+
root@controller:~# openstack endpoint create --region RegionOne
compute internal http://controller:8774/v2.1/%(tenant_id)s
+--------------+-------------------------------------------+
| Field        | Value                                     |
+--------------+-------------------------------------------+
| enabled      | True                                      |
| id           | a0f623ed345e4bdb8fced929b7fe6b3f          |
| interface    | internal                                  |
| region       | RegionOne                                 |
| region_id    | RegionOne                                 |
| service_id   | 04132edd7f654f56ba0cc23ac182c9aa          |
| service_name | nova                                      |
| service_type | compute                                   |
| url          | http://controller:8774/v2.1/%(tenant_id)s |
```

```
+----------------+---------------------------------------------+
root@controller:~# openstack endpoint create --region RegionOne
compute admin http://controller:8774/v2.1/%(tenant_id)s
+----------------+---------------------------------------------+
| Field          | Value                                       |
+----------------+---------------------------------------------+
| enabled        | True                                        |
| id             | 3964db0d281545acbaa6c18abc44a216            |
| interface      | admin                                       |
| region         | RegionOne                                   |
| region_id      | RegionOne                                   |
| service_id     | 04132edd7f654f56ba0cc23ac182c9aa            |
| service_name   | nova                                        |
| service_type   | compute                                     |
| url            | http://controller:8774/v2.1/%(tenant_id)s |
+----------------+---------------------------------------------+
root@controller:~#
```

4. Install the Nova packages that will provide the API, the conductor, the console, and the scheduler services:

```
root@controller:~# apt install nova-api nova-conductor nova-consoleauth nova-novncproxy nova-scheduler
```

5. Create the Nova configuration file:

```
root@controller:~# cat /etc/nova/nova.conf
[DEFAULT]
dhcpbridge_flagfile=/etc/nova/nova.conf
dhcpbridge=/usr/bin/nova-dhcpbridge
log-dir=/var/log/nova
state_path=/var/lib/nova
force_dhcp_release=True
verbose=True
ec2_private_dns_show_ip=True
enabled_apis=osapi_compute,metadata
transport_url = rabbit://openstack:lxcpassword@controller
auth_strategy = keystone
my_ip = 10.208.132.45
use_neutron = True
firewall_driver = nova.virt.firewall.NoopFirewallDriver

[database]
connection = mysql+pymysql://nova:lxcpassword@controller/nova

[api_database]
connection = mysql+pymysql://nova:lxcpassword@controller/nova_api
```

```
[oslo_concurrency]
lock_path = /var/lib/nova/tmp

[libvirt]
use_virtio_for_bridges=True

[wsgi]
api_paste_config=/etc/nova/api-paste.ini

[keystone_authtoken]
auth_uri = http://controller:5000
auth_url = http://controller:35357
memcached_servers = controller:11211
auth_type = password
project_domain_name = default
user_domain_name = default
project_name = service
username = nova
password = lxcpassword

[vnc]
vncserver_listen = $my_ip
vncserver_proxyclient_address = $my_ip

[glance]
api_servers = http://controller:9292
root@controller:~#
```

6. Create the database tables:

```
root@controller:~# su -s /bin/sh -c "nova-manage api_db sync" nova
...
root@controller:~# su -s /bin/sh -c "nova-manage db sync" nova
...
root@controller:~#
```

7. Start the Nova services:

```
root@controller:~# service nova-api restart
root@controller:~# service nova-consoleauth restart
root@controller:~# service nova-scheduler restart
root@controller:~# service nova-conductor restart
root@controller:~# service nova-novncproxy restart
root@controller:~#
```

8. Install the nova-compute service, which will provision KVM instances:

```
root@controller:~# apt install nova-compute
```

9. Update the Nova configuration file, as follows:

```
root@controller:~# cat /etc/nova/nova.conf
[DEFAULT]
dhcpbridge_flagfile=/etc/nova/nova.conf
dhcpbridge=/usr/bin/nova-dhcpbridge
log-dir=/var/log/nova
state_path=/var/lib/nova
force_dhcp_release=True
verbose=True
ec2_private_dns_show_ip=True
enabled_apis=osapi_compute,metadata
transport_url = rabbit://openstack:lxcpassword@controller
auth_strategy = keystone
my_ip = 10.208.132.45
use_neutron = True
firewall_driver = nova.virt.firewall.NoopFirewallDriver
compute_driver = libvirt.LibvirtDriver

[database]
connection = mysql+pymysql://nova:lxcpassword@controller/nova

[api_database]
connection = mysql+pymysql://nova:lxcpassword@controller/nova_api

[oslo_concurrency]
lock_path = /var/lib/nova/tmp

[libvirt]
use_virtio_for_bridges=True

[wsgi]
api_paste_config=/etc/nova/api-paste.ini

[keystone_authtoken]
auth_uri = http://controller:5000
auth_url = http://controller:35357
memcached_servers = controller:11211
auth_type = password
project_domain_name = default
user_domain_name = default
project_name = service
username = nova
password = lxcpassword

[vnc]
enabled = True
vncserver_listen = $my_ip
```

```
vncserver_proxyclient_address = $my_ip
novncproxy_base_url = http://controller:6080/vnc_auto.html

[glance]
api_servers = http://controller:9292

root@controller:~#
```

10. Specify the virtualization driver to be used:

```
root@controller:~# cat /etc/nova/nova-compute.conf
[DEFAULT]
compute_driver=libvirt.LibvirtDriver
[libvirt]
virt_type=kvm
root@controller:~#
```

11. Restart the `nova-compute` service and list the available services:

```
root@controller:~# service nova-compute restart
root@controller:~# openstack compute service list
+----+------------------+------------+----------+---------+-------
+---------------------+
| ID | Binary           | Host       | Zone     | Status  | State |
Updated At           |
+----+------------------+------------+----------+---------+-------
+---------------------+
| 8  | nova-consoleauth | controller | internal | enabled | up    |
2017-04-26T17:58      |
| 9  | nova-scheduler   | controller | internal | enabled | up    |
2017-04-26T17:58      |
| 10 | nova-conductor   | controller | internal | enabled | up    |
2017-04-26T17:58      |
| 15 | nova-compute     | controller | nova     | enabled | up    |
None                  |
+----+------------------+------------+----------+---------+-------
+---------------------+
root@controller:~# pgrep -lf nova | uniq -f1
14110 nova-consoleaut
14176 nova-conductor
14239 nova-novncproxy
20877 nova-api
20994 nova-scheduler
21065 nova-compute
root@controller:~#
```

How it works...

In steps 1 and 2, we create the Nova database and user in MariaDB. In step 3, we create the service and endpoints that we can use to send API calls to.

In steps 4 and 5, we install the packages for the Nova services and proceed to create a simple configuration file.

We create the database table schemas in step 6 and start the Nova services in step 7.

For this example deployment, we are using a single node to run all of the OpenStack services we are interested in. However, you can use a second node just for the nova-compute service that will provision the KVM virtual machines. We install the nova-compute service in step 8, update the configuration file, and examine the nova-compute service external configuration in steps 9 and 10.

We finish the recipe by making sure that all Nova services have been configured and running in step 11.

Installing and configuring the OpenStack Neutron networking service

The OpenStack Neutron project provides networking as a service to manage the networking between virtual instances. It is responsible for setting up virtual interfaces, configuring a software bridge, creating routes, and managing IP addressing.

> For more information on the various Neutron services, refer to `https://d ocs.openstack.org/security-guide/networking/architecture.html`.

In this recipe, we are going to install and configure the following Neutron components:

- `neutron-server`: This is the service that provides API to dynamically request and configure virtual networks
- `neutron-plugin-ml2`: This is the framework that enables the use of various network technologies, such as the Linux Bridge, Open vSwitch, GRE, and VXLAN, that we saw in earlier chapters

- `neutron-linuxbridge-agent`: This is the service that provides the Linux bridge plugin agent
- `neutron-l3-agent`: This is the daemon that performs forwarding and NAT functionality between software-defined networks, by creating virtual routers
- `neutron-dhcp-agent`: This is the service that controls the DHCP daemon, which assigns IP addresses to the instances running on the compute nodes
- `neutron-metadata-agent`: This is the service that passes instance metadata to Neutron

In earlier recipes, we configured and used the Linux bridge and Open vSwitch manually and later delegated the management of the networking to libvirt. OpenStack Neutron integrates with libvirt and automates this process even further by exposing API calls that other services like Nova can utilize.

Getting ready

For this recipe, we are going to need:

- An Ubuntu server with great virtualization capabilities
- Access to the internet for package installation
- A database server, a message queue, and `memcached` installed and configured, as described in the *Preparing the host for the OpenStack deployment* recipe
- The Keystone service we deployed in the *Installing and configuring the OpenStack Keystone identity service* recipe
- The Nova services we configured in the *Installing and configuring the OpenStack Nova compute service* recipe

How to do it...

To install, configure, and create a network managed by Neutron, execute the following steps:

1. Create the Neutron database:

```
root@controller:~# mysql -u root -plxcpassword
MariaDB [(none)]> CREATE DATABASE neutron;
Query OK, 1 row affected (0.00 sec)
MariaDB [(none)]> GRANT ALL PRIVILEGES ON neutron.* TO
'neutron'@'localhost' IDENTIFIED BY 'lxcpassword';
```

```
Query OK, 0 rows affected (0.00 sec)
MariaDB [(none)]> GRANT ALL PRIVILEGES ON neutron.* TO
'neutron'@'%' IDENTIFIED BY 'lxcpassword';
Query OK, 0 rows affected (0.00 sec)
MariaDB [(none)]> exit
Bye
root@controller:~#
```

2. Create the Neutron user and add it to the admin role in Keystone:

```
root@controller:~# openstack user create --domain default --
password-prompt neutron
User Password:
Repeat User Password:
+--------------------+----------------------------------+
| Field              | Value                            |
+--------------------+----------------------------------+
| domain_id          | default                          |
| enabled            | True                             |
| id                 | 02934ad74c94461482b95fff32d36894 |
| name               | neutron                          |
| password_expires_at | None                            |
+--------------------+----------------------------------+
root@controller:~# openstack role add --project service --user
neutron admin
root@controller:~#
```

3. Create the Neutron service and endpoints:

```
root@controller:~# openstack service create --name neutron --
description "OpenStack Networking" network
+-------------+----------------------------------+
| Field       | Value                            |
+-------------+----------------------------------+
| description | OpenStack Networking             |
| enabled     | True                             |
| id          | 24b32d32d4b54e3ab2d785a1817b8e7e |
| name        | neutron                          |
| type        | network                          |
+-------------+----------------------------------+
root@controller:~# openstack endpoint create --region RegionOne
network public http://controller:9696
+-------------+----------------------------------+
| Field       | Value                            |
+-------------+----------------------------------+
| enabled     | True                             |
| id          | 544821d511e04847869fc601f2ebf0f7 |
| interface   | public                           |
```

```
| region       | RegionOne                        |
| region_id    | RegionOne                        |
| service_id   | 24b32d32d4b54e3ab2d785a1817b8e7e |
| service_name | neutron                          |
| service_type | network                          |
| url          | http://controller:9696           |
+--------------+----------------------------------+
root@controller:~# openstack endpoint create --region RegionOne
network internal http://controller:9696
+--------------+----------------------------------+
| Field        | Value                            |
+--------------+----------------------------------+
| enabled      | True                             |
| id           | 05e276ec603f424f85be8705ce7fe86a |
| interface    | internal                         |
| region       | RegionOne                        |
| region_id    | RegionOne                        |
| service_id   | 24b32d32d4b54e3ab2d785a1817b8e7e |
| service_name | neutron                          |
| service_type | network                          |
| url          | http://controller:9696           |
+--------------+----------------------------------+
root@controller:~# openstack endpoint create --region RegionOne
network admin http://controller:9696
+--------------+----------------------------------+
| Field        | Value                            |
+--------------+----------------------------------+
| enabled      | True                             |
| id           | 836b4309186146fb9143544490cd0bc1 |
| interface    | admin                            |
| region       | RegionOne                        |
| region_id    | RegionOne                        |
| service_id   | 24b32d32d4b54e3ab2d785a1817b8e7e |
| service_name | neutron                          |
| service_type | network                          |
| url          | http://controller:9696           |
+--------------+----------------------------------+
root@controller:~#
```

4. Install the Neutron packages:

```
root@controller:~# apt install neutron-server neutron-plugin-ml2
neutron-linuxbridge-agent neutron-l3-agent neutron-dhcp-agent
neutron-metadata-agent
...
root@controller:~#
```

5. Create the Neutron configuration file:

```
root@controller:~# cat /etc/neutron/neutron.conf
[DEFAULT]
core_plugin = ml2
service_plugins = router
allow_overlapping_ips = True
transport_url = rabbit://openstack:lxcpassword@controller
auth_strategy = keystone
notify_nova_on_port_status_changes = True
notify_nova_on_port_data_changes = True

[agent]
root_helper = sudo /usr/bin/neutron-rootwrap
/etc/neutron/rootwrap.conf

[cors]
[cors.subdomain]
[database]
connection = mysql+pymysql://neutron:lxcpassword@controller/neutron

[keystone_authtoken]
auth_uri = http://controller:5000
auth_url = http://controller:35357
memcached_servers = controller:11211
auth_type = password
project_domain_name = default
user_domain_name = default
project_name = service
username = neutron
password = lxcpassword

[matchmaker_redis]
[nova]
auth_url = http://controller:35357
auth_type = password
project_domain_name = default
user_domain_name = default
region_name = RegionOne
project_name = service
username = nova
password = lxcpassword

[oslo_concurrency]
[oslo_messaging_amqp]
[oslo_messaging_notifications]
[oslo_messaging_rabbit]
[oslo_messaging_zmq]
```

```
[oslo_policy]
[qos]
[quotas]
[ssl]
root@controller:~#
```

6. Define the network type and extensions that we are going to use with Neutron:

```
root@controller:~# cat /etc/neutron/plugins/ml2/ml2_conf.ini
[DEFAULT]
[ml2]
type_drivers = flat,vlan,vxlan
tenant_network_types = vxlan
mechanism_drivers = linuxbridge,l2population
extension_drivers = port_security

[ml2_type_flat]
flat_networks = provider

[ml2_type_geneve]
[ml2_type_gre]
[ml2_type_vlan]
[ml2_type_vxlan]
vni_ranges = 1:1000

[securitygroup]
enable_ipset = True
root@controller:~#
```

7. Define the interface that will be added to the software bridge and the IP the
   bridge will be bound to, replacing the IP address and interface name (eth1 in this
   example) as needed:

```
root@controller:~# cat
/etc/neutron/plugins/ml2/linuxbridge_agent.ini
[DEFAULT]
[agent]
[linux_bridge]
physical_interface_mappings = provider:eth1

[securitygroup]
enable_security_group = True
firewall_driver =
neutron.agent.linux.iptables_firewall.IptablesFirewallDriver

[vxlan]
enable_vxlan = True
local_ip = 10.208.132.45
```

```
l2_population = True
root@controller:~#
```

8. Configure the Layer 3 agent as follows:

```
root@controller:~# cat /etc/neutron/l3_agent.ini
[DEFAULT]
interface_driver =
neutron.agent.linux.interface.BridgeInterfaceDriver

[AGENT]
root@controller:~#
```

9. Configure the DHCP agent:

```
root@controller:~# cat /etc/neutron/dhcp_agent.ini
[DEFAULT]
interface_driver =
neutron.agent.linux.interface.BridgeInterfaceDriver
dhcp_driver = neutron.agent.linux.dhcp.Dnsmasq
enable_isolated_metadata = True

[AGENT]
root@controller:~#
```

10. Create a configuration for the metadata agent:

```
root@controller:~# cat /etc/neutron/metadata_agent.ini
[DEFAULT]
nova_metadata_ip = controller
metadata_proxy_shared_secret = lxcpassword

[AGENT]
[cache]
root@controller:~#
```

11. Update the configuration file for the Nova services to include Neutron. A completely minimal working example follows to look as the following:

```
root@controller:~# cat /etc/nova/nova.conf
[DEFAULT]
dhcpbridge_flagfile=/etc/nova/nova.conf
dhcpbridge=/usr/bin/nova-dhcpbridge
log-dir=/var/log/nova
state_path=/var/lib/nova
force_dhcp_release=True
verbose=True
ec2_private_dns_show_ip=True
```

```
enabled_apis=osapi_compute,metadata
transport_url = rabbit://openstack:lxcpassword@controller
auth_strategy = keystone
my_ip = 10.208.132.45
use_neutron = True
firewall_driver = nova.virt.firewall.NoopFirewallDriver
compute_driver = libvirt.LibvirtDriver
scheduler_default_filters = RetryFilter, AvailabilityZoneFilter,
RamFilter, ComputeFilter, ComputeCapabilitiesFilter,
ImagePropertiesFilter, ServerGroupAntiAffinityFilter,
ServerGroupAffinityFilter

[database]
connection = mysql+pymysql://nova:lxcpassword@controller/nova

[api_database]
connection = mysql+pymysql://nova:lxcpassword@controller/nova_api

[oslo_concurrency]
lock_path = /var/lib/nova/tmp

[libvirt]
use_virtio_for_bridges=True

[wsgi]
api_paste_config=/etc/nova/api-paste.ini

[keystone_authtoken]
auth_uri = http://controller:5000
auth_url = http://controller:35357
memcached_servers = controller:11211
auth_type = password
project_domain_name = default
user_domain_name = default
project_name = service
username = nova
password = lxcpassword

[vnc]
enabled = True
vncserver_listen = $my_ip
vncserver_proxyclient_address = $my_ip
novncproxy_base_url = http://controller:6080/vnc_auto.html

[glance]
api_servers = http://controller:9292

[libvirt]
```

```
virt_type = kvm

[neutron]
url = http://controller:9696
auth_url = http://controller:35357
auth_type = password
project_domain_name = default
user_domain_name = default
region_name = RegionOne
project_name = service
username = neutron
password = lxcpassword
service_metadata_proxy = True
metadata_proxy_shared_secret = lxcpassword
root@controller:~#
```

12. Populate the Neutron databases:

```
root@controller:~# su -s /bin/sh -c "neutron-db-manage --config-
file /etc/neutron/neutron.conf --config-file
/etc/neutron/plugins/ml2/ml2_conf.ini upgrade head" neutron
INFO [alembic.runtime.migration] Context impl MySQLImpl.
INFO [alembic.runtime.migration] Will assume non-transactional DDL.
 Running upgrade for neutron ...
INFO [alembic.runtime.migration] Context impl MySQLImpl.
INFO [alembic.runtime.migration] Will assume non-transactional DDL.
INFO [alembic.runtime.migration] Running upgrade -> kilo,
kilo_initial
...
root@controller:~#
```

13. Restart all Neutron services and Nova:

```
root@controller:~# service neutron-server restart
root@controller:~# service neutron-linuxbridge-agent restart
root@controller:~# service neutron-dhcp-agent restart
root@controller:~# service neutron-metadata-agent restart
root@controller:~# service neutron-l3-agent restart
root@controller:~# service nova-api restart
root@controller:~# service nova-compute restart
root@controller:~#
```

14. Verify that the Neutron services have been registered:

```
root@controller:~# openstack network agent list
+------------------------------------------+--------------------+------
+--------------------+-------+-------+----------------------------+
| ID | Agent Type | Host | Availability Zone | Alive | State |
```

```
Binary |
+------------------------------------+---------------------+------
+--------------------+-------+-------+----------------------------+
| 9242d71d-de25-4b3e-8aa8-62691ef72001 | Linux bridge agent | kvm2
| None | True | UP | neutron-linuxbridge-agent |
| 92b601de-06df-4b10-88c7-8f27bc48f6ab | L3 agent | kvm2 | nova |
True | UP | neutron-l3-agent |
| d249f986-9b26-4c5d-8ea5-311daf3b395d | DHCP agent | kvm2 | nova |
True | UP | neutron-dhcp-agent |
| f3cac79b-a7c3-4672-b846-9268f2d58706 | Metadata agent | kvm2 |
None | True | UP | neutron-metadata-agent |
+------------------------------------+---------------------+------
+--------------------+-------+-------+----------------------------+
root@controller:~#
```

15. Create a new network:

```
root@controller:~# openstack network create nat
+----------------------------+-------------------------------------
+
| Field                      | Value
|
+----------------------------+-------------------------------------
+
| admin_state_up             | UP
|
| availability_zone_hints    |
|
| availability_zones         |
|
| created_at                 | 2017-04-26T18:17:24Z
|
| description                |
|
| headers                    |
|
| id                         | b7ccb514-21fc-4ced-b74f-026e7e358bba
|
| ipv4_address_scope         | None
|
| ipv6_address_scope         | None
|
| mtu                        | 1450
|
| name                       | nat
|
| port_security_enabled      | True
|
```

```
| project_id              | 123c1e6f33584dd1876c0a34249a6e11
|
| project_id              | 123c1e6f33584dd1876c0a34249a6e11
|
| provider:network_type   | vxlan
|
| provider:physical_network | None
|
| provider:segmentation_id  | 37
|
| revision_number         | 3
|
| router:external         | Internal
|
| shared                  | False
|
| status                  | ACTIVE
|
| subnets                 |
|
| tags                    | []
|
| updated_at              | 2017-04-26T18:17:24Z
|
+----------------------------+------------------------------------
+
root@controller:~#
```

16. Define the DNS server, the default gateway, and the subnet range that will be assigned to the guests:

```
root@controller:~# openstack subnet create --network nat --dns-
nameserver 8.8.8.8 --gateway 192.168.0.1 --subnet-range
192.168.0.0/24 nat
+--------------------+------------------------------------------+
| Field              | Value                                    |
+--------------------+------------------------------------------+
| allocation_pools   | 192.168.0.2-192.168.0.254                |
| cidr               | 192.168.0.0/24                           |
| created_at         | 2017-04-26T18:17:41Z                     |
| description        |                                          |
| dns_nameservers    | 8.8.8.8                                  |
| enable_dhcp        | True                                     |
| gateway_ip         | 192.168.0.1                              |
| headers            |                                          |
| host_routes        |                                          |
| id                 | 296250a7-f241-4f84-adbb-64a45c943094     |
| ip_version         | 4                                        |
```

```
| ipv6_address_mode  | None                                 |
| ipv6_ra_mode       | None                                 |
| name               | nat                                  |
| network_id         | b7ccb514-21fc-4ced-b74f-026e7e358bba |
| project_id         | 123c1e6f33584dd1876c0a34249a6e11     |
| project_id         | 123c1e6f33584dd1876c0a34249a6e11     |
| revision_number    | 2                                    |
| service_types      | []                                   |
| subnetpool_id      | None                                 |
| updated_at         | 2017-04-26T18:17:41Z                 |
+--------------------+--------------------------------------+
root@controller:~#
```

17. Update the subnet information in Neutron:

```
root@controller:~# neutron net-update nat --router:external
Updated network: nat
root@controller:~#
```

18. Create a new software router:

```
root@controller:~# openstack router create router

+-------------------------+--------------------------------------+
| Field                   | Value                                |
+-------------------------+--------------------------------------+
| admin_state_up          | UP                                   |
| availability_zone_hints |                                      |
| availability_zones      |                                      |
| created_at              | 2017-04-26T18:18:05Z                 |
| description             |                                      |
| external_gateway_info   | null                                 |
| flavor_id               | None                                 |
| headers                 |                                      |
| id                      | f9cd8c96-a53c-4585-ad21-0e409f3b4d70 |
| name                    | router                               |
| project_id              | 10a92eccbad9439d9e56c4edda6b211f     |
| project_id              | 10a92eccbad9439d9e56c4edda6b211f     |
| revision_number         | 3                                    |
| routes                  |                                      |
| status                  | ACTIVE                               |
| updated_at              | 2017-04-26T18:18:05Z                 |
+-------------------------+--------------------------------------+
root@controller:~#
```

19. As the admin user, add the subnet we created earlier to the router as an interface:

```
root@controller:~# . rc.admin
root@controller:~# neutron router-interface-add router nat
Added interface 2e1e2fd3-1819-489b-a21f-7005862f9de7 to router
router.
root@controller:~#
```

20. List the network namespaces that Neutron created:

```
root@controller:~# ip netns
qrouter-f9cd8c96-a53c-4585-ad21-0e409f3b4d70
qdhcp-b7ccb514-21fc-4ced-b74f-026e7e358bba
root@controller:~#
```

21. List the ports on the software router:

```
root@controller:~# neutron router-port-list router
+----------------------------------------+------+--------------------
+----------------------------------------------------------------+
| id | name | mac_address | fixed_ips |
+----------------------------------------+------+--------------------
+----------------------------------------------------------------+
| 2e1e2fd3-1819-489b-a21f-7005862f9de7 | | fa:16:3e:0e:db:14 |
{"subnet_id": "296250a7-f241-4f84-adbb-64a45c943094", "ip_address":
"192.168.0.1"} |
+----------------------------------------+------+--------------------
+----------------------------------------------------------------+
root@controller:~#
```

22. List the Neutron networks and ensure that the one we created earlier is present:

```
root@controller:~# openstack network list
+----------------------------------------+------+--------------------
+----------------------------------------------------------------+
| ID                                     | Name | Subnets
|
+----------------------------------------+------+--------------------
+----------------------------------------------------------------+
| b7ccb514-21fc-4ced-b74f-026e7e358bba | nat  | 296250a7-f241-4f84-
adbb-64a45c943094 |
+----------------------------------------+------+--------------------
+----------------------------------------------------------------+
root@controller:~#
```

How it works...

We start this recipe by creating a new database for Neutron in step 1. We then proceed to create the user for the Neutron service and add it to the admin role for the service. In steps 2 and 3, we define the service endpoints that will be exposed for Nova to use. In steps 4 and 5, we install the Neutron packages and create a basic configuration file. In step 6, we select the VXLAN type of networking for this example deployment. In steps 7, 8, 9, and 10, we configure the bridge agent, the layer 3 agent, the DHCP agent, and the metadata agent.

In step 11, we update the Nova configuration file to contain a section about the Neutron service. In step 12, we create the database schema and restart all Neutron services in step 13, including `nova-api` and `nova-compute`.

In step 14, we verify that the Neutron services have been registered and proceed to create a new network in step 15.

In step 18, we define a new software router. We add the subnet we created earlier to it in step 19, then verify the new route configuration in step 21.

The last step 22 ensures that the network we defined earlier is active.

Building and inspecting KVM instances with OpenStack

In this recipe, we are going to build our first KVM instance using the OpenStack infrastructure we put in place in the previous recipes. Building a new KVM instance consists of the following steps:

1. We send an API call to the `nova-api` service.
2. The `nova-api` service requests a target compute host from the nova-scheduler service.
3. `nova-scheduler` picks an available compute host, based on the configured filters, such as available memory, disk, and CPU utilization.
4. Once the `nova-scheduler` selects an appropriate host, the `nova-compute` service on the selected host, requests the image from the Glance repository, if not already cached locally. Once the image is on the new server, `nova-compute` builds the new KVM instance.

Getting ready

For this recipe, we are going to need the following things:

- A database server, a message queue, and `memcached` installed and configured, as described in the *Preparing the host for the OpenStack deployment* recipe.
- The Glance service with an available image. For more information on how to deploy Glance and add a new image, refer to the *Installing and configuring the OpenStack Glance image service* recipe.
- The Keystone service we deployed in the *Installing and configuring the OpenStack Keystone identity service* recipe.
- The Nova services we configured in the *Installing and configuring the OpenStack Nova compute service* recipe.
- The Neutron service that was deployed in the *Installing and configuring the OpenStack Neutron networking service* recipe.

How to do it...

To build a new KVM instance using the OpenStack **command-line interface** (**CLI**), perform the following steps:

1. Ensure that we have an available Glance image to use:

```
root@controller:~# openstack image list
+--------------------------------------+--------------+--------+
| ID                                   | Name         | Status |
+--------------------------------------+--------------+--------+
| abce08d2-2f9f-4545-a414-32019d41c0cd | ubuntu_16.04 | active |
+--------------------------------------+--------------+--------+
root@controller:~#
```

2. Create a new instance flavor type:

```
root@controller:~# openstack flavor create --id 0 --vcpus 1 --ram
1024 --disk 5000 kvm.medium
+----------------------------+------------+
| Field                      | Value      |
+----------------------------+------------+
| OS-FLV-DISABLED:disabled   | False      |
| OS-FLV-EXT-DATA:ephemeral  | 0          |
| disk                       | 5000       |
| id                         | 0          |
| name                       | kvm.medium |
```

```
| os-flavor-access:is_public | True        |
| properties                 |             |
| ram                        | 1024        |
| rxtx_factor                | 1.0         |
| swap                       |             |
| vcpus                      | 1           |
+----------------------------+-------------+
root@controller:~#
root@controller:~# openstack flavor list
+----+------------+------+------+-----------+-------+-----------+
| ID | Name       | RAM  | Disk | Ephemeral | VCPUs | Is Public |
+----+------------+------+------+-----------+-------+-----------+
| 0  | kvm.medium | 1024 | 5000 | 0         | 1     | True      |
+----+------------+------+------+-----------+-------+-----------+
root@controller:~#
```

3. Create a new SSH key-pair:

```
root@controller:~# openstack keypair create --public-key
~/.ssh/kvm_rsa.pub kvmkey
+-------------+-------------------------------------------------+
| Field       | Value                                           |
+-------------+-------------------------------------------------+
| fingerprint | e9:7e:e6:05:8b:a4:31:c3:5e:41:65:0e:29:23:eb:2a |
| name        | kvmkey                                          |
| user_id     | cc14c5dbbd654c438e52d38efaf4f1a6               |
+-------------+-------------------------------------------------+
root@controller:~# openstack keypair list
+--------+-------------------------------------------------+
| Name   | Fingerprint                                     |
+--------+-------------------------------------------------+
| kvmkey | e9:7e:e6:05:8b:a4:31:c3:5e:41:65:0e:29:23:eb:2a |
+--------+-------------------------------------------------+
root@controller:~#
```

4. Define the security group rules that allow SSH and ICMP access:

```
root@controller:~# openstack security group rule create --proto
icmp default

+----------------------+----------------------------+
| Field                | Value                      |
+----------------------+----------------------------+
| created_at           | 2017-04-26T18:17:13Z       |
| description          |                            |
| direction            | ingress                    |
| ethertype            | IPv4                       |
| headers              |                            |
```

```
| id                | ca28501a-1b3b-448f-8c1b-0fa6f9fa9263 |
| port_range_max    | None                                 |
| port_range_min    | None                                 |
| project_id        | 123c1e6f33584dd1876c0a34249a6e11     |
| project_id        | 123c1e6f33584dd1876c0a34249a6e11     |
| protocol          | icmp                                 |
| remote_group_id   | None                                 |
| remote_ip_prefix  | 0.0.0.0/0                            |
| revision_number   | 1                                    |
| security_group_id | 050b8174-d961-4706-ab63-1cdd2a25fbdd |
| updated_at        | 2017-04-26T18:17:13Z                 |
+-------------------+--------------------------------------+
root@controller:~#
root@controller:~# openstack security group rule create --proto tcp
--dst-port 22 default

+-------------------+--------------------------------------+
| Field             | Value                                |
+-------------------+--------------------------------------+
| created_at        | 2017-04-26T18:17:18Z                 |
| description       |                                      |
| direction         | ingress                              |
| ethertype         | IPv4                                 |
| headers           |                                      |
| id                | 334130c3-42b2-4f1b-aba6-c46e91ad203e |
| port_range_max    | 22                                   |
| port_range_min    | 22                                   |
| project_id        | 123c1e6f33584dd1876c0a34249a6e11     |
| project_id        | 123c1e6f33584dd1876c0a34249a6e11     |
| protocol          | tcp                                  |
| remote_group_id   | None                                 |
| remote_ip_prefix  | 0.0.0.0/0                            |
| revision_number   | 1                                    |
| security_group_id | 050b8174-d961-4706-ab63-1cdd2a25fbdd |
| updated_at        | 2017-04-26T18:17:18Z                 |
+-------------------+--------------------------------------+
root@controller:~#
```

5. List the available networks, we defined earlier:

```
root@controller:~# openstack network list
+--------------------------------------+------+--------------------
--------------------+
| ID                                   | Name | Subnets
|
+--------------------------------------+------+--------------------
--------------------+
| b7ccb514-21fc-4ced-b74f-026e7e358bba | nat  | 296250a7-f241-4f84-
```

```
adbb-64a45c943094 |
+-----------------------------------+------+--------------------
------------------+
root@controller:~#
```

6. Build a new KVM instance and list its status:

```
root@controller:~# openstack server create --flavor kvm.medium --
image ubuntu_16.04 --nic net-id=b7ccb514-21fc-4ced-
b74f-026e7e358bba --security-group default --key-name kvmkey
ubuntu_instance
+-----------------------------------+--------------------------
----------------+
| Field                             | Value
|
+-----------------------------------+--------------------------
----------------+
| OS-DCF:diskConfig                 | MANUAL
|
| OS-EXT-AZ:availability_zone        |
|
| OS-EXT-SRV-ATTR:host              | None
|
| OS-EXT-SRV-ATTR:hypervisor_hostname | None
|
| OS-EXT-SRV-ATTR:instance_name      |
|
| OS-EXT-STS:power_state            | NOSTATE
|
| OS-EXT-STS:task_state             | scheduling
|
| OS-EXT-STS:vm_state               | building
|
| OS-SRV-USG:launched_at            | None
|
| OS-SRV-USG:terminated_at          | None
|
| accessIPv4                        |
|
| accessIPv6                        |
|
| addresses                         |
|
| adminPass                         | Z23yEuDLBjLe
|
| config_drive                      |
|
| created                           | 2017-04-26T19:11:23Z
```

```
|
| flavor                              | kvm.medium (0)
|
| hostId                              |
|
| id                                  |
0f4745b1-9d4b-4e8a-82f7-9eaa1f9bb08f    |
| image                               | ubuntu_16.04 (abce08d2-
a414-32019d41c0cd) |
| key_name                            | kvmkey
|
| name                                | ubuntu_instance
|
| os-extended-volumes:volumes_attached | []
|
| progress                            | 0
|
| project_id                          |
123c1e6f33584dd1876c0a34249a6e11        |
| properties                          |
|
| security_groups                     | [{u'name': u'default'}]
|
| status                              | BUILD
|
| updated                             | 2017-04-26T19:11:23Z
|
| user_id                             |
cc14c5dbbd654c438e52d38efaf4f1a6        |
+---------------------------------------+----------------------------
-----------------+
root@controller:~# openstack server list
+--------------------+-----------------+----------+------------------
--+---------------+
| ID                 | Name            | Status   | Networks
| Image Name   |
+--------------------+-----------------+----------+------------------
--+---------------+
| 0f4745b1-...-9bb08f | ubuntu_instance | BUILD    |
nat=192.168.0.11 | ubuntu_16.04 |
+--------------------+-----------------+----------+------------------
--+---------------+
root@controller:~#
```

7. Ensure that the container was started successfully:

```
root@controller:~# pgrep -lfa qemu
23388 /usr/bin/qemu-system-x86_64 -name instance-00000005 -S -
machine pc-i440fx-xenial,accel=kvm,usb=off -cpu Haswell-
noTSX,+abm,+pdpe1gb,+rdrand,+f16c,+osxsave,+dca,+pdcm,+xtpr,+tm2,+e
st,+smx,+vmx,+ds_cpl,+monitor,+dtes64,+pbe,+tm,+ht,+ss,+acpi,+ds,+v
me -m 1024 -realtime mlock=off -smp 1,sockets=1,cores=1,threads=1 -
uuid 0f4745b1-9d4b-4e8a-82f7-9eaa1f9bb08f -smbios
type=1,manufacturer=OpenStack Foundation,product=OpenStack
Nova,version=14.0.4,serial=6d6366d9-4569-6233-
dad6-4927587cc79f,uuid=0f4745b1-9d4b-4e8a-82f7-9eaa1f9bb08f,family=
Virtual Machine -no-user-config -nodefaults -chardev
socket,id=charmonitor,path=/var/lib/libvirt/qemu/domain-
instance-00000005/monitor.sock,server,nowait -mon
chardev=charmonitor,id=monitor,mode=control -rtc
base=utc,driftfix=slew -global kvm-pit.lost_tick_policy=discard -
no-hpet -no-shutdown -boot strict=on -device piix3-usb-
uhci,id=usb,bus=pci.0,addr=0x1.0x2 -drive
file=/var/lib/nova/instances/0f4745b1-9d4b-4e8a-82f7-9eaa1f9bb08f/d
isk,format=qcow2,if=none,id=drive-virtio-disk0,cache=none -device
virtio-blk-pci,scsi=off,bus=pci.0,addr=0x4,drive=drive-virtio-
disk0,id=virtio-disk0,bootindex=1 -netdev
tap,fd=26,id=hostnet0,vhost=on,vhostfd=28 -device virtio-net-
pci,netdev=hostnet0,id=net0,mac=fa:16:3e:3c:c0:0f,bus=pci.0,addr=0x
3 -chardev
file,id=charserial0,path=/var/lib/nova/instances/0f4745b1-9d4b-4e8a
-82f7-9eaa1f9bb08f/console.log -device isa-
serial,chardev=charserial0,id=serial0 -chardev pty,id=charserial1 -
device isa-serial,chardev=charserial1,id=serial1 -device usb-
tablet,id=input0 -vnc 0.0.0.0:0 -k en-us -device cirrus-
vga,id=video0,bus=pci.0,addr=0x2 -device virtio-balloon-
pci,id=balloon0,bus=pci.0,addr=0x5 -msg timestamp=on
root@controller:~# openstack server list
+------------------------+-----------------+--------+------------
--------+--------------+
| ID                     | Name            | Status | Networks
| Image Name   |
+------------------------+-----------------+--------+------------
--------+--------------+
| 0f4745b1-...-9eaa1f9bb08f | ubuntu_instance | ACTIVE |
nat=192.168.0.11 | ubuntu_16.04 |
+------------------------+-----------------+--------+------------
--------+--------------+
root@controller:~#
```

8. Inspect the KVM instance:

```
root@controller:~# openstack server show ubuntu_instance
+------------------------------------+------------------------------------
-----------------+
| Field                              | Value
|
+------------------------------------+------------------------------------
-----------------+
| OS-DCF:diskConfig                  | MANUAL
|
| OS-EXT-AZ:availability_zone        | nova
|
| OS-EXT-SRV-ATTR:host               | controller
|
| OS-EXT-SRV-ATTR:hypervisor_hostname | controller
|
| OS-EXT-SRV-ATTR:instance_name      | instance-00000001
|
| OS-EXT-STS:power_state             | Running
|
| OS-EXT-STS:task_state              | None
|
| OS-EXT-STS:vm_state                | active
|
| OS-SRV-USG:launched_at             | 2017-04-26T19:11:37.000000
|
| OS-SRV-USG:terminated_at           | None
|
| accessIPv4                         |
|
| accessIPv6                         |
|
| addresses                          | nat=192.168.0.11
|
| config_drive                       |
|
| created                            | 2017-04-26T19:11:23Z
|
| flavor                             | kvm.medium (0)
|
| hostId                             |
c8d0t2jgdlkasdjg0iu4kjdg3o43045t             |
| id                                 |
0f4745b1-9d4b-4e8a-82f7-9eaa1f9bb08f         |
| image                              | ubuntu_16.04 (abce08d2-
a414-32019d41c0cd) |
| key_name                           | kvmkey
```

```
|
| name                                  | ubuntu_instance
|
| os-extended-volumes:volumes_attached  | []
|
| progress                              | 0
|
| project_id                            |
123c1e6f33584dd1876c0a34249a6e11       |
| properties                            |
|
| security_groups                       | [{u'name': u'default'}]
|
| status                                | ACTIVE
|
| updated                               | 2017-04-26T19:11:23Z
|
| user_id                               |
cc14c5dbbd654c438e52d38efaf4f1a6       |
+---------------------------------------+---------------------------
----------------+
root@controller:~#
```

How it works...

We start the recipe by ensuring that we have an available Glance image to choose from. We list all available images in Glance in step 1. In step 2, we create a new instance flavor; we specify the allocated CPU, memory, and disk resources for the new instance type. In step 3, although it is not mandatory, we create a new SSH key pair that can later be used to SSH to the new instance. In step 4, we create two new security group rules that allow SSH and ICMP traffic. This is handy if we would like to ping and SSH to the new instance. Before we build the instance, we need to list the available networks in Neutron, which the guest will be part of; we do this in step 5.

With all of the earlier prerequisites in place, we build a new KVM instance in step 6, by specifying the instance flavor, the Glance image, the network, the security group, and the SSH key. We then proceed to list the status of the instance. Notice how the task state shows as scheduling, meaning that the `nova-scheduler` is selecting a host to provision the instance on and the status is BUILD. Since we are only using a single host for this example deployment, the instance is going to be provisioned on the same compute server. From the output of the build command, we can also see the IP address that was assigned to the new instance.

In step 7, we can see that the new instance was successfully provisioned, its status now shows as ACTIVE and a new QEMU process has been started.

Finally, in step 8, we examine the running instance; note that the power state field now shows Running and the status field displays active.

Stopping KVM instances with OpenStack

In this short recipe, we are going to stop a running KVM instance, we provisioned in the last recipe, using the familiar `openstack` command syntax.

Getting ready

For this recipe, we are going to need the following:

- A database server, a message queue, and `memcached` installed and configured, as described in the *Preparing the host for the OpenStack deployment* recipe.
- The Glance service with an available image. For more information on how to deploy Glance and add a new image, refer to the *Installing and configuring the OpenStack Glance image service* recipe.
- The Keystone service we deployed in the *Installing and configuring the OpenStack Keystone identity service* recipe.
- The Nova services we configured in the *Installing and configuring the OpenStack Nova compute service* recipe.
- The Neutron service that was deployed in the *Installing and configuring the OpenStack Neutron networking service* recipe.
- A running KVM instance, provisioned with OpenStack.

How to do it...

To stop a running KVM guest using OpenStack, perform the following simple steps:

1. List the provisioned OpenStack instances:

```
root@controller:~# openstack server list
+---------------------------+------------------+--------+-----------
-------+---------------+
| ID                        | Name             | Status | Networks
| Image Name |
```

```
+--------------------------------+------------------+--------+-----------
-------+--------------+
| 0f4745b1-...-9eaa1f9bb08f | ubuntu_instance | ACTIVE |
nat=192.168.0.11 | ubuntu_16.04 |
+--------------------------------+------------------+--------+-----------
-------+--------------+
root@controller:~#
```

2. Stop the instance:

```
root@controller:~# openstack server stop ubuntu_instance
root@controller:~#
```

3. List the KVM guests using libvirt:

```
root@controller:~# virsh list --all
 Id Name               State
---------------------------------------------------------
 -   instance-00000001 shut off

root@controller:~#
```

4. Ensure that the QEMU process for the instance has terminated:

```
root@controller:~# pgrep -lfa qemu
root@controller:~#
```

5. Check the status of the KVM guest:

```
root@controller:~# openstack server list
+--------------------------------+------------------+--------+-----------
-------+--------------+
| ID                          | Name             | Status | Networks
| Image Name   |
+--------------------------------+------------------+--------+-----------
-------+--------------+
| 0f4745b1-...-9eaa1f9bb08f | ubuntu_instance | SHUTOFF|
nat=192.168.0.11 | ubuntu_16.04 |
+--------------------------------+------------------+--------+-----------
-------+--------------+
root@controller:~#
```

How it works...

We start by listing the available KVM instances, provisioned with OpenStack in step 1. In step 2, we stop the instance by specifying its name. Please note that we can also use the instance ID to stop it. Since OpenStack uses the libvirt to manage the lifecycle of the KVM instances, in step 3, we see that the instance has been indeed destroyed. In step 4, we ensure that the QEMU process for the guest has also been terminated. In the last step, we can see that the instance state is now SHUTOFF instead of ACTIVE. Instances in this state can be started again by executing the following command:

```
root@controller:~# openstack server start ubuntu_instance
root@controller:~# openstack server list
+--------------------------+------------------+--------+-------------------
+---------------+
| ID                       | Name             | Status | Networks          |
Image Name     |
+--------------------------+------------------+--------+-------------------
+---------------+
| 0f4745b1-...-9eaa1f9bb08f | ubuntu_instance | ACTIVE | nat=192.168.0.11 |
ubuntu_16.04   |
+--------------------------+------------------+--------+-------------------
+---------------+
root@controller:~#
```

Terminating KVM instances with OpenStack

In this recipe, we are going to terminate a KVM instance provisioned with OpenStack. Terminating the instance will undefine it through libvirt, release the allocated CPU memory and disk resources back to the pool of available resource, for the compute host, and mark its IP address as available in the Neutron database.

Getting ready

For this recipe, we are going to need the following:

- A database server, a message queue, and memcached installed and configured, as described in the *Preparing the host for the OpenStack deployment* recipe.
- The Glance service with an available image. For more information on how to deploy Glance and add a new image, refer to the *Installing and configuring the OpenStack Glance image service* recipe.

- The Keystone service we deployed in the *Installing and configuring the OpenStack Keystone identity service* recipe.
- The Nova services we configured in the *Installing and configuring the OpenStack Nova compute service* recipe.
- The Neutron service that was deployed in the *Installing and configuring the OpenStack Neutron networking service* recipe.
- A running KVM instance, provisioned with OpenStack.

How to do it...

To terminate a running instance, perform the following steps:

1. Obtain the name or ID of the instance to be terminated:

```
root@controller:~# openstack server start ubuntu_instance
root@controller:~# openstack server list
+------------------------------+------------------+--------+-----------
-------+---------------+
| ID                           | Name             | Status | Networks
| Image Name    |
+------------------------------+------------------+--------+-----------
-------+---------------+
| 0f4745b1-...-9eaa1f9bb08f | ubuntu_instance | ACTIVE |
nat=192.168.0.11 | ubuntu_16.04 |
+------------------------------+------------------+--------+-----------
-------+---------------+
root@controller:~#
```

2. Delete the instance by providing the name:

```
root@controller:~# openstack server delete ubuntu_instance
root@controller:~#
```

3. Ensure that the instance was undefined:

```
root@controller:~# openstack server list

root@controller:~# virsh list --all
 Id    Name    State
------------------------------------------------------------

root@controller:~#
```

4. Examine the `nova-api`, `neutron-server`, and `nova-compute` logs:

```
root@controller:~# cat /var/log/nova/nova-api.log | grep -i delete
2017-05-04 15:30:07.733 20915 INFO nova.osapi_compute.wsgi.server
[req-54dbe80f-9942-43d8-949a-d80daa2440a9
cc14c5dbbd654c438e52d38efaf4f1a6 123c1e6f33584dd1876c0a34249a6e11 -
default default] 10.184.226.74 "DELETE
/v2.1/123c1e6f33584dd1876c0a34249a6e11/servers/0f4745b1-9d4b-4e8a-8
2f7-9eaa1f9bb08f HTTP/1.1" status: 204 len: 339 time: 0.1859989
root@controller:~#
root@controller:~# cat /var/log/neutron/neutron-server.log | grep -
i delete
2017-05-04 15:30:08.402 17910 INFO neutron.wsgi [req-5c9674d6-
c596-4b17-b975-54625ac7adb2 cc14c5dbbd654c438e52d38efaf4f1a6
123c1e6f33584dd1876c0a34249a6e11 - - -] 10.184.226.74 - -
[04/May/2017 15:30:08] "DELETE /v2.0/ports/fdaf6ea1-b76a-4895-a028-
db15831132fa.json HTTP/1.1" 204 173 0.320351
root@controller:~#
root@controller:~# cat /var/log/nova/nova-compute.log
...
2017-05-04 15:30:07.747 21065 INFO nova.compute.manager
[req-54dbe80f-9942-43d8-949a-d80daa2440a9
cc14c5dbbd654c438e52d38efaf4f1a6 123c1e6f33584dd1876c0a34249a6e11 -
- -] [instance: 0f4745b1-9d4b-4e8a-82f7-9eaa1f9bb08f] Terminating
instance
2017-05-04 15:30:07.952 21065 INFO nova.virt.libvirt.driver [-]
[instance: 0f4745b1-9d4b-4e8a-82f7-9eaa1f9bb08f] Instance destroyed
successfully.
2017-05-04 15:30:07.953 21065 INFO os_vif
[req-54dbe80f-9942-43d8-949a-d80daa2440a9
cc14c5dbbd654c438e52d38efaf4f1a6 123c1e6f33584dd1876c0a34249a6e11 -
- -] Successfully unplugged vif
VIFBridge(active=True,address=fa:16:3e:3c:c0:0f,bridge_name='brqb7c
cb514-21',has_traffic_filtering=True,id=fdaf6ea1-b76a-4895-a028-
db15831132fa,network=Network(b7ccb514-21fc-4ced-
b74f-026e7e358bba),plugin='linux_bridge',port_profile=<?>,preserve_
on_delete=False,vif_name='tapfdaf6ea1-b7')
2017-05-04 15:30:07.970 21065 INFO nova.virt.libvirt.driver
[req-54dbe80f-9942-43d8-949a-d80daa2440a9
cc14c5dbbd654c438e52d38efaf4f1a6 123c1e6f33584dd1876c0a34249a6e11 -
- -] [instance: 0f4745b1-9d4b-4e8a-82f7-9eaa1f9bb08f] Deleting
instance files
/var/lib/nova/instances/0f4745b1-9d4b-4e8a-82f7-9eaa1f9bb08f_del
2017-05-04 15:30:07.974 21065 INFO nova.virt.libvirt.driver
[req-54dbe80f-9942-43d8-949a-d80daa2440a9
cc14c5dbbd654c438e52d38efaf4f1a6 123c1e6f33584dd1876c0a34249a6e11 -
- -] [instance: 0f4745b1-9d4b-4e8a-82f7-9eaa1f9bb08f] Deletion of
/var/lib/nova/instances/0f4745b1-9d4b-4e8a-82f7-9eaa1f9bb08f_del
```

```
complete
. . .
root@controller:~#
```

How it works...

We begin by listing all instances that Nova knows about in step 1, noting the name of the instance we would like to delete.

In step 2, we delete the instance by specifying its name. Note that we can also use its ID instead. In step 3, we confirm that the instance has been undefined by libvirt and is no longer available in OpenStack.

In step 4, we can see the API calls that were sent to the nova-api, neutron-server, and nova-compute services and the action that those services took.

7
Using Python to Build and Manage KVM Instances

In this chapter, we are going to cover the following topics:

- Installing and using the Python libvirt library
- Defining KVM instances with Python
- Starting, stopping, and deleting KVM instances with Python
- Inspecting KVM instances with Python
- Building a simple REST API server with libvirt and bottle

Introduction

The `libvirt` library exposes a virtualization agnostic interface for controlling the full lifecycle of KVM (and other technologies, such as XEN and LXC) instances. Using the Python bindings we can define, start, destroy, and delete virtual guests, along with anything else the `virsh` userspace tool implements. In fact, we can see that the `virsh` command uses various libvirt shared libraries, by running:

```
root@kvm:~# ldd /usr/bin/virsh | grep libvirt
libvirt-lxc.so.0 => /usr/lib/x86_64-linux-gnu/libvirt-lxc.so.0
(0x00007fd050d88000)
libvirt-qemu.so.0 => /usr/lib/x86_64-linux-gnu/libvirt-qemu.so.0
(0x00007fd050b84000)
libvirt.so.0 => /usr/lib/x86_64-linux-gnu/libvirt.so.0 (0x00007fd050394000)
root@kvm:~#
```

The Python libvirt module, also provides methods to monitor and report the use of CPU, memory, storage, and network resources on the hypervisor node and other capabilities depending on the type of hypervisor driver in use.

In this chapter, we are going to use a small subset of the Python libvirt API to define, start, inspect, and stop a KVM instance.

> For a complete list of functions, classes, and methods that the Python libvirt module provides, execute:
> ```
> root@kvm:~# pydoc libvirt
> ```

Installing and using the Python libvirt library

In this recipe we are going to install the Python libvirt module and its dependencies, create a new virtual environment, and install the `iPython` command shell for interactive computing.

Getting ready

For this recipe we are going to need the following:

- An Ubuntu host, with libvirt and QEMU installed and configured
- The `debian.img` raw image file we built in the *Installing custom OS on the image with debootstrap* recipe from Chapter 1, *Getting Started with QEMU and KVM*
- The Python 2.7 interpreter, usually provided by the `python2.7` package

How to do it...

To install the Python libvirt module, the `iPython` utility, and to create a new virtual environment for our tests, follow these steps:

1. Install the Python development packages `pip` and `virtualenv`:

```
root@kvm:~# apt-get install python-pip python-dev pkg-config build-
essential autoconf libvirt-dev
root@kvm:~# pip install virtualenv
Downloading/unpacking virtualenv
  Downloading virtualenv-15.1.0-py2.py3-none-any.whl (1.8MB): 1.8MB
```

```
downloaded
Installing collected packages: virtualenv
Successfully installed virtualenv
Cleaning up...
root@kvm:~#
```

2. Create a new Python virtual environment and activate it:

```
root@kvm:~# mkdir kvm_python
root@kvm:~# virtualenv kvm_python/
New python executable in /root/kvm_python/bin/python
Installing setuptools, pip, wheel...done.
root@kvm:~# source kvm_python/bin/activate
(kvm_python) root@kvm:~# cd kvm_python/
(kvm_python) root@kvm:~/kvm_python# ls -la
total 28
drwxr-xr-x 6 root root 4096 May 9 17:28 .
drwx------ 8 root root 4096 May 9 17:28 ..
drwxr-xr-x 2 root root 4096 May 9 17:28 bin
drwxr-xr-x 2 root root 4096 May 9 17:28 include
drwxr-xr-x 3 root root 4096 May 9 17:28 lib
drwxr-xr-x 2 root root 4096 May 9 17:28 local
-rw-r--r-- 1 root root 60 May 9 17:28 pip-selfcheck.json
(kvm_python) root@kvm:~/kvm_python#
```

3. Install the libvirt module:

```
(kvm_python) root@kvm:~/kvm_python# pip install libvirt-python
Collecting libvirt-python
  Using cached libvirt-python-3.3.0.tar.gz
Building wheels for collected packages: libvirt-python
  Running setup.py bdist_wheel for libvirt-python ... done
  Stored in directory:
/root/.cache/pip/wheels/67/f0/5c/c939bf8fcce5387a36efca53eab34ba8e9
4a28f244fd1757c1
Successfully built libvirt-python
Installing collected packages: libvirt-python
Successfully installed libvirt-python-3.3.0
(kvm_python) root@kvm:~/kvm_python# pip freeze
appdirs==1.4.3
libvirt-python==3.3.0
packaging==16.8
pyparsing==2.2.0
six==1.10.0
(kvm_python) root@kvm:~/kvm_python# python --version
Python 2.7.6
(kvm_python) root@kvm:~/kvm_python#
```

4. Install `iPython` and start it:

```
(kvm_python) root@kvm:~/kvm_python# apt-get install ipython
...
(kvm_python) root@kvm:~/kvm_python# ipython
Python 2.7.6 (default, Oct 26 2016, 20:30:19)
Type "copyright", "credits" or "license" for more information.

IPython 1.2.1 -- An enhanced Interactive Python.
? -> Introduction and overview of IPython's features.
%quickref -> Quick reference.
help -> Python's own help system.
object? -> Details about 'object', use 'object??' for extra
details.

In [1]:
```

How it works...

We start by installing the dependency packages in step 1. Since we are going to use a Python virtual environment for our development, we install the `virtualenv` package as well. The Python libvirt module is going to be installed in the virtual environment with the `pip` package manager, since we don't want to pollute the host with extra packages.

In step 2, we create and activate a new Python virtual environment and install the Python libvirt module in step 3.

Finally in step 4, we install and start the `iPython` development tool, which we are going to use throughout this chapter.

Defining KVM instances with Python

In this recipe we are going to define a new KVM instance using the Python libvirt module we installed in the previous recipe. We are going to use a virtual environment and the `iPython` development tool for the following examples.

Getting ready

For this recipe we are going to need the following:

- An Ubuntu host, with libvirt and QEMU installed and configured
- The `debian.img` raw image file we built in the *Installing custom OS on the image with debootstrap* recipe from Chapter 1, *Getting Started with QEMU and KVM*
- Python 2.7, the `iPython` tool, and the virtual environment we created in the *Installing and using the Python libvirt library* recipe in this chapter

How to do it...

To define a new KVM instance, using the Python libvirt module follow these instructions:

1. In the iPython interpreter, import the `libvirt` module:

```
In [1]: import libvirt

In [2]:
```

2. Create the instance definition string:

```
In [2]: xmlconfig = """
<domain type='kvm' id='1'>
 <name>kvm_python</name>
 <memory unit='KiB'>1048576</memory>
 <currentMemory unit='KiB'>1048576</currentMemory>
 <vcpu placement='static'>1</vcpu>
 <resource>
   <partition>/machine</partition>
 </resource>
 <os>
   <type arch='x86_64' machine='pc-i440fx-trusty'>hvm</type>
   <boot dev='hd'/>
 </os>
 <features>
   <acpi/>
   <apic/>
   <pae/>
 </features>
 <clock offset='utc'/>
 <on_poweroff>destroy</on_poweroff>
 <on_reboot>restart</on_reboot>
 <on_crash>restart</on_crash>
```

```
    <devices>
      <emulator>/usr/bin/qemu-system-x86_64</emulator>
      <disk type='file' device='disk'>
        <driver name='qemu' type='raw'/>
        <source file='/tmp/debian.img'/>
        <backingStore/>
        <target dev='hda' bus='ide'/>
        <alias name='ide0-0-0'/>
        <address type='drive' controller='0' bus='0' target='0'
  unit='0'/>
      </disk>
      <controller type='usb' index='0'>
        <alias name='usb'/>
        <address type='pci' domain='0x0000' bus='0x00' slot='0x01'
  function='0x2'/>
      </controller>
      <controller type='pci' index='0' model='pci-root'>
        <alias name='pci.0'/>
      </controller>
      <controller type='ide' index='0'>
        <alias name='ide'/>
        <address type='pci' domain='0x0000' bus='0x00' slot='0x01'
  function='0x1'/>
      </controller>
      <interface type='network'>
        <mac address='52:54:00:da:02:01'/>
        <source network='default' bridge='virbr0'/>
        <target dev='vnet0'/>
        <model type='rtl8139'/>
        <alias name='net0'/>
        <address type='pci' domain='0x0000' bus='0x00' slot='0x03'
  function='0x0'/>
      </interface>
      <serial type='pty'>
        <source path='/dev/pts/5'/>
        <target port='0'/>
        <alias name='serial0'/>
      </serial>
      <console type='pty' tty='/dev/pts/5'>
        <source path='/dev/pts/5'/>
        <target type='serial' port='0'/>
        <alias name='serial0'/>
      </console>
      <input type='mouse' bus='ps2'/>
      <input type='keyboard' bus='ps2'/>
      <graphics type='vnc' port='5900' autoport='yes'
  listen='0.0.0.0'>
        <listen type='address' address='0.0.0.0'/>
```

```
      </graphics>
      <video>
        <model type='cirrus' vram='16384' heads='1'/>
        <alias name='video0'/>
        <address type='pci' domain='0x0000' bus='0x00' slot='0x02'
function='0x0'/>
      </video>
      <memballoon model='virtio'>
        <alias name='balloon0'/>
        <address type='pci' domain='0x0000' bus='0x00' slot='0x04'
function='0x0'/>
      </memballoon>
   </devices>
</domain>
"""


In [3]:
```

3. Obtain a connection to the hypervisor:

```
In [3]: conn = libvirt.open('qemu:///system')

In [4]:
```

4. Define the new instance without starting it:

```
In [4]: instance = conn.defineXML(xmlconfig)

In [5]:
```

5. List the defined instances on the host:

```
In [5]: instances = conn.listDefinedDomains()

In [6]: print 'Defined instances: {}'.format(instances)
Defined instances: ['kvm_python']

In [7]:
```

6. Ensure the instance has been defined, using the `virsh` command:

```
(kvm_python) root@kvm:~/kvm_python# virsh list --all
 Id   Name           State
-----------------------------------------------------------
  -    kvm_python    shut off

(kvm_python) root@kvm:~/kvm_python#
```

How it works...

In this recipe, we are using the pre-existing raw Debian image we created in Chapter 1, *Getting Started with QEMU and KVM*, to define the KVM instance.

In step 1, we import the libvirt package and proceed to define the new KVM instance. We assign the XML formatted string to the xmlconfig variable in step 2. Notice that the definition contains the name of the new instance and the location of the image file.

In step 3, we obtain a connection object and assign it to the conn variable. We can now use the available methods to define the KVM guest.

> *To list all available methods for an object in iPython, type the variable name followed by . and press the Tab key twice:*
> *In [7]: conn.*
> *Display all 117 possibilities? (y or n)*
> ```
> conn.allocPages                          conn.getURI
> conn.nodeDeviceLookupByName
> conn.baselineCPU                         conn.getVersion
> conn.nodeDeviceLookupSCSIHostByWWN
> conn.c_pointer                           conn.interfaceDefineXML
> conn.numOfDefinedDomains     conn.interfaceLookupByMACString
> conn.numOfDefinedInterfaces
> ...
> ```
>
> *In [7]: conn.*

TIP

> *To obtain help on a method, append the question mark character at the end of the method:*
> ```
> In [7]: conn.defineXML?
> Type: instancemethod
> String Form:<bound method virConnect.defineXML of
> <libvirt.virConnect object at 0x7fc5e57dc350>>
> File: /root/kvm_python/lib/python2.7/site-
> packages/libvirt.py
> Definition: conn.defineXML(self, xml)
> Docstring:
> Define a domain, but does not start it.
> This definition is persistent, until explicitly undefined
> with
> virDomainUndefine(). A previous definition for this domain
> would be
> ```

overridden if it already exists.

*Some hypervisors may prevent this operation if there is a current
block copy operation on a transient domain with the same ID as the
domain being defined; in that case, use* virDomainBlockJobAbort() *to
stop the block copy first.*

*virDomainFree should be used to free the resources after the
domain object is no longer needed.*

In [7]:

In step 4, we use the defineXML() method on the libvirt.virConnect connection
object, passing the XML definition string and assign it to the instance variable. We can see
the type of the new object by running:

```
In [7]: type(instance)
Out[7]: libvirt.virDomain

In [8]:
```

In step 5, we list the defined instances on the host, by using the listDefinedDomains()
method and we confirm the result by using the virsh command in step 6.

There's more...

Let's add some simple error checking to the preceding Python code and write all of it to a
new file. We are going to be adding to this file in the subsequent recipes:

```
(kvm_python) root@kvm:~/kvm_python# cat kvm.py
import libvirt

xmlconfig = """
<domain type='kvm' id='1'>
 <name>kvm_python</name>
 <memory unit='KiB'>1048576</memory>
 <currentMemory unit='KiB'>1048576</currentMemory>
 <vcpu placement='static'>1</vcpu>
 <resource>
   <partition>/machine</partition>
 </resource>
 <os>
   <type arch='x86_64' machine='pc-i440fx-trusty'>hvm</type>
   <boot dev='hd'/>
```

```
    </os>
    <features>
      <acpi/>
      <apic/>
      <pae/>
    </features>
    <clock offset='utc'/>
    <on_poweroff>destroy</on_poweroff>
    <on_reboot>restart</on_reboot>
    <on_crash>restart</on_crash>
    <devices>
      <emulator>/usr/bin/qemu-system-x86_64</emulator>
      <disk type='file' device='disk'>
        <driver name='qemu' type='raw'/>
        <source file='/tmp/debian.img'/>
        <backingStore/>
        <target dev='hda' bus='ide'/>
        <alias name='ide0-0-0'/>
        <address type='drive' controller='0' bus='0' target='0' unit='0'/>
      </disk>
      <controller type='usb' index='0'>
        <alias name='usb'/>
        <address type='pci' domain='0x0000' bus='0x00' slot='0x01'
function='0x2'/>
      </controller>
      <controller type='pci' index='0' model='pci-root'>
        <alias name='pci.0'/>
      </controller>
      <controller type='ide' index='0'>
        <alias name='ide'/>
        <address type='pci' domain='0x0000' bus='0x00' slot='0x01'
function='0x1'/>
      </controller>
      <interface type='network'>
        <mac address='52:54:00:da:02:01'/>
        <source network='default' bridge='virbr0'/>
        <target dev='vnet0'/>
        <model type='rtl8139'/>
        <alias name='net0'/>
        <address type='pci' domain='0x0000' bus='0x00' slot='0x03'
function='0x0'/>
      </interface>
      <serial type='pty'>
        <source path='/dev/pts/5'/>
        <target port='0'/>
        <alias name='serial0'/>
      </serial>
      <console type='pty' tty='/dev/pts/5'>
```

```
      <source path='/dev/pts/5'/>
      <target type='serial' port='0'/>
      <alias name='serial0'/>
    </console>
    <input type='mouse' bus='ps2'/>
    <input type='keyboard' bus='ps2'/>
    <graphics type='vnc' port='5900' autoport='yes' listen='0.0.0.0'>
      <listen type='address' address='0.0.0.0'/>
    </graphics>
    <video>
      <model type='cirrus' vram='16384' heads='1'/>
      <alias name='video0'/>
      <address type='pci' domain='0x0000' bus='0x00' slot='0x02'
function='0x0'/>
    </video>
    <memballoon model='virtio'>
      <alias name='balloon0'/>
      <address type='pci' domain='0x0000' bus='0x00' slot='0x04'
function='0x0'/>
    </memballoon>
  </devices>
</domain>
"""

conn = libvirt.open('qemu:///system')
if conn == None:
  print 'Failed to connecto to the hypervizor'
  exit(1)

instance = conn.defineXML(xmlconfig)
if instance == None:
  print 'Failed to define the instance'
  exit(1)

instances = conn.listDefinedDomains()
print 'Defined instances: {}'.format(instances)

conn.close()

(kvm_python) root@kvm:~/kvm_python#
```

To execute the script, ensure that the python_kmv instance has been undefined first, then run:

```
(kvm_python) root@kvm:~/kvm_python# python kvm.py
Defined instances: ['kvm_python']
(kvm_python) root@kvm:~/kvm_python#
```

Starting, stopping, and deleting KVM instances with Python

In this recipe we are going to use the `create()` method on the instance object we defined in the previous recipe to start it and the `destroy()` method to stop it.

To obtain more information on the `create()` method, run:

```
In [1]: instance.create?
Type: instancemethod
String Form:<bound method virDomain.create of <libvirt.virDomain object at
0x7fc5d9b97d90>>
File: /root/kvm_python/lib/python2.7/site-packages/libvirt.py
Definition: instance.create(self)
Docstring:
Launch a defined domain. If the call succeeds the domain moves from the
defined to the running domains pools. The domain will be paused only
if restoring from managed state created from a paused domain. For more
control, see virDomainCreateWithFlags().

In [2]:
```

Getting ready

For this recipe we are going to need the following:

- An Ubuntu host, with libvirt and QEMU installed and configured
- The `debian.img` raw image file we built in the Installing custom OS on the image with debootstrap recipe from `Chapter 1`, *Getting Started with QEMU and KVM*
- Python 2.7, the iPython tool, and the virtual environment we created in the *Installing and using the Python libvirt library* recipe in this chapter
- The instance object we created in the *Defining KVM instances with Python* recipe in this chapter

How to do it...

To start the KVM instance that was defined earlier, to obtain its status and finally to stop it, use the following Python code:

1. Invoke the `create()` method on the instance object:

    ```
    In [1]: instance.create()
    Out[1]: 0

    In [2]:
    ```

2. Ensure the instance is in a running state by calling the `isActive()` method on the instance object:

    ```
    In [2]: instance.isActive()
    Out[2]: 1

    In [3]:
    ```

3. Check the status of the KVM instance from the host OS:

    ```
    (kvm_python) root@kvm:~/kvm_python# virsh list --all
     Id    Name           State
    ------------------------------------------------------------
     5     kvm_python     running

    (kvm_python) root@kvm:~/kvm_python#
    ```

4. Stop the instance with the `destroy()` method:

    ```
    In [3]: instance.destroy()
    Out[3]: 0

    In [4]:
    ```

5. Ensure the instance has been destroyed:

    ```
    In [4]: instance.isActive()
    Out[4]: 0

    In [5]:
    ```

6. Delete the instance and list all defined guests:

```
In [5]: instance.undefine()
Out[5]: 0

In [6]: conn.listDefinedDomains()
Out[6]: []

In [7]:
```

How it works...

In step 1, we call the `create()` method to launch the defined instance. If successful the guest will transition from shut off state to running as we can see in the output of the command in step 3. In step 2, we use the `isActive()` method, to check the status of the instance. An output of 1 indicates that the instance is running.

In step 4, we stop the instance using the `destroy()` method and confirm in step 5.

Finally in step 6, we delete the instance using the `undefine()` method and list all defined instances with the `listDefinedDomains()` call.

There's more...

Let's add the new code to the Python script we started in the *Defining KVM instances with Python* recipe. The updated script should look like the following:

```
(kvm_python) root@kvm:~/kvm_python# cat kvm.py
import libvirt
import time

xmlconfig = """
<domain type='kvm' id='1'>
 <name>kvm_python</name>
 <memory unit='KiB'>1048576</memory>
 <currentMemory unit='KiB'>1048576</currentMemory>
 <vcpu placement='static'>1</vcpu>
 <resource>
   <partition>/machine</partition>
 </resource>
 <os>
   <type arch='x86_64' machine='pc-i440fx-trusty'>hvm</type>
   <boot dev='hd'/>
```

```
  </os>
  <features>
    <acpi/>
    <apic/>
    <pae/>
  </features>
  <clock offset='utc'/>
  <on_poweroff>destroy</on_poweroff>
  <on_reboot>restart</on_reboot>
  <on_crash>restart</on_crash>
  <devices>
    <emulator>/usr/bin/qemu-system-x86_64</emulator>
    <disk type='file' device='disk'>
      <driver name='qemu' type='raw'/>
      <source file='/tmp/debian.img'/>
<backingStore/>
      <target dev='hda' bus='ide'/>
      <alias name='ide0-0-0'/>
      <address type='drive' controller='0' bus='0' target='0' unit='0'/>
    </disk>
    <controller type='usb' index='0'>
      <alias name='usb'/>
      <address type='pci' domain='0x0000' bus='0x00' slot='0x01'
function='0x2'/>
    </controller>
    <controller type='pci' index='0' model='pci-root'>
      <alias name='pci.0'/>
    </controller>
    <controller type='ide' index='0'>
      <alias name='ide'/>
      <address type='pci' domain='0x0000' bus='0x00' slot='0x01'
function='0x1'/>
    </controller>
    <interface type='network'>
      <mac address='52:54:00:da:02:01'/>
      <source network='default' bridge='virbr0'/>
      <target dev='vnet0'/>
      <model type='rtl8139'/>
      <alias name='net0'/>
      <address type='pci' domain='0x0000' bus='0x00' slot='0x03'
function='0x0'/>
    </interface>
    <serial type='pty'>
      <source path='/dev/pts/5'/>
      <target port='0'/>
      <alias name='serial0'/>
    </serial>
    <console type='pty' tty='/dev/pts/5'>
```

```
            <source path='/dev/pts/5'/>
            <target type='serial' port='0'/>
            <alias name='serial0'/>
         </console>
         <input type='mouse' bus='ps2'/>
         <input type='keyboard' bus='ps2'/>
         <graphics type='vnc' port='5900' autoport='yes' listen='0.0.0.0'>
            <listen type='address' address='0.0.0.0'/>
         </graphics>
         <video>
            <model type='cirrus' vram='16384' heads='1'/>
            <alias name='video0'/>
            <address type='pci' domain='0x0000' bus='0x00' slot='0x02'
function='0x0'/>
         </video>
         <memballoon model='virtio'>
            <alias name='balloon0'/>
<address type='pci' domain='0x0000' bus='0x00' slot='0x04' function='0x0'/>
         </memballoon>
      </devices>
</domain>
"""

conn = libvirt.open('qemu:///system')
if conn == None:
    print 'Failed to connecto to the hypervizor'
    exit(1)

instance = conn.defineXML(xmlconfig)
if instance == None:
    print 'Failed to define the instance'
    exit(1)

instances = conn.listDefinedDomains()
print 'Defined instances: {}'.format(instances)

time.sleep(5)

if instance.create() < 0:
    print 'Failed to start the {} instance'.format(instance.name())
exit(1)

if instance.isActive():
    print 'The instance {} is running'.format(instance.name())
else:
    print 'The instance {} is not running'.format(instance.name())

time.sleep(5)
```

```
if instance.destroy() < 0:
  print 'Failed to stop the {} instance'.format(instance.name())
  exit(1)
else:
  print 'The instance {} has been destroyed'.format(instance.name())

if instance.undefine() < 0:
  print 'Failed to remove the {} instance'.format(instance.name())
  exit(1)
else:
  print 'The instance {} has been undefined'.format(instance.name())

conn.close()

(kvm_python) root@kvm:~/kvm_python#
```

Starting the script should define a new instance, start it, stop it, and finally remove it:

```
(kvm_python) root@kvm:~/kvm_python# python kvm.py
Defined instances: ['kvm1', 'kvm_python']
The instance kvm_python is running
The instance kvm_python has been destroyed
The instance kvm_python has been undefined
(kvm_python) root@kvm:~/kvm_python#
```

In the preceding script, we used the `instance.name()` method to get the name of the KVM guest and print it. We also clean up, by closing the connection to the hypervisor with the `conn.close()` call.

Inspecting KVM instances with Python

In this recipe we are going to collect instance information, using methods from the `libvirt.virDomain` class.

> For more information on the libvirt Python API, please refer to the official documentation at: `http://libvirt.org/docs/libvirt-appdev-guide-python/en-US/html/index.html`.

Getting ready

For this recipe we are going to need the following:

- An Ubuntu host, with libvirt and QEMU installed and configured
- The `debian.img` raw image file we built in the *Installing custom OS on the image with debootstrap* recipe from `Chapter 1`, *Getting Started with QEMU and KVM*
- Python 2.7, the `iPython` tool, and the virtual environment we created in the *Installing and using the Python libvirt library* recipe in this chapter
- The `instance` object we created in the *Defining KVM instances with Python* recipe in this chapter, representing the KVM guest

How to do it...

To collect CPU, memory, and state information about a running instance, use the following Python methods:

1. Get the name of the instance:

   ```
   In [1]: instance.name()
   Out[1]: 'kvm_python'

   In [2]:
   ```

2. Ensure the instance is running:

   ```
   In [2]: instance.isActive()
   Out[2]: 1

   In [3]:
   ```

3. Collect resource statistics on the KVM instance:

   ```
   In [3]: instance.info()
   Out[3]: [1, 1048576L, 1048576L, 1, 10910000000L]

   In [4]:
   ```

4. Retrieve the maximum amount of physical memory allocated to the instance:

   ```
   In [4]: instance.maxMemory()
   Out[4]: 1048576L
   ```

```
In [5]:
```

5. Extract CPU statistics for the instance:

```
In [5]: instance.getCPUStats(1)
Out[5]:
[{'cpu_time': 10911545901L,
 'system_time': 1760000000L,
 'user_time': 1560000000L}]

In [6]:
```

6. Check if the virtual machine is using hardware acceleration:

```
In [6]: instance.OSType()
Out[6]: 'hvm'

In [7]:
```

7. Collect the instance state:

```
In [82]: state, reason = instance.state()

In [83]: if state == libvirt.VIR_DOMAIN_NOSTATE:
    ....:           print('The state is nostate')
    ....: elif state == libvirt.VIR_DOMAIN_RUNNING:
    ....:           print('The state is running')
    ....: elif state == libvirt.VIR_DOMAIN_BLOCKED:
    ....:           print('The state is blocked')
    ....: elif state == libvirt.VIR_DOMAIN_PAUSED:
    ....:           print('The state is paused')
    ....: elif state == libvirt.VIR_DOMAIN_SHUTDOWN:
    ....:           print('The state is shutdown')
    ....: elif state == libvirt.VIR_DOMAIN_SHUTOFF:
    ....:           print('The state is shutoff')
    ....: elif state == libvirt.VIR_DOMAIN_CRASHED:
    ....:           print('The state is crashed')
    ....: elif state == libvirt.VIR_DOMAIN_PMSUSPENDED:
    ....:            print('The state is suspended')
    ....: else:
    ....:           print('The state is unknown')
    ....:
The state is running

In [84]:
```

How it works...

In this recipe, we used a few new methods from the `libvirt.virDomain` class. Let's see what they do in more detail and then add them to the simple `kvm.py` Python script we started in the *Defining KVM instances with Python* recipe.

In steps 1 and 2, we get the name of the KVM instance and ensure it's in a running state.

In step 3, we collect the following instance information, returned as a Python list:

- **state**: The state of the instance, as defined in the *virDomainState* enumerated type at `https://libvirt.org/html/libvirt-libvirt-domain.html#virDomainState`
- **maxMemory**: The maximum memory used by the guest
- **memory**: The current amount of memory used by the instance
- **nbVirtCPU**: The number of allocated virtual CPUs
- **cpuTime**: The time used by the instance (in nanoseconds)

In step 4, we collect the memory allocated to the instance. Notice how it matches the output of the function from step 3.

In step 5, we collect information about the CPU of the guest instance. We can see the CPU, system, and user times.

The `hvm` output of the `OSType()` method in step 6, indicates that the guest OS is designed to run on bare metal, requiring full virtualization, such as KVM.

In the last step of this recipe, we call the `state()` method to return the current instance state.

There's more...

Let's finish up this chapter with a complete example script, containing all of the methods we have used so far:

```
(kvm_python) root@kvm:~/kvm_python# cat kvm.py
import libvirt
import time


def main():

  xmlconfig = """
```

```
<domain type='kvm' id='1'>
<name>kvm_python</name>
<memory unit='KiB'>1048576</memory>
<currentMemory unit='KiB'>1048576</currentMemory>
<vcpu placement='static'>1</vcpu>
<resource>
  <partition>/machine</partition>
</resource>
<os>
  <type arch='x86_64' machine='pc-i440fx-trusty'>hvm</type>
  <boot dev='hd'/>
</os>
<features>
<acpi/>
  <apic/>
  <pae/>
</features>
<clock offset='utc'/>
<on_poweroff>destroy</on_poweroff>
<on_reboot>restart</on_reboot>
<on_crash>restart</on_crash>
<devices>
  <emulator>/usr/bin/qemu-system-x86_64</emulator>
  <disk type='file' device='disk'>
    <driver name='qemu' type='raw'/>
    <source file='/tmp/debian.img'/>
    <backingStore/>
    <target dev='hda' bus='ide'/>
    <alias name='ide0-0-0'/>
    <address type='drive' controller='0' bus='0' target='0' unit='0'/>
  </disk>
  <controller type='usb' index='0'>
    <alias name='usb'/>
    <address type='pci' domain='0x0000' bus='0x00' slot='0x01'
function='0x2'/>
  </controller>
  <controller type='pci' index='0' model='pci-root'>
    <alias name='pci.0'/>
  </controller>
  <controller type='ide' index='0'>
    <alias name='ide'/>
    <address type='pci' domain='0x0000' bus='0x00' slot='0x01'
function='0x1'/>
  </controller>
  <interface type='network'>
    <mac address='52:54:00:da:02:01'/>
    <source network='default' bridge='virbr0'/>
    <target dev='vnet0'/>
```

```
        <model type='rt18139'/>
        <alias name='net0'/>
        <address type='pci' domain='0x0000' bus='0x00' slot='0x03'
function='0x0'/>
      </interface>
      <serial type='pty'>
        <source path='/dev/pts/5'/>
        <target port='0'/>
        <alias name='serial0'/>
      </serial>
      <console type='pty' tty='/dev/pts/5'>
        <source path='/dev/pts/5'/>
 <target type='serial' port='0'/>
        <alias name='serial0'/>
      </console>
      <input type='mouse' bus='ps2'/>
      <input type='keyboard' bus='ps2'/>
      <graphics type='vnc' port='5900' autoport='yes' listen='0.0.0.0'>
        <listen type='address' address='0.0.0.0'/>
      </graphics>
      <video>
        <model type='cirrus' vram='16384' heads='1'/>
        <alias name='video0'/>
        <address type='pci' domain='0x0000' bus='0x00' slot='0x02'
function='0x0'/>
      </video>
      <memballoon model='virtio'>
        <alias name='balloon0'/>
        <address type='pci' domain='0x0000' bus='0x00' slot='0x04'
function='0x0'/>
      </memballoon>
    </devices>
    </domain>
    """

    conn = libvirt.open('qemu:///system')
    if conn == None:
      print 'Failed to connecto to the hypervizor'
exit(1)

    instance = conn.defineXML(xmlconfig)
    if instance == None:
      print 'Failed to define the instance'
      exit(1)

    instances = conn.listDefinedDomains()
    print 'Defined instances: {}'.format(instances)
```

```
  time.sleep(5)

  if instance.create() < 0:
    print 'Failed to start the {} instance'.format(instance.name())
    exit(1)

  if instance.isActive():
    print 'The instance {} is running'.format(instance.name())
  else:
    print 'The instance {} is not running'.format(instance.name())

  print 'The instance state, max memory, current memory, CPUs and time is
{}'.format(instance.info())

  print 'The CPU, system and user times are
{}'.format(instance.getCPUStats(1))

print 'The OS type for the {} instance is {}'.format(instance.name(),
instance.OSType())

  time.sleep(5)

  if instance.destroy() < 0:
    print 'Failed to stop the {} instance'.format(instance.name())
    exit(1)
  else:
    print 'The instance {} has been destroyed'.format(instance.name())

  if instance.undefine() < 0:
    print 'Failed to remove the {} instance'.format(instance.name())
    exit(1)
  else:
    print 'The instance {} has been undefined'.format(instance.name())

  conn.close()

if __name__ == "__main__":
  main()

(kvm_python) root@kvm:~/kvm_python#
```

Executing it provides the following output, assuming the kvm_python instance has been undefined first:

```
(kvm_python) root@kvm:~/kvm_python# python kvm.py
Defined instances: ['kvm_python']
The instance kvm_python is running
The instance state, max memory, current memory, CPUs and time is [1,
1048576L, 1048576L, 1, 40000000L]
The CPU, system and user times are [{'cpu_time': 42349077L, 'system_time':
0L, 'user_time': 30000000L}]
The OS type for the kvm_python instance is hvm
The instance kvm_python has been destroyed
The instance kvm_python has been undefined
(kvm_python) root@kvm:~/kvm_python#
```

Building a simple REST API server with libvirt and bottle

In this recipe, we are going to use all of the libvirt methods we saw in the earlier recipes to build a simple RESTfull API server, leveraging the bottle micro framework for Python.

Bottle is described as a fast and simple **Web Server Gateway Interface** (**WSGI**) micro web-framework for Python, which is distributed as a single module file.

> For more information on the bottle micro framework please visit the official website at: https://bottlepy.org/docs/dev/.

The simple API server we are implementing, will accept the following requests:

- **list**: get method that lists all defined libvirt instances.
- **define**: post method used to define a new KVM instance. We are going to provide the XML definition as a header in the post request.
- **start**: post method to start an instance. The name of the instance will be provided in the header of the request.
- **stop**: post method to spot a KVM instance.
- **undefine**: post method to delete the instance.

Getting ready

For this recipe we are going to need the following:

- An Ubuntu host, with libvirt and QEMU installed and configured
- The debian.img raw image file we built in the *Installing custom OS on the image with debootstrap* recipe from Chapter 1, *Getting Started with QEMU and KVM*
- Python 2.7 and the virtual environment we created in the *Installing and using the Python libvirt library* recipe in this chapter
- The curl command line tool for transferring data with URL syntax, usually provided by the curl package

How to do it...

The following steps describe how to install the bottle module and the simple RESTfull API server written in Python:

1. Install the bottle module:

```
(kvm_python) root@kvm:~/kvm_python# pip install bottle
Collecting bottle
...
 Downloading bottle-0.12.13.tar.gz (70kB)
 100% |████████████████████████████████| 71kB
4.5MB/s
...
Successfully installed bottle-0.12.13
(kvm_python) root@kvm:~/kvm_python#
```

2. Create a new file, import the libvirt and bottle modules and write the libvirt connection method:

```
(kvm_python) root@kvm:~/kvm_python# vim kvm_api.py
import libvirt
from bottle import run, request, get, post, HTTPResponse

def libvirtConnect():
  try:
    conn = libvirt.open('qemu:///system')
  except libvirt.libvirtError:
    conn = None

  return conn
```

3. Implement /define the API route and function:

```
def defineKVMInstance(template):
  conn = libvirtConnect()

  if conn == None:
    return HTTPResponse(status=500, body='Error defining
instance\n')
  else:
    try:
      conn.defineXML(template)
      return HTTPResponse(status=200, body='Instance defined\n')
    except libvirt.libvirtError:
      return HTTPResponse(status=500, body='Error defining
instance\n')


@post('/define')
def build():
  template = str(request.headers.get('X-KVM-Definition'))
  status = defineKVMInstance(template)

  return status
```

4. Implement /undefine the API route and function:

```
def undefineKVMInstance(name):
  conn = libvirtConnect()

  if conn == None:
    return HTTPResponse(status=500, body='Error undefining
instance\n')
  else:
    try:
      instance = conn.lookupByName(name)
      instance.undefine()
      return HTTPResponse(status=200, body='Instance undefined\n')
    except libvirt.libvirtError:
      return HTTPResponse(status=500, body='Error undefining
instance\n')


@post('/undefine')
def build():
  name = str(request.headers.get('X-KVM-Name'))
  status = undefineKVMInstance(name)

  return status
```

5. Implement /start the API route and function:

```
def startKVMInstance(name):
  conn = libvirtConnect()

  if conn == None:
    return HTTPResponse(status=500, body='Error starting
instance\n')
  else:
    try:
      instance = conn.lookupByName(name)
      instance.create()
      return HTTPResponse(status=200, body='Instance started\n')
    except libvirt.libvirtError:
      return HTTPResponse(status=500, body='Error starting
instance\n')


@post('/start')
def build():
  name = str(request.headers.get('X-KVM-Name'))
  status = startKVMInstance(name)

  return status
```

6. Implement /stop the API route and function:

```
def stopKVMInstance(name):
  conn = libvirtConnect()

  if conn == None:
    return HTTPResponse(status=500, body='Error stopping
instance\n')
  else:
    try:
      instance = conn.lookupByName(name)
      instance.destroy()
      return HTTPResponse(status=200, body='Instance stopped\n')
    except libvirt.libvirtError:
      return HTTPResponse(status=500, body='Error stopping
instance\n')


@post('/stop')
def build():
  name = str(request.headers.get('X-KVM-Name'))
  status = stopKVMInstance(name)
```

```
        return status
```

7. Implement /list the API route and function:

```
def getLibvirtInstances():
  conn = libvirtConnect()

  if conn == None:
    return HTTPResponse(status=500, body='Error listing
instances\n')
  else:
    try:
      instances = conn.listDefinedDomains()
      return instances
    except libvirt.libvirtError:
      return HTTPResponse(status=500, body='Error listing
instances\n')


@get('/list')
def list():
  kvm_list = getLibvirtInstances()

  return "List of KVM instances: {}\n".format(kvm_list)
```

8. Invoke the run() method to start the WSGI server when the script is executed:

```
run(host='localhost', port=8080, debug=True)
```

How it works...

Let's look at the code in more detail. First, save the preceding changes in a file and execute the script:

```
(kvm_python) root@kvm:~/kvm_python# python kvm_api.py
Bottle v0.12.13 server starting up (using WSGIRefServer())...
Listening on http://localhost:8080/
Hit Ctrl-C to quit.
```

In a separate terminal, define a new instance, passing the following XML definition, as a header:

```
(kvm_python) root@kvm:~/kvm_python# curl -s -i -XPOST localhost:8080/define
--header "X-KVM-Definition: <domain type='kvm'><name>kvm_api</name><memory
unit='KiB'>1048576</memory><vcpu >1</vcpu><os><type arch='x86_64'
```

```
machine='pc-i440fx-trusty'>hvm</type></os><devices><emulator>/usr/bin/qemu-
system-x86_64</emulator><disk type='file' device='disk'><driver name='qemu'
type='raw'/><source file='/tmp/debian.img'/><target dev='hda'
bus='ide'/></disk><interface type='network'><mac
address='52:54:00:da:02:01'/><source network='default'
bridge='virbr0'/><target dev='vnet0'/></interface><graphics type='vnc'
port='5900' autoport='yes' listen='0.0.0.0'><listen type='address'
address='0.0.0.0'/></graphics></devices></domain>"
HTTP/1.0 200 OK
Date: Fri, 12 May 2017 20:29:14 GMT
Server: WSGIServer/0.1 Python/2.7.6
Content-Length: 17
Content-Type: text/html; charset=UTF-8

Instance defined
(kvm_python) root@kvm:~/kvm_python#
```

We are using the raw Debian image we created in Chapter 1, *Getting Started with QEMU and KVM*. The XML definition should look familiar as well; we've been using it in most of the recipes in this chapter.

We should now have a new KVM instance defined. Let's use the /list route to list all instances and confirm with the virsh command:

```
(kvm_python) root@kvm:~/kvm_python# curl localhost:8080/list
List of KVM instances: ['kvm_api']
(kvm_python) root@kvm:~/kvm_python# virsh list --all
 Id    Name        State
----------------------------------------------------
 -     kvm_api     shut off

(kvm_python) root@kvm:~/kvm_python#
```

Now that we have a defined instance, let's start it using the /start route and ensure it's running:

```
(kvm_python) root@kvm:~/kvm_python# curl -s -i -XPOST localhost:8080/start
--header "X-KVM-Name: kvm_api"
HTTP/1.0 200 OK
Date: Fri, 12 May 2017 20:29:38 GMT
Server: WSGIServer/0.1 Python/2.7.6
Content-Length: 17
Content-Type: text/html; charset=UTF-8

Instance started
(kvm_python) root@kvm:~/kvm_python# virsh list --all
 Id    Name        State
```

```
--------------------------------------------------------
 1     kvm_api    running

(kvm_python) root@kvm:~/kvm_python#
```

To stop the instance and remove it completely, we use the /stop and /undefine routes from the script:

```
(kvm_python) root@kvm:~/kvm_python# curl -s -i -XPOST localhost:8080/stop -
-header "X-KVM-Name: kvm_api"
HTTP/1.0 200 OK
Date: Fri, 12 May 2017 20:29:52 GMT
Server: WSGIServer/0.1 Python/2.7.6
Content-Length: 17
Content-Type: text/html; charset=UTF-8

Instance stopped
(kvm_python) root@kvm:~/kvm_python#
(kvm_python) root@kvm:~/kvm_python# virsh list --all
 Id    Name        State
--------------------------------------------------------
 -     kvm_api    shut off

(kvm_python) root@kvm:~/kvm_python#
(kvm_python) root@kvm:~/kvm_python# curl -s -i -XPOST
localhost:8080/undefine --header "X-KVM-Name: kvm_api"
HTTP/1.0 200 OK
Date: Fri, 12 May 2017 20:30:09 GMT
Server: WSGIServer/0.1 Python/2.7.6
Content-Length: 19
Content-Type: text/html; charset=UTF-8

Instance undefined
(kvm_python) root@kvm:~/kvm_python#
(kvm_python) root@kvm:~/kvm_python# virsh list --all
 Id Name State
--------------------------------------------------------

(kvm_python) root@kvm:~/kvm_python#
```

Let us go through the code in more detail.

In step 1, we install the bottle module in the Python virtual environment.

After importing the libvirt and bottle packages in step 2, we define the libvirtConnect() method. The functions in our program will use it to connect to the hypervisor.

In step 3, we implement the /define route and its functionality. The @post decorator links the code from the following function to a URL path. In our example the /define route is bound to the build() function. Passing the /define route to the curl command will execute the function, which in turn will call the defineKVMInstance() method to define the instance.

We use the same code pattern in steps 4, 5, and 6 to start, stop, and undefine the instance.

In step 7, we use the @get decorator to implement a function to list all defined instances on the host.

In step 8, we use the run class which provides the run() method we use to start a built-in server. In our example the server will be listening on localhost, port 8080.

As we saw earlier, executing the script will start a listening socket on port 8080, which we can interact with, using the curl command.

There's more...

The full code implementation follows:

```
import libvirt
from bottle import run, request, get, post, HTTPResponse

def libvirtConnect():
  try:
    conn = libvirt.open('qemu:///system')
  except libvirt.libvirtError:
    conn = None

  return conn


def getLibvirtInstances():
  conn = libvirtConnect()

  if conn == None:
    return HTTPResponse(status=500, body='Error listing instances\n')
  else:
    try:
      instances = conn.listDefinedDomains()
      return instances
    except libvirt.libvirtError:
      return HTTPResponse(status=500, body='Error listing instances\n')
```

```python
def defineKVMInstance(template):
  conn = libvirtConnect()

  if conn == None:
    return HTTPResponse(status=500, body='Error defining instance\n')
  else:
    try:
      conn.defineXML(template)
      return HTTPResponse(status=200, body='Instance defined\n')
    except libvirt.libvirtError:
      return HTTPResponse(status=500, body='Error defining instance\n')


def undefineKVMInstance(name):
  conn = libvirtConnect()

  if conn == None:
    return HTTPResponse(status=500, body='Error undefining instance\n')
  else:
    try:
      instance = conn.lookupByName(name)
      instance.undefine()
      return HTTPResponse(status=200, body='Instance undefined\n')
    except libvirt.libvirtError:
      return HTTPResponse(status=500, body='Error undefining instance\n')


def startKVMInstance(name):
  conn = libvirtConnect()

  if conn == None:
    return HTTPResponse(status=500, body='Error starting instance\n')
  else:
    try:
      instance = conn.lookupByName(name)
      instance.create()
      return HTTPResponse(status=200, body='Instance started\n')
    except libvirt.libvirtError:
      return HTTPResponse(status=500, body='Error starting instance\n')


def stopKVMInstance(name):
  conn = libvirtConnect()

  if conn == None:
    return HTTPResponse(status=500, body='Error stopping instance\n')
  else:
    try:
```

```
      instance = conn.lookupByName(name)
      instance.destroy()
      return HTTPResponse(status=200, body='Instance stopped\n')
    except libvirt.libvirtError:
      return HTTPResponse(status=500, body='Error stopping instance\n')


@post('/define')
def build():
  template = str(request.headers.get('X-KVM-Definition'))
  status = defineKVMInstance(template)

  return status


@post('/undefine')
def build():
  name = str(request.headers.get('X-KVM-Name'))
  status = undefineKVMInstance(name)

  return status


@get('/list')
def list():
  kvm_list = getLibvirtInstances()

  return "List of KVM instances: {}\n".format(kvm_list)


@post('/start')
def build():
  name = str(request.headers.get('X-KVM-Name'))
  status = startKVMInstance(name)

  return status


@post('/stop')
def build():
  name = str(request.headers.get('X-KVM-Name'))
  status = stopKVMInstance(name)

  return status


run(host='localhost', port=8080, debug=True)
```

8
Kernel Tuning for KVM Performance

In this chapter, we are going to cover the following performance tuning recipes:

- Tuning the kernel for low I/O latency
- Memory tuning for KVM guests
- CPU performance options
- NUMA tuning with libvirt
- Tuning the kernel for network performance

Introduction

In this chapter, we are going to explore various configuration options and tools that can help improve the performance of the host OS and the KVM instances running on it.

When running KVM virtual machines, it's important to understand that from the host perspective, they are regular processes. We can see that KVM guests are Linux processes by examining the process tree on the hypervisor:

```
root@kvm:~# virsh list
 Id  Name State
 ------------------------------------------------
 16  kvm  running

root@kvm:~# pgrep -lfa qemu
19913 /usr/bin/qemu-system-x86_64 -name kvm -S -machine pc-i440fx-
trusty,accel=kvm,usb=off -m 1024 -realtime mlock=off -smp
1,sockets=1,cores=1,threads=1 -uuid 283c6653-9981-9396-efb4-fb864d87f769 -
```

```
no-user-config -nodefaults -chardev
socket,id=charmonitor,path=/var/lib/libvirt/qemu/domain-
kvm/monitor.sock,server,nowait -mon
chardev=charmonitor,id=monitor,mode=control -rtc base=utc -no-shutdown -
boot strict=on -device piix3-usb-uhci,id=usb,bus=pci.0,addr=0x1.0x2 -drive
file=/tmp/debian.img,format=raw,if=none,id=drive-ide0-0-0 -device ide-
hd,bus=ide.0,unit=0,drive=drive-ide0-0-0,id=ide0-0-0,bootindex=1 -netdev
tap,fd=26,id=hostnet0 -device
rtl8139,netdev=hostnet0,id=net0,mac=52:54:00:2f:df:93,bus=pci.0,addr=0x3 -
chardev pty,id=charserial0 -device isa-
serial,chardev=charserial0,id=serial0 -vnc 0.0.0.0:0 -device cirrus-
vga,id=video0,bus=pci.0,addr=0x2 -device virtio-balloon-
pci,id=balloon0,bus=pci.0,addr=0x4 -msg timestamp=on
root@kvm:~#
```

The virtual CPUs allocated to the KVM guests are Linux threads, managed by the host scheduler:

```
root@kvm:~# ps -eLf
UID PID PPID LWP C NLWP STIME TTY TIME CMD
...
libvirt+ 19913 1 19913 0 3 14:02 ? 00:00:00 /usr/bin/qemu-system-x86_64 -
name kvm -S -machine pc-i440fx-trusty,accel=kvm,usb=off -m 1024 -realtime
mlock=off -smp 1,sockets=1,cores=1,threads=1 -uuid 283c6653-9981-9396-efb4-
fb864d87f769 -no-user-config -nodefaul
libvirt+ 19913 1 19914 0 3 14:02 ? 00:00:08 /usr/bin/qemu-system-x86_64 -
name kvm -S -machine pc-i440fx-trusty,accel=kvm,usb=off -m 1024 -realtime
mlock=off -smp 1,sockets=1,cores=1,threads=1 -uuid 283c6653-9981-9396-efb4-
fb864d87f769 -no-user-config -nodefaul
libvirt+ 19913 1 19917 0 3 14:02 ? 00:00:00 /usr/bin/qemu-system-x86_64 -
name kvm -S -machine pc-i440fx-trusty,accel=kvm,usb=off -m 1024 -realtime
mlock=off -smp 1,sockets=1,cores=1,threads=1 -uuid 283c6653-9981-9396-efb4-
fb864d87f769 -no-user-config -nodefaul
...
root@kvm:~#
```

Depending on the type of I/O scheduler, the libvirt network driver, and memory configuration, the performance of the virtual machine can vary greatly. Before making any changes to the earlier-mentioned components, it is important to understand the type of work the guest OS will be performing. Tuning the host and guest OS for memory-intensive work will be different from I/O or CPU bound loads.

Because all KVM instances are just regular Linux processes, the QEMU driver can apply any of the following **Control Group** (**cgroup**) controllers: `cpuset`, `cpu`, `memory`, `blkio`, and device controllers. Using the cgroup controllers provides more granular control over the allowed CPU, memory, and I/O resources, as we are going to see in more detail in the following recipes.

Perhaps the most important point when tuning and optimizing any system is to establish the performance baseline prior to making any adjustments. Start by measuring the baseline performance of a subsystem, such as memory or I/O, make small incremental adjustments, then measure the impact of the changes again. Repeat as necessary until a desired effect is reached.

The recipes in this chapter are meant to give the reader a starting point for what can be tuned on the host and the virtual machines to improve performance, or account for the side effects of running different workloads on the same host/VM and the effects of multitenancy. All resources should be adjusted based on the type of workload, hardware setup, and other variables.

Tuning the kernel for low I/O latency

In this recipe, we are going to cover some of the disk performance optimization techniques by selecting an I/O scheduler and tuning the block I/O using Linux control groups, for the virtual guest and the host.

There are three I/O schedulers to choose from on the host OS and in the KVM instance:

- `noop`: This is one of the simplest kernel schedulers; it works by inserting all incoming I/O requests into a simple **FIFO** (**First In, First Out**) queue. This scheduler is useful when the host OS should not attempt to reorder I/O requests when multiple virtual machines are running.
- `deadline`: This scheduler imposes a deadline on all I/O operations to prevent starvation of requests, giving priority to read requests, due to processes usually blocking on read operations.
- `cfq`: The main goal of **Completely Fair Queuing** (**CFQ**) is to maximize the overall CPU utilization while allowing better interactive performance.

Selecting the right I/O scheduler on the host and guests greatly depends on the workloads and the underlying hardware storage.

As a general rule, selecting the `noop` scheduler for the guest OS allows the host hypervisor to better optimize the I/O requests, because it is aware of all requests coming from the virtual guests. However, if the underlying storage for the KVM machines is iSCSI volumes or any other remote storage such as GlusterFS, using the deadline scheduler, might yield better results.

On most modern Linux kernels, the `deadline` scheduler is the default, and it might be sufficient for hosts running multiple KVM virtual machines. As with any system tuning, testing is required when changing the schedulers on the host and guest OS.

Getting ready

For this recipe, we are going to need the following:

- An Ubuntu host, with libvirt and QEMU installed and configured
- A running KVM virtual machine

How to do it...

To change the I/O scheduler on the host and the KVM instance and set an I/O weight, perform the following steps:

1. On the host OS, list the I/O scheduler currently in use, substituting the block device with whatever is appropriate for your system:

   ```
   root@kvm:~# cat /sys/block/sda/queue/scheduler
   noop deadline [cfq]
   root@kvm:~#
   ```

2. Change the I/O scheduler on demand and ensure it is in use by running:

   ```
   root@kvm:~# echo deadline > /sys/block/sda/queue/scheduler
   root@kvm:~# cat /sys/block/sda/queue/scheduler
   noop [deadline] cfq
   root@kvm:~#
   ```

3. To make the change persistent across server restarts, add the following line to the GRUB default configuration and update:

   ```
   root@kvm:~# echo 'GRUB_CMDLINE_LINUX="elevator=deadline"' >>
   /etc/default/grub
   root@kvm:~# tail -1 /etc/default/grub
   ```

```
GRUB_CMDLINE_LINUX="elevator=deadline"
root@kvm:~# update-grub2
Generating grub configuration file ...
Found linux image: /boot/vmlinuz-3.13.0-107-generic
Found initrd image: /boot/initrd.img-3.13.0-107-generic
done
root@kvm:~# cat /boot/grub/grub.cfg | grep elevator
 linux /boot/vmlinuz-3.13.0-107-generic root=/dev/md126p1 ro
elevator=deadline rd.fstab=no acpi=noirq noapic
cgroup_enable=memory swapaccount=1 quiet
 linux /boot/vmlinuz-3.13.0-107-generic root=/dev/md126p1 ro
elevator=deadline rd.fstab=no acpi=noirq noapic
cgroup_enable=memory swapaccount=1 quiet
 linux /boot/vmlinuz-3.13.0-107-generic root=/dev/md126p1 ro
recovery nomodeset elevator=deadline
root@kvm:~#
```

4. For the KVM instance, set up the noop I/O scheduler persistently:

```
root@kvm:~# virsh console kvm1
Connected to domain kvm1
Escape character is ^]
root@kvm1:~# echo 'GRUB_CMDLINE_LINUX="elevator=noop"' >>
/etc/default/grub
root@kvm1:~# tail -1 /etc/default/grub
GRUB_CMDLINE_LINUX="elevator=noop"
root@kvm1:~# update-grub2
Generating grub configuration file ...
Found linux image: /boot/vmlinuz-3.13.0-107-generic
Found initrd image: /boot/initrd.img-3.13.0-107-generic
done
root@kvm1:~# cat /boot/grub/grub.cfg | grep elevator
 linux /boot/vmlinuz-3.13.0-107-generic root=/dev/md126p1 ro
elevator=noop rd.fstab=no acpi=noirq noapic cgroup_enable=memory
swapaccount=1 quiet
 linux /boot/vmlinuz-3.13.0-107-generic root=/dev/md126p1 ro
elevator=noop rd.fstab=no acpi=noirq noapic cgroup_enable=memory
swapaccount=1 quiet
 linux /boot/vmlinuz-3.13.0-107-generic root=/dev/md126p1 ro
recovery nomodeset elevator=noop
root@kvm1:~#
```

5. Set a weight of 100 for the KVM instance using the `blkio` cgroup controller:

```
root@kvm:~# virsh blkiotune --weight 100 kvm

root@kvm:~# virsh blkiotune kvm
weight : 100
```

```
device_weight :
device_read_iops_sec:
device_write_iops_sec:
device_read_bytes_sec:
device_write_bytes_sec:

root@kvm:~#
```

6. Find the `cgroup` directory hierarchy on the host:

```
root@kvm:~# mount | grep cgroup
none on /sys/fs/cgroup type tmpfs (rw)
systemd on /sys/fs/cgroup/systemd type cgroup
(rw,noexec,nosuid,nodev,none,name=systemd)
root@kvm:~#
```

7. Ensure that the cgroup for the KVM instance contains the weight that we set up earlier on the `blkio` controller:

```
root@kvm:~# cat /sys/fs/cgroup/blkio/machine/kvm.libvirt-
qemu/blkio.weight
100
root@kvm:~#
```

> For a detailed explanation on how Linux cgroups work, refer to the *Containerization with LXC* book from Packt publishing at `https://www.pac ktpub.com/virtualization-and-cloud/containerization-lxc`.

How it works...

We can see what I/O scheduler the kernel is currently using by examining the `scheduler` file in the `/sys` virtual filesystem. In step 1, we see that it's the `cfq` scheduler. We then proceed to change the I/O scheduler on the running system in step 2. Please keep in mind that changing the scheduler on demand like that will not persist server restarts. In steps 3 and 4, we modify the GRUB configuration which will append the new scheduler information to the kernel boot instructions. Restarting the server or the virtual machine will now select the new I/O scheduler.

If running multiple virtual machines on the same host, it might be useful to give more I/O priority to some of them based on certain criteria, such as time of day and VM workload. In step 5, we use the blkio cgroup controller to set a weight for the KVM guest. Lower weight will give better I/O priority. In steps 6 and 7, we can see that the correct cgroup hierarchy has been created and the blkio.weight file contains the new weight we set with the virsh command.

Memory tuning for KVM guests

When it comes to memory tuning of KVM guests there are few options available, depending on the workload of the virtual machine. One such option is Linux HugePages.

Most Linux hosts by default address memory in 4 KB segments, named pages. However, the kernel is capable of using larger page sizes. Using HugePages (pages bigger than 4 KB) may improve performance by increasing the CPU cache hits against the transaction **Lookaside Buffer (TLB)**. The TLB is a memory cache that stores recent translations of virtual memory to physical addresses for quick retrieval.

In this recipe, we are going to enable and set HugePages on the hypervisor and the KVM guest, then examine the tuning options that the virsh command provides.

Getting ready

For this recipe, we are going to need the following:

- An Ubuntu host, with libvirt and QEMU installed and configured
- A running KVM virtual machine

How to do it...

To enable and set HugePages on the hypervisor and the KVM guest and use the virsh command to set various memory options, follow these steps:

1. Check the current HugePages settings on the host OS:

```
root@kvm:~# cat /proc/meminfo | grep -i huge
AnonHugePages: 509952 kB
HugePages_Total: 0
HugePages_Free: 0
```

```
HugePages_Rsvd: 0
HugePages_Surp: 0
Hugepagesize: 2048 kB
root@kvm:~#
```

2. Connect to the KVM guest and check the current HugePages settings:

```
root@kvm1:~# cat /proc/meminfo | grep -i huge
HugePages_Total: 0
HugePages_Free: 0
HugePages_Rsvd: 0
HugePages_Surp: 0
Hugepagesize: 2048 kB
root@kvm1:~#
```

3. Increase the size of the pool of HugePages from 0 to 25000 on the hypervisor and verify the following:

```
root@kvm:~# sysctl vm.nr_hugepages=25000
vm.nr_hugepages = 25000
root@kvm:~# cat /proc/meminfo | grep -i huge
AnonHugePages: 446464 kB
HugePages_Total: 25000
HugePages_Free: 24484
HugePages_Rsvd: 0
HugePages_Surp: 0
Hugepagesize: 2048 kB
root@kvm:~# cat /proc/sys/vm/nr_hugepages
25000
root@kvm:~#
```

4. Check whether the hypervisor CPU supports 2 MB and 1 GB HugePages sizes:

```
root@kvm:~# cat /proc/cpuinfo | egrep -i "pse|pdpe1" | tail -1
flags : fpu vme de pse tsc msr pae mce cx8 apic sep mtrr pge mca
cmov pat pse36 clflush dts acpi mmx fxsr sse sse2 ss ht tm pbe
syscall nx pdpe1gb rdtscp lm constant_tsc arch_perfmon pebs bts
rep_good nopl xtopology nonstop_tsc aperfmperf eagerfpu pni
pclmulqdq dtes64 monitor ds_cpl vmx smx est tm2 ssse3 fma cx16 xtpr
pdcm pcid dca sse4_1 sse4_2 x2apic movbe popcnt tsc_deadline_timer
aes xsave avx f16c rdrand lahf_lm abm arat epb xsaveopt pln pts
dtherm tpr_shadow vnmi flexpriority ept vpid fsgsbase tsc_adjust
bmi1 avx2 smep bmi2 erms invpcid
root@kvm:~#
```

5. Set 1 GB HugePages size by editing the default GRUB configuration and rebooting:

```
root@kvm:~# cat /etc/default/grub
...
GRUB_CMDLINE_LINUX_DEFAULT="rd.fstab=no acpi=noirq noapic
cgroup_enable=memory swapaccount=1 quiet hugepagesz=1GB
hugepages=1"
...
root@kvm:~# update-grub
Generating grub configuration file ...
Found linux image: /boot/vmlinuz-3.13.0-107-generic
Found initrd image: /boot/initrd.img-3.13.0-107-generic
done
root@kvm:~# cat /boot/grub/grub.cfg | grep -i huge
  linux /boot/vmlinuz-3.13.0-107-generic root=/dev/md126p1 ro
elevator=deadline rd.fstab=no acpi=noirq noapic
cgroup_enable=memory swapaccount=1 quiet hugepagesz=1GB hugepages=1
  linux /boot/vmlinuz-3.13.0-107-generic root=/dev/md126p1 ro
elevator=deadline rd.fstab=no acpi=noirq noapic
cgroup_enable=memory swapaccount=1 quiet hugepagesz=1GB hugepages=1
root@kvm:~# reboot
```

6. Install the HugePages package:

```
root@kvm:~# apt-get install hugepages
```

7. Check the current HugePages size:

```
root@kvm:~# hugeadm --pool-list
 Size       Minimum Current Maximum Default
 2097152    25000   25000   25000    *
root@kvm:~#
```

8. Enable HugePages support for KVM:

```
root@kvm:~# sed -i 's/KVM_HUGEPAGES=0/KVM_HUGEPAGES=1/g'
/etc/default/qemu-kvm
root@kvm:~# root@kvm:~# /etc/init.d/libvirt-bin restart
libvirt-bin stop/waiting
libvirt-bin start/running, process 16257
root@kvm:~#
```

9. Mount the HugeTable virtual filesystem on the host OS:

```
root@kvm:~# mkdir /hugepages
root@kvm:~# echo "hugetlbfs /hugepages hugetlbfs mode=1770,gid=2021
0 0" >> /etc/fstab
root@kvm:~# mount -a
root@kvm:~# mount | grep hugepages
hugetlbfs on /hugepages type hugetlbfs (rw,mode=1770,gid=2021)
root@kvm:~#
```

10. Edit the configuration for the KVM guest and enable HugePages:

```
root@kvm:~# virsh destroy kvm1
Domain kvm1 destroyed

root@kvm:~# virsh edit kvm1
...
  <memoryBacking>
    <hugepages/>
  </memoryBacking>
...
Domain kvm1 XML configuration edited.

root@kvm:~# virsh start kvm1
Domain kvm1 started

root@kvm:~#
```

If you see the following error when starting the KVM instance: `error: internal error: hugetlbfs filesystem is not mounted or disabled by administrator config`, make sure that the HugePages virtual filesystem was mounted successfully in step 9.

If you see the following error when starting the KVM instance: `error: internal error: process exited while connecting to monitor: file_ram_alloc: can't mmap RAM pages: Cannot allocate memory`, you need to increase the HugePages pool in step 3.

11. Update the memory hard limit for the KVM instance and verify, as follows:

```
root@kvm:~# virsh memtune kvm1
hard_limit : unlimited
soft_limit : unlimited
swap_hard_limit: unlimited

root@kvm:~# virsh memtune kvm1 --hard-limit 2GB
```

```
root@kvm:~# virsh memtune kvm1
hard_limit : 1953125
soft_limit : unlimited
swap_hard_limit: unlimited

root@kvm:~#
```

How it works...

Libvirt and KVM support and take advantage of HugePages. Please be aware that not every workload will benefit of having pages larger than the default. Instances running databases and memory bound KVM instances are good use cases. As always, before enabling this feature, measure the performance of your application inside the virtual machine to ensure that it will benefit from HugePages.

In this recipe, we enabled HugePages on the host and the guest OS and set a hard limit on the usable memory for the guest. Let's go through the steps in more detail.

In steps 1 and 2, we check the current state of HugePages. From the output, we can see that there's no HugePages pool currently allocated, indicated by the HugePages_Total field and the current size of the HugePages of 2 MB.

In step 3, we increase the HugePages pool size to 25000. The change is on demand and will not persist server reboot. To make it persistent, you can add it to the /etc/sysctl.conf file.

In order to use the HugePages feature, we need to ensure that the CPU of the host server has hardware support for it, as indicated by the pse and pdpe1 flags, as shown in step 4.

In step 5, we configure the GRUB bootloader to start the kernel with HugePages support and a set size of 1 GB.

Although we can work directly with the files exposed by the /proc virtual filesystem, in step 6, we install the HugePages package, which provides a few useful userspace tools to list and manage various memory settings. We use the hugeadm command in step 7 to list the size of the HugePages pool.

To enable HugePages support for KVM, we update the /etc/default/qemu-kvm file in step 8, mount the virtual filesystem for it in step 9, and finally reconfigure the KVM virtual machine to use HugePages by adding the <hugepages/> stanza for the <memoryBacking> object.

Libvirt provides a convenient way to manage the amount of allocated memory for the KVM guests. In step 11, we set a hard limit of 2 GB for the `kvm1` virtual machine.

CPU performance options

There are a few methods to control CPU allocation and the available CPU cycles for KVM machines-using cgroups and the libvirt-provided CPU pinning and affinity functions, we are going to explore in this recipe. CPU affinity is a scheduler property that connects a process to a given set of CPUs on the host OS.

When provisioning virtual machines with libvirt, the default behavior is to provision the guests on any available CPU cores. In some cases, **Non-Uniform Memory Access** (**NUMA**) is a good example of when we need to designate a core per KVM instance (as we are going to see in the next recipe), that it's better to assign the virtual machine to a specified CPU core. Since each KVM virtual machine is a kernel process (`qemu-system-x86_64` more specifically in our examples), we can do this using tools such as `taskset` or the `virsh` command. We can also use the cgroups CPU subsystem to manage CPU cycle allocation, which provides more granular control over CPU resource utilization per virtual machine.

Getting ready

For this recipe, we are going to need the following:

- An Ubuntu host, with libvirt and QEMU installed and configured
- A running KVM virtual machine

How to do it...

To pin a KVM virtual machine to a specific CPU and to change the CPU shares, perform the following:

1. Obtain information about the available CPU cores on the hypervisor:

```
root@kvm:~# virsh nodeinfo
CPU model: x86_64
CPU(s): 40
CPU frequency: 2593 MHz
CPU socket(s): 1
Core(s) per socket: 10
```

```
Thread(s) per core: 2
NUMA cell(s): 2
Memory size: 131918328 KiB

root@kvm:~#
```

2. Get information about the CPU allocation for the KVM guest:

```
root@kvm:~# virsh vcpuinfo kvm1
VCPU: 0
CPU: 2
State: running
CPU time: 9.1s
CPU Affinity: yyyyyyyyyyyyyyyyyyyyyyyyyyyyyyyyyyyyyyyyyyyy

root@kvm:~#
```

3. Pin the KVM instance CPU (VCPU: 0) to the first hypervisor CPU (CPU: 0) and display the result:

```
root@kvm:~# virsh vcpupin kvm1 0 0 --live

root@kvm:~# virsh vcpuinfo kvm1
VCPU: 0
CPU: 0
State: running
CPU time: 9.3s
CPU Affinity: y---------------------------------------

root@kvm:~#
```

4. List the share of runtime that is assigned to a KVM instance:

```
root@kvm:~# virsh schedinfo kvm1
Scheduler : posix
cpu_shares : 1024
vcpu_period : 100000
vcpu_quota : -1
emulator_period: 100000
emulator_quota : -1

root@kvm:~#
```

5. Modify the current CPU weight of a running virtual machine:

```
root@kvm:~# virsh schedinfo kvm cpu_shares=512
Scheduler : posix
cpu_shares : 512
vcpu_period : 100000
vcpu_quota : -1
emulator_period: 100000
emulator_quota : -1

root@kvm:~#
```

6. Check the CPU shares in the CPU cgroups subsystem:

```
root@kvm:~# cat /sys/fs/cgroup/cpu/machine/kvm1.libvirt-
qemu/cpu.shares
512
root@kvm:~#
```

7. Examine the updated XML instance definition:

```
root@kvm:~# virsh dumpxml kvm1
. . .
 <vcpu placement='static'>1</vcpu>
 <cputune>
   <shares>512</shares>
   <vcpupin vcpu='0' cpuset='0'/>
 </cputune>
 . . .
root@kvm:~#
```

How it works...

We begin by gathering information about the CPU resources available on the hypervisor. From the output in step 1, we can see that the host OS has 40 CPUs on one socket.

In step 2, we collect information about the virtual machine CPU and its affinity with the host CPUs. In this example, the KVM guest has one virtual CPU, denoted by the VCPU: 0 record and affinity to all 40 hypervisor processors, as indicated by the CPU Affinity: yyyyyyyyyyyyyyyyyyyyyyyyyyyyyyyyyyyyyyyy field.

In step 3, we pin/bind the virtual CPU to the first physical processor on the hypervisor. Note the change in the affinity output: CPU Affinity: y------------------------- -------------.

From the output of the `virsh` command in step 4, we can observe that the CPU shares allocated to the KVM instance are set to 1024. This value is a ratio, meaning that if another guest has 512 shares, it will have twice fewer CPU runtime than that of an instance with 1024 shares. We reduce that value in step 5.

In steps 6 and 7, we confirm that the CPU shares were correctly set in the CPU cgroup subsystem on the host OS. As we mentioned earlier, CPU shares are configured using cgroups and can be adjusted directly or by the provided libvirt functionality, by means of the `virsh` command.

NUMA tuning with libvirt

NUMA is a technology that allows the system memory to be divided into zones, also named nodes. The NUMA nodes are then allocated to particular CPUs or sockets. In contrast to the traditional monolithic memory approach, where each CPU/core can access all the memory regardless of its locality, usually resulting in larger latencies, NUMA bound processes can access memory that is local to the CPU they are being executed on. In most cases, this is much faster than the memory connected to the remote CPUs on the system.

Libvirt uses the `libnuma` library to enable NUMA functionality for virtual machines, as we can see here:

```
root@kvm:~# ldd /usr/sbin/libvirtd | grep numa
  libnuma.so.1 => /usr/lib/x86_64-linux-gnu/libnuma.so.1
(0x00007fd12d49e000)
root@kvm:~#
```

Libvirt NUMA supports the following memory allocation policies to place virtual machines to NUMA nodes:

- **strict**: The placement will fail if the memory cannot be allocated on the target node
- **interleave**: Memory pages are allocated in a round-robin fashion
- **preferred**: This policy allows the hypervisor to provide memory from other nodes in case there's not enough memory available from the specified nodes

In this recipe, we are going to enable NUMA access for a KVM instance and explore its impact on the overall system performance.

Getting ready

For this recipe, we are going to need the following:

- An Ubuntu host, with libvirt and QEMU installed and configured
- A running KVM virtual machine
- The `numastat` utility

How to do it...

To enable a KVM virtual machine to run on a given NUMA node and CPU using the strict NUMA policy, perform the following steps:

1. Install the `numactl` package and check the hardware configuration of the hypervisor:

```
root@kvm:~# apt-get install numactl
...
root@kvm:~# numactl --hardware
available: 2 nodes (0-1)
node 0 cpus: 0 1 2 3 4 5 6 7 8 9 20 21 22 23 24 25 26 27 28 29
node 0 size: 64317 MB
node 0 free: 3173 MB
node 1 cpus: 10 11 12 13 14 15 16 17 18 19 30 31 32 33 34 35 36 37
38 39
node 1 size: 64509 MB
node 1 free: 31401 MB
node distances:
node 0 1
  0: 10 21
  1: 21 10
root@kvm:~#
```

2. Display the current NUMA placement for the KVM guest:

```
root@kvm:~# numastat -c kvm1

Per-node process memory usage (in MBs) for PID 22395 (qemu-system-
x86)
                Node 0      Node 1      Total
                ------      ------      -----
Huge                 0           0          0
Heap                 1           1          2
Stack                2           2          4
```

```
Private          39        21        59
-------        ------    ------    -----
Total            42        23        65
root@kvm:~#
```

3. Edit the XML instance definition, set the memory mode to strict, and select the second NUMA node (indexing starts from 0, so the second NUMA node is labeled as 1), then restart the guest:

```
root@kvm:~# virsh edit kvm1
...
<vcpu placement='static' cpuset='10-11'>2</vcpu>
<numatune>
 <memory mode='strict' nodeset='1'/>
</numatune>
...
Domain kvm1 XML configuration edited.

root@kvm:~# virsh destroy kvm1
Domain kvm1 destroyed

root@kvm:~# virsh start kvm1
Domain kvm1 started

root@kvm:~#
```

4. Get the NUMA parameters for the KVM instance:

```
root@kvm:~# virsh numatune kvm1
numa_mode : strict
numa_nodeset : 1

root@kvm:~#
```

5. Print the current virtual CPU affinity:

```
root@kvm:~# virsh vcpuinfo kvm1
VCPU: 0
CPU: 11
State: running
CPU time: 8.4s
CPU Affinity: ----------yy-----------------------------

VCPU: 1
CPU: 10
State: running
CPU time: 0.3s
CPU Affinity: ----------yy-----------------------------
```

```
root@kvm:~#
```

6. Print the NUMA node placement for the KVM instance:

```
root@kvm:~# numastat -c kvm1

Per-node process memory usage (in MBs) for PID 22395 (qemu-system-
x86)
                Node 0      Node 1      Total
                ------      ------      -----
Huge                 0           0          0
Heap                 0           3          3
Stack                0           2          2
Private              0         174        174
-------         ------      ------      -----
Total                0         179        179
root@kvm:~#
```

How it works...

We start by examining the NUMA setup on the host OS. From the output of the `numactl` command in step 1, we can observe that the hypervisor has two NUMA nodes: node 0 and node 1. Each node manages a list of CPUs. In this case, NUMA node 1 contains CPUs from 10 to 19 and from 30 to 39 and contains 64 GB of memory. This means that 64 GB of RAM is going to be local to those CPUs and access to the memory from those CPUs is going to be much faster than from CPUs that are part of node 0. To improve memory access latencies for a KVM guest, we need to pin the virtual CPUs assigned to the virtual machine to CPUs that are a part of the same NUMA node.

In step 2, we can see that the KVM instance uses memory from both NUMA nodes, which is not ideal.

In step 3, we edit the guest XML definition and pin the guest on the 10th and 11th CPUs, which are a part of the NUMA node 1, using the `cpuset='10-11'` parameter. We also specify the strict NUMA node and the second NUMA node with the `<memory mode='strict' nodeset='1'/>` parameter.

After restarting the instance, in step 4, we confirm that the KVM guest is now running using the strict NUMA mode on node 1. We also confirm that the CPU pinning is indeed what we specified in step 5. Note that the CPU affinity is flagged on the 10th and 11th elements of the CPU affinity element.

From the output in step 6, we can see that the KVM guest is now using memory only from the NUMA node 1 as desired.

If you run a memory intensive application before and after the NUMA adjustment and test, you will most likely see significant performance gains when accessing large amounts of memory inside the KVM guest, thanks to the CPU and memory locality that NUMA provides.

There is more...

In this recipe, we saw examples on how to manually assign a KVM process to a NUMA node by editing the XML definition of the guest. Some Linux distributions such as RHEL/CentOS 7 and Ubuntu 16.04 provide the numad (NUMA daemon) service, which aims at automatically balancing processes between NUMA nodes by monitoring the current memory topology:

1. To install the service on Ubuntu 16.04, run:

```
root@kvm:~# lsb_release -a
No LSB modules are available.
Distributor ID: Ubuntu
Description: Ubuntu 16.04.2 LTS
Release: 16.04
Codename: xenial
root@kvm2:~# apt install numad
...
root@kvm:~#
```

2. To start the service, execute the following code:

```
root@kvm:~# service numad start
root@kvm2:~# pgrep -lfa numad
12601 /usr/bin/numad -i 15
root@kvm:~#
```

3. To manage a specific KVM guest with numad, pass the process ID of the KVM instance:

```
root@kvm:~# numad -S 0 -p $(pidof qemu-system-x86_64)
root@kvm:~#
```

4. The service will log any NUMA rebalancing attempts:

```
root@kvm:~# tail /var/log/numad.log
Thu May 25 21:06:42 2017: Changing THP scan time in
/sys/kernel/mm/transparent_hugepage/khugepaged/scan_sleep_millisecs
from 10000 to 1000 ms.
Thu May 25 21:06:42 2017: Registering numad version 20150602 PID
12601
Thu May 25 21:09:25 2017: Adding PID 4601 to inclusion PID list
Thu May 25 21:09:25 2017: Scanning only explicit PID list processes
root@kvm:~#
```

The numad service can be helpful on OpenStack compute nodes, where manual NUMA balancing may be too involving.

Tuning the kernel for network performance

Most modern Linux kernels ship sufficiently tuned for various network workloads. Some distributions provide predefined tuning services (a good example is tuned for Red Hat/CentOS), which include a set of profiles based on the server role.

Let's go over the steps taken during data transmission and reception, on a typical Linux host, before we delve into how to tune the hypervisor:

1. The application first writes the data to a socket, which in turn is put in the transmit buffer.
2. The kernel encapsulates the data into a **Protocol Data Unit** (**PDU**).
3. The PDU is then moved onto the per-device transmit queue.
4. The **Network Interface Cards** (**NIC**) driver then pops the PDU from the transmit queue and copies it to the NIC.
5. The NIC sends the data and raises a hardware interrupt.
6. On the other end of the communication channel, the NIC receives the frame, copies it on the receive buffer, and raises hard interrupt.
7. The kernel in turn handles the interrupt and raises a soft interrupt to process the packet.
8. Finally, the kernel handles the soft interrupt and moves the packet up the TCP/IP stack for decapsulation, and puts it in a receive buffer for a process to read from.

In this recipe, we are going to examine a few best practices for tuning the Linux kernel, usually resulting in better network performance, on multitenant KVM hosts.

> Please make sure that you establish a baseline before making any configuration changes, by measuring the host performance first. Make small incremental changes, then measure the impact again.
> The examples in this recipe are not meant to be copied/pasted without prior understanding of the possible positive or negative impact they might make. Use the examples presented as a guide as to what can be tuned-the actual values must be carefully considered, based on the server type and the entire environment.

Getting ready

For this recipe, we are going to need the following:

- An Ubuntu host, with libvirt and QEMU installed and configured
- A running KVM virtual machine

How to do it...

To tune the kernel for better network performance, execute the following steps (for more information on what the kernel tunables are, read the *How it works...* section):

1. Increase the max TCP send and receive socket buffer size:

```
root@kvm:~# sysctl net.core.rmem_max
net.core.rmem_max = 212992
root@kvm:~# sysctl net.core.wmem_max
net.core.wmem_max = 212992
root@kvm:~# sysctl net.core.rmem_max=33554432
net.core.rmem_max = 33554432
root@kvm:~# sysctl net.core.wmem_max=33554432
net.core.wmem_max = 33554432
root@kvm:~#
```

2. Increase the TCP buffer limits: min, default, and max number of bytes. Set max to 16 MB for 1 GE NIC, and 32 M or 54 M for 10 GE NIC:

```
root@kvm:~# sysctl net.ipv4.tcp_rmem
net.ipv4.tcp_rmem = 4096 87380 6291456
root@kvm:~# sysctl net.ipv4.tcp_wmem
```

```
net.ipv4.tcp_wmem = 4096 16384 4194304
root@kvm:~# sysctl net.ipv4.tcp_rmem="4096 87380 33554432"
net.ipv4.tcp_rmem = 4096 87380 33554432
root@kvm:~# sysctl net.ipv4.tcp_wmem="4096 65536 33554432"
net.ipv4.tcp_wmem = 4096 65536 33554432
root@kvm:~#
```

3. Ensure that TCP window scaling is enabled:

```
root@kvm:~# sysctl net.ipv4.tcp_window_scaling
net.ipv4.tcp_window_scaling = 1
root@kvm:~#
```

4. To help increase TCP throughput with 1 GB NICs or larger, increase the length of the transmit queue of the network interface. For paths with more than 50 ms RTT, a value of 5000-10000 is recommended:

```
root@kvm:~# ifconfig eth0 txqueuelen 5000
root@kvm:~#
```

5. Reduce the `tcp_fin_timeout` value:

```
root@kvm:~# sysctl net.ipv4.tcp_fin_timeout
net.ipv4.tcp_fin_timeout = 60
root@kvm:~# sysctl net.ipv4.tcp_fin_timeout=30
net.ipv4.tcp_fin_timeout = 30
root@kvm:~#
```

6. Reduce the `tcp_keepalive_intvl` value:

```
root@kvm:~# sysctl net.ipv4.tcp_keepalive_intvl
net.ipv4.tcp_keepalive_intvl = 75
root@kvm:~# sysctl net.ipv4.tcp_keepalive_intvl=30
net.ipv4.tcp_keepalive_intvl = 30
root@kvm:~#
```

7. Enable fast recycling of TIME_WAIT sockets. The default value is 0 (disabled):

```
root@kvm:~# sysctl net.ipv4.tcp_tw_recycle
net.ipv4.tcp_tw_recycle = 0
root@kvm:~# sysctl net.ipv4.tcp_tw_recycle=1
net.ipv4.tcp_tw_recycle = 1
root@kvm:~#
```

8. Enable the reusing of sockets in the `TIME_WAIT` state for new connections. The default value is 0 (disabled):

```
root@kvm:~# sysctl net.ipv4.tcp_tw_reuse
net.ipv4.tcp_tw_reuse = 0
root@kvm:~# sysctl net.ipv4.tcp_tw_reuse=1
net.ipv4.tcp_tw_reuse = 1
root@kvm:~#
```

9. Starting with kernel version 2.6.13, Linux supports pluggable congestion control algorithms. The congestion control algorithm used is set using the `sysctl` variable `net.ipv4.tcp_congestion_control`, which is set to bic/cubic by default on Ubuntu. To get a list of congestion control algorithms that are available in your kernel (if you are running 2.6.20 or higher), run the following:

```
root@kvm:~# sysctl net.ipv4.tcp_available_congestion_control
net.ipv4.tcp_available_congestion_control = cubic reno
root@kvm:~#
```

10. To enable more pluggable congestion control algorithms, load the kernel modules:

```
root@kvm:~# modprobe tcp_htcp
root@kvm:~# modprobe tcp_bic
root@kvm:~# modprobe tcp_vegas
root@kvm:~# modprobe tcp_westwood
root@kvm:~# sysctl net.ipv4.tcp_available_congestion_control
net.ipv4.tcp_available_congestion_control = cubic reno htcp bic
vegas westwood
root@kvm:~#
```

11. For long, fast paths, it is usually better to use cubic or htcp algorithms. Cubic is the default for a number of Linux distributions, but if it is not the default on your system, you can do the following:

```
root@kvm:~# sysctl net.ipv4.tcp_congestion_control
net.ipv4.tcp_congestion_control = cubic
root@kvm:~#
```

12. If the hypervisor is overwhelmed with SYN connections, the following options might help in reducing the impact:

```
root@kvm:~# sysctl net.ipv4.tcp_max_syn_backlog
net.ipv4.tcp_max_syn_backlog = 2048
root@kvm:~# sysctl net.ipv4.tcp_max_syn_backlog=16384
net.ipv4.tcp_max_syn_backlog = 16384
root@kvm:~# sysctl net.ipv4.tcp_synack_retries
net.ipv4.tcp_synack_retries = 5
root@kvm:~# sysctl net.ipv4.tcp_synack_retries=1
net.ipv4.tcp_synack_retries = 1
root@kvm:~#
```

13. Having a sufficient number of available file descriptors is quite important, since pretty much everything on Linux is a file. Each network connection uses a file descriptor/socket. To check your current max and available file descriptors, run the following code:

```
root@kvm:~# sysctl fs.file-nr
fs.file-nr = 1280 0 13110746
root@kvm:~#
```

14. To increase the max file descriptors, execute the following:

```
root@kvm:~# sysctl fs.file-max=10000000
fs.file-max = 10000000
root@kvm:~# sysctl fs.file-nr
fs.file-nr = 1280 0 10000000
root@kvm:~#
```

15. If your hypervisor is using stateful iptable rules, the `nf_conntrack` kernel module might run out of memory for connection tracking and an error will be logged: `nf_conntrack: table full, dropping packet`. In order to raise that limit and therefore allocate more memory, you need to calculate how much RAM each connection uses. You can get that information from the proc file `/proc/slabinfo`. The `nf_conntrack` entry shows the active entries, how big each object is, and how many fit in a slab (each slab fits in one or more kernel page, usually 4 K if not using HugePages). Accounting for the overhead of the kernel page size, you can see from the `slabinfo` that each `nf_conntrack` object takes about 316 bytes (this will differ on different systems). So to track 1 M connections, you'll need to allocate roughly 316 MB of memory:

```
root@kvm:~# sysctl net.netfilter.nf_conntrack_count
net.netfilter.nf_conntrack_count = 23
root@kvm:~# sysctl net.netfilter.nf_conntrack_max
```

```
net.netfilter.nf_conntrack_max = 65536
root@kvm:~# sysctl -w net.netfilter.nf_conntrack_max=1000000
net.netfilter.nf_conntrack_max = 1000000
root@kvm:~# echo 250000 >
/sys/module/nf_conntrack/parameters/hashsize # hashsize =
nf_conntrack_max / 4
root@kvm:~#
```

How it works...

In step 1, we increase the maximum send and receive socket buffers. This will allocate more memory to the TCP stack, but on servers with a large amount of memory and many TCP connections, it will ensure that the buffer sizes will be sufficient. A good starting point for selecting the default values is the **Bandwidth Delay Product** (**BDP**) based on a measured delay, for example, multiply the bandwidth of the link to the average round trip time to some host.

In step 2, we increase the min, default, and max number of bytes used by TCP to regulate send buffer sizes. TCP dynamically adjusts the size of the send buffer from the default values.

In step 3, we make sure that window scaling is enabled. TCP window scaling automatically increases the receive window size.

> For more information on window scaling, please refer to https://en.wikipedia.org/wiki/TCP_window_scale_option.

In step 5, we reduce the `tcp_fin_timeout` value which specifies how many seconds to wait for a final FIN packet before the socket is forcibly closed. In steps 6 and 7, we reduce the number of seconds between TCP keep-alive probes and fast recycling of sockets in the `TIME_WAIT` state.

As a refresher, the following diagram shows the various TCP states a connection can be in:

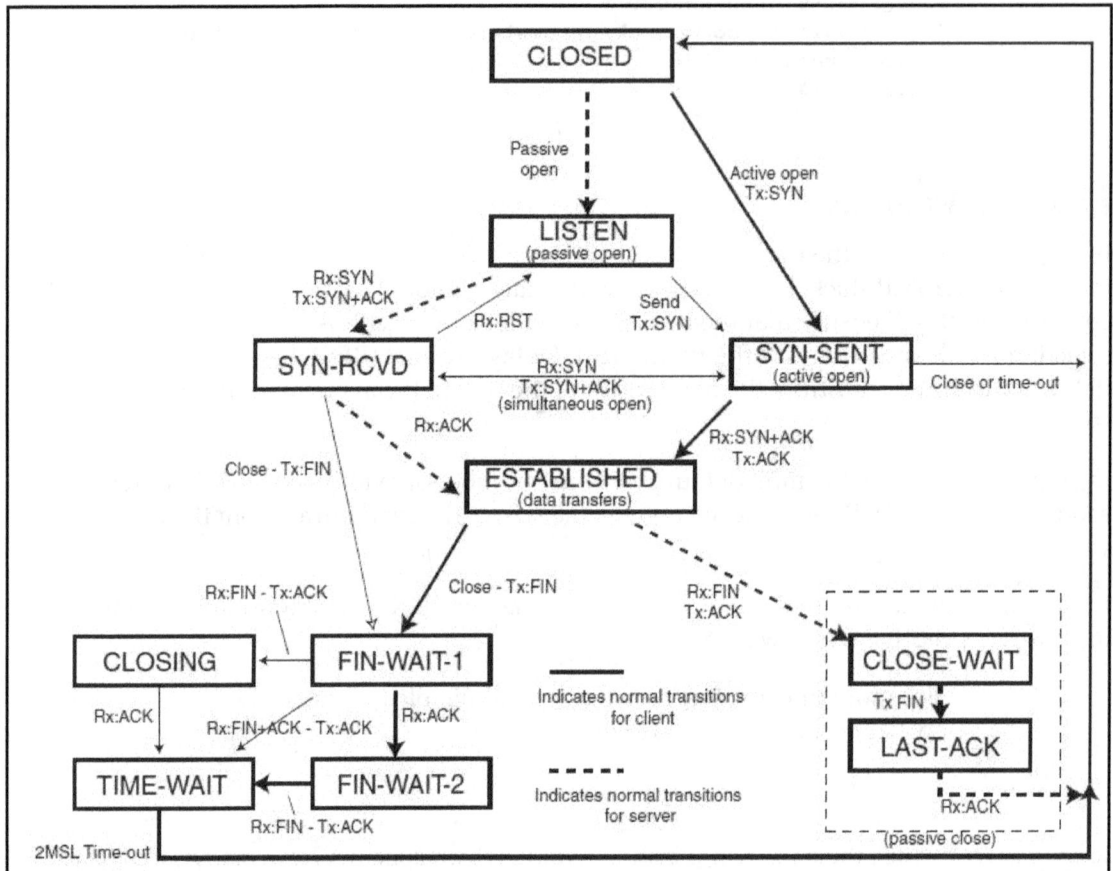

TCP state diagram

In step 8, we enable the reuse of sockets in the `TIME_WAIT` state only for new connections. On hosts with large numbers of KVM instances, this might have a significant impact on how fast new connections can be established.

In steps 9 and 10, we enable various congestion control algorithms. The choice of congestion control algorithms is selected when the kernel is built. In step 11, we select the cubic algorithm, in which the window is a cubic function of time since the last congestion event, with the inflection point set to the window prior to that event.

> For more information about network congestion-avoidance algorithms, please refer to `https://en.wikipedia.org/wiki/TCP_congestion_contr ol`.

On systems experiencing an overwhelming amount of SYN requests, adjusting the maximum number of queued connection requests that have still not received an acknowledgement from the connecting client, using the `tcp_max_syn_backlog` and `tcp_synack_retries` options, might help. We do that in step 12.

In steps 13 and 14, we increase the maximum number of file descriptors on the system. This helps when a large number of network connections are present because each connection requires a file descriptor.

In the last step, we have the `nf_conntrack_max` option. This is useful if we are tracking connections on the hypervisor using the `nf_conntrack` kernel module.

Index

A

Access Control Lists (ACLs) 105
Advanced Message Queuing Protocol (AMQP)
177
AppArmor 48

B

block devices
attaching, to virtual machines 71, 75
bottle micro framework
reference 280
bridged network
configuring 118, 120, 121

C

CentOS images
reference 33
command-line interface (CLI) 242
Content Addressable Memory (CAM) 96
custom OS
installing, on image with debootstrap 17, 21

D

Debian images
reference 33
debootstrap
used, for custom OS installation on image 17, 22
directories
sharing, between running VM and host OS 75, 79
disk image formats
dmg 13
nbd 13
qcow 13
qcow2 12
raw 12

vdi 13
vhdx 13
vmdk 13
disk images
managing, with qemu-img 10

F

Fedora images
reference 33

I

identity tokens
reference 213
image preparation, for OS installation
qemu-nbd, using 13, 16
image
resizing 23, 29
iSCSI storage pool
used, for performing manual offline migration
132, 140, 144

K

Kernel-based Virtual Machine (KVM)
about 8
CPU and memory resources, managing 66, 71
QEMU VM, starting 37, 40
KVM backups
rsync, using 181, 183
tar, using 181, 183
KVM configs
editing 58, 62
inspecting 58, 62
KVM instances
autostarting 79
building, with OpenStack 241, 245, 249
building, with virt install command 62, 66

console, using 62
defining 49, 52
defining, with Python 260, 264, 267
deleting, with Python 268, 270
inspecting, with OpenStack 241, 245, 249
inspecting, with Python 273, 276
migrating 131
monitoring, with Sensu 169, 173, 174, 177, 181
removing 55
starting 55
starting, with Python 270
stopping 55
stopping, with OpenStack 250, 252
stopping, with Python 268, 270
terminating, with OpenStack 252, 255

L

libvirt Python API
  reference 273
libvirt
  about 257
  configuring 46
  configuring file 48
  installing 46, 48
  libvirt.conf file 48
  qemu.conf file 48
  source code, download link 46
  used, for resource usage collection 160, 168
Linux bridge
  about 96
  creating 96, 98, 101, 103, 105
local image
  used, for performing offline migration 154, 156
Logical Volume Management (LVM) 29

M

manual offline migration
  GlusterFS shared volumes, using 144, 149
  performing, with iSCSI storage pool 132, 141,
    144

N

Network Address Translation (NAT) forwarding
  network
  configuring 111, 114, 117, 118

Network Block Device (NBD) 18
Network Interface Card (NIC) 121
network interfaces
  manipulating 126, 127, 129

O

offline migration
  performing, virsh command used 154
  performing, with local image 154
online migration
  performing, virsh command used 156
  performing, with local image 156
  performing, with virsh command with shared
    storage 149, 153
Open vSwitch (OVS) 95
Open vSwitch (OVS) bridge
  about 105
  creating 106, 109, 110
OpenStack deployment
  host, preparing 202, 203, 204, 205
OpenStack Glance image service
  configuring 214, 215, 218, 220
  installing 214, 215, 218, 220
OpenStack Keystone identity service
  configuring 205, 208, 209, 213
  installing 205, 208, 209, 213
OpenStack Neutron networking service
  configuring 228, 233, 236, 240
  installing 228, 231, 236, 240
  reference 228
OpenStack Nova compute service
  configuring 221, 224
  installing 221, 224, 228
  reference 221
OpenStack
  about 201
  reference 202
  used, for building KVM Instances 241, 247, 249
  used, for inspecting KVM Instances 241, 248,
    249
  used, for stopping KVM instances 250, 252
  used, for terminating KVM instances 252, 255
openSUSE images
  reference 33
OVS

reference 110

P

PCI passthrough network
    configuring 121, 125, 126
Peripheral Component Interconnect Express
    (PCIe) 121
pre-existing images
    using 30, 32
Python libvirt library
    installing 258, 260
    using 258, 260
Python libvrit module 258
Python
    used, for defining KVM instances 260, 264
    used, for deleting KV M instances 268, 273
    used, for inspecting KVM instances 273
    used, for starting KVM instances 268, 273
    used, for stopping KVM instances 268, 273

Q

QEMU Copy-On-Write (QCOW2) 184
QEMU VM
    starting, with KVM support 38, 40
qemu-img
    used, for managing disk images 10
qemu-nbd
    used, for image preparation for OS installation
    13, 16
Quality of Service (QoS) 105
Quick Emulator (QEMU)
    about 7
    configuring 8
    installing 8
    source code, download link 8
    used, for executing virtual machines 33, 37

R

RADOS Block Device (RBD) backend 82
Remote Frame Buffer (RFB) 41
Remote Procedure Calls (RPC) 109
resource usage
    collecting, with libvirt 160, 167
REST API server
    building, with bottle 280, 284, 287

building, with libvirt 280, 284, 287
rsync
    used, for KVM backups 181, 183
running VM, and hostOS
    directories, sharing 75

S

secrets
    managing 92
Sensu
    deployment, setting up 170
    reference 172
    used, for monitoring KVM instances 169, 174,
    177, 181
Service-Level Agreements (SLAs) 159
Single Root I/O Virtualization (SR-IOV) 121
snapshots
    creating 184, 187, 189
    deleting 197, 199
    editing 194
    inspecting 191, 194
    internal snapshot 189
    listing 190, 191
    reverting 195, 197
Software-defined Networking (SDN) 95
Spanning Tree Protocol (STP) 99
standard output (stdout)
    configuration file, reference 59
storage management
    reference 87
storage pools
    working with 82, 86

T

tar
    used, for KVM backups 181, 183

U

Ubuntu images
    reference 33
Uchiwa 172

V

virsh command, with shared storage

used, for online migration 149

virsh command

used, for performing offline migration 154, 156

Virtual Functions (VFs) 125

virtual machines

block devices, attaching 71, 75

executing, with QEMU 33, 37

Virtual Network Computing (VNC)

about 41

used, for connecting to running instance 40

VM, and hostOS

directories, sharing 79

volumes

managing 88, 91

W

Web Server Gateway Interface (WSGI) 210, 280

X

XML attributes

reference 126

XML format

reference 52

www.ingramcontent.com/pod-product-compliance
Lightning Source LLC
Chambersburg PA
CBHW082106220326
41598CB00066BA/5607